CHASTE CINEMATICS

CHASTE CINEMATICS

VICTOR J. VITANZA

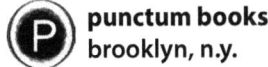
punctum books
brooklyn, n.y.

CHASTE CINEMATICS
© 2015 Victor J. Vitanza

http://creativecommons.org/licenses/by-nc-sa/4.0/

This work carries a Creative Commons BY-NC-SA 4.0 International license, which means that you are free to copy and redistribute the material in any medium or format, and you may also remix, transform and build upon the material, as long as you clearly attribute the work to the authors (but not in a way that suggests the authors or punctum endorses you and your work), you do not use this work for commercial gain in any form whatsoever, and that for any remixing and transformation, you distribute your rebuild under the same license.

First published in 2015 by
punctum books
Brooklyn, New York
http://punctumbooks.com

punctum books is an independent, open-access publisher dedicated to radically creative modes of intellectual inquiry and writing across a whimsical para-humanities assemblage. We solicit and pimp quixotic, sagely mad engagements with textual thought-bodies. We provide shelters for intellectual vagabonds.

ISBN-13: 978-0692541555
ISBN-10: 0692541551

Facing-page drawing: Heather Masciandaro.
Cover and book designed by Chris Piuma.

Before you start to read this book,

take this moment to think about making a donation to **punctum books**, an independent non-profit press,

@ http://punctumbooks.com/about/

If you're reading the e-book, you can click on the image below to go directly to our donations site. Any amount, no matter the size, is appreciated and will help us to keep our ship of fools afloat. Contributions from dedicated readers will also help us to keep our commons open and to cultivate new work that can't find a welcoming port elsewhere. Our adventure is not possible without your support.

Vive la open-access.

Fig. 1. Hieronymus Bosch, *Ship of Fools* (1490-1500)

"Nothing is ever to be posited that is not also reversed and caught up again in the supplementarity of this reversal [reversement]. To put it another way: there would no longer be either a right side or a wrong side of discourse, or even of texts, but each passing from one to the other would make audible and comprehensible even what resists the recto-verso structure that shores up common sense. If this is to be practiced for every meaning posited—for every word, utterance, sentence, but also of course for every phoneme, every letter—we need to proceed in such a way that linear reading is no longer possible."

>   Luce Irigaray, This Sex
>   (79–80, Irigaray's emphasis; Cf. "Invisible")

"Long ago I started putting to myself a question: Where are the beginning and the end of the novel? I have found some answers while writing my books. Long ago I came to understand that the arts are 'reversible' and 'nonreversible.' Some arts are reversible and enable the recipient to approach the work from various sides, or even to go around it and have a good look at it, changing the spot of the perspective, and the direction of his [more so, her] looking at it according to his [more so, her] own preference, as is the case with architecture, sculpture, or painting. Others, nonreversible arts, such as music and literature, look like one-way roads on which everything moves from the beginning to the end, from birth to death. I have always wished to make literature, which is a nonreversible art, a reversible one. Therefore, my novels have no end in the classical meaning of the word."

>   Milorad Pavić, "The Beginning and the End
>   of Reading—The Beginning and the End
>   of the Novel" (142)

TABLE OF CONTENTS
(OR, DVD MENU)

Preamble · Behind the Ob-Scenes (or, Confronting the Preamble)   page xiii

Logos (λόγος) · The Obtuse Sense of the Scene · Methodos (μέθοδος) · A Background Check · A Program Without a Program · Dedication · Acknowledgments · Image Permissions

Chaste Cinema I?   page 1

Short Cuts: Cut to One. Cut to Two. Cut to Three · Scanning the Cuts: Installation 1, or Imagined Interviews, DVD One (Shaffer and Forman, *Amadeus*, Canonization). Installation 2, DVD Two (Hal Hartley, *Henry Fool*, Pedagogy). Installation 3, DVD Three+ (John Waters, *Multiple Maniacs*, Chaste Rape in Divine Places) · Cut To Paste: Writing flux aside flux on "a Riemann surface"

Chaste Cinema II?   page 69

Helke Sander's *Liberators Take Liberties*: Research (Facts, Statistics, Testimony). Further Testimony (German and Russian). The Master Narrative (A Pre-meditation). Resistance. Counter-Resistance. Meditations · Pagan Meditations (Eros) · Aphrodite, The Shadow Narrative I · Virginie Despentes and Coralie Trinh Thi's *Baise-Moi*, The Shadow Narrative II · Alain Resnais's *Hiroshima Mon Amour*, The Mourning Narrative: Eros Redux. Exemplars of "A Life." Sensation (or "Bicycle-less neo-realism"). Unmourning. Antimemory.

Chaste Cinema III+?   page 153

Reading and Writing Revenge Fantasies: Wendy Hesford (Margie Strosser's *Rape Stories*) · At First Viewing · Subsequent Viewings · Interruptions as Other Viewings (*Memento*) · A Peculiar (Now Impertinent) Reading

Excursus · The Assessment-Test Event   page 187

Alternate Endings with Rebeginnings?   page 199

Irreversibility (Gaspar Noé's *Irréversible*) · Reversible Destiny · Multiply Principles, Fly towards Transversals

Easter Eggs   page 209

Dominique Laporte's The Irreparable, as the object of loss. · Giorgio Agamben's The Irreparable, as hope in what is without remedy.

Deleted Scenes   page 215

Works Cited   page 219

PREAMBLE
BEHIND THE OB-SCENES
(OR, CONFRONTING THE PREAMBLE)

Logos (λόγος)

Ob scene: 1590s, "offensive to the senses, or to taste and refinement," from M.Fr. obscène, from L. obscenus "offensive," especially to modesty, originally "boding ill, inauspicious," perhaps from ob "onto" (see ob-) + caenum "filth." Meaning "offensive to modesty or decency" is attested from 1590s.

Online Etymology Dictionary

When we read, it is not ours to absorb all that is written. Our thoughts are jealous and they constantly blank out the thoughts of others, for there is not room enough in us for two scents at one time.

Milorad Pavić, *Dictionary of the Khazars*

As historians are well aware...the passage from promiscuity to modesty cannot occur without a refinement of the sense of smell that entails a lowering of the threshold of tolerance for certain odors.

Dominique Laporte, *Histoire de la merdre (Prologue)*

The Obtuse Sense of the Scene
(the writer's attempts and expectations)

This book—based on an *imagined* DVD list of extras (i.e., supplements) rather than a traditional book's table of contents (i.e., discontents)—is composed of a series of beginnings.[1] Transversally arranged. Both vertically and horizontally. But obtusely. At different angles. The general theme is *cinema* (cinematics) *and sexual violence* (rape).[2] And yet, the theme—a general economy of a theme—is to

---

1 This work is a sequel, if not also a prequel, to *Sexual Violence in Western Thought and Writing: Chaste Rape* (Palgrave, 2011).

2 On the matter of "cinema (cinematics)," I have in mind a number of citations, but especially Weiss' *Cinematics*. As Harry Rand points out, Weiss's novelistic discussion with "virtual co-authors" makes the "conversation … strange" (349). Rand interrupts much of his discussion with statements made by five of his colleague-friends (at times as many as three on a page) without even bothering to counter-argue the charges against him. I admire this approach. Rand, however, writes: "One wonders what pangs of intellectual integrity or masochism moved Weiss to include this remark, without acting to rectify the lacunae that prompted it" (349; cf. Berleant). Additionally, see Steigler, *Technics and Time,* 3; Doane; Shaviro, *Cinematic Body*. As for Post Cinematics (without or with a hyphen), I have in mind Shaviro's *Post Cinematic Affect*. Also, see "Roundtable Discussion. The Post-Cinematic in Paranormal Activity and Paranormal Activity 2. With Julia Leyda, Nicholas Rombes, Steven Shaviro, and Therese Grisham (moderator)" at <http://www.lafuriaumana.it/index.php/locchio-che-uccide/385-roundtable-discussion-about-post-cinematic>. Kittler, "Man as a Drunken Town-Musician," discusses various national and methodical senses on the word "cinematics." Also, there is its opposite: "acinematic" (Lyotard, "Acinema"; e.g., see James Cahill; Ramdas).

On the matter of "sexual violence (rape)," I work, here, with Monique Plaza's "Our Damages." (Cf. Hengehold's "Immodest" and Žižek's *Violence* 1–8; cf. Ann Cahill, 15–49.) My approach, therefore, is a wide scope, including *harassment, assault, rape,* and most assuredly *torture*. My understanding of *rape* and *torture* as sexual violence is informed not only by Plaza but even more so by Kate Millett's thinking in *The Basement*, which I discuss at length in the introduction and in chapter two in *Sexual Violence*.

begin again with a remix of such assemblages as *Chaste Rape / Divine Filth*, as well as Sacred / Profane.³ All folded and wrapped up in the name of *Chaste Cinematics*. These are paradoxes that are exceptionally perverse, when described in detail.⁴

Intermittently, I have imagined this book as a *shooting script with voluminous production notes and imaginary storyboards* toward a film that is, in fact, produced and yet

---

3 Which are not binaries. Alone. For they remix together. Yet, traditional philosophy would keep these proximities widely separate. Simply recall the basic principles of traditional philosophy: identification, not-contradiction, and the excluded third. As Henry Miller writes, however, "I love everything that flows" together (*Tropic* 257-58).

To begin again: *Chaste Rape* refers to a book by Stephanie Jed, titled *Chaste Thinking*, which is about Humanists and their Chaste Thinking about rape. (*Chaste Thinking*, consequently, becomes *Chaste Rape* as the subtitle of my most recent book *Sexual Violence*.) *Divine Filth* is the title of a book by Bataille (a collection of notes, introduced and translated by Mark Sptizer). In "'The Old Mole'," Bataille adds to the dichotomy the "eagle" and the "mole" (see *Visions* 32-44). Within each title, as well as in other dichotomies, there is a dialectical tension. However, this tension is not merely "dialectical" with its vertical drive but also "diatactical" with a horizontal drive bringing about reflexive thinking (see White, *Tropics* 4). The diatactical resists any third toward a synthesis or transcendence. As for the *Sacred* and *Profane*, I have in mind Mircea Eliade, but also Emile Durkheim's earlier work, *Elementary Forms*, and Giorgio Agamben's later works, *Homo Sacer* and *Profanations*.

Wonderfully complicating what is generally said here, however, is Nancy, who writes: "The sacred ... signifies the separate, what is set aside, removed, cut off. In one sense, then, religion and the sacred are opposed, as the bond is opposed to the cut. In another sense, religions can no doubt be represented as securing a bond with the separated sacred. But in yet another sense, the sacred is what it is only through its separation, and there is no bond with it. There is then, strictly speaking, no religion of the sacred. The sacred is what, of itself, remains set apart, at a distance, and with which one forms no bond (or only a very paradoxical one). It is what one cannot touch (or only by a touch without contact).... One attempt to form a bond with the sacred occurs in sacrifice.... Where sacrifice ceases, so does religion" (*Ground* 1; cf. 3-4).

4 See Zoe Gross on "Excremental Ecstasy [and] Divine Defecation." Cf. Kristeva's discussion of abjection in *Powers of Horror*.

never released in any form for public or private viewing.⁵ In its absence, however, I think that *the film* is nonetheless *imagined* and *meditated* on and casuistically sketched into the form of a fugue in constant flux. After all, my *imagined* task here is *meditation* through *remediation*. I say "imagined" as in images—film images—a third sense of filmic images. Present, yet k/not (see Barthes, "Third").

This book implicitly deals with my attempts, therefore, to understand further how I might rethink what has been thought and disseminated on sexual violence, this time around, in cinema. Previously, I have interrogated why *Western* thinkers have continued to embrace the myths of pagan gods, raping mortal women, as founding *representative anecdotes* for the establishment of city states, nations, and eventually psychoanalysis.⁶ With all based on a series of templates for an original trauma. Apparently, the dis-

---

5   The exemplary, suppressed film that I have in mind is *The Day the Clown Cried*, which was produced (1972), yet never released. Jerry Lewis plays Helmut Doork, a clown in the Holocaust and finally in a Nazi concentration camp, leading children to their death. According to lore, Lewis is the only one who has a copy. View, however, a discussion about the film <http://www.youtube.com/watch?v=U2nUgPvgO18>. And the shooting script <http://www.dailyscript.com/scripts/the_day_the_clown_cried.html>.

6   E.g., as stated in the Preface to *Sexual Violence*, I have in mind: The rape of Korê and the wandering of Demeter, leading to the founding of Athens; the rape of Leda, giving us Helen and Clytemnestra; the rape of Helen, giving us Aeneas and Livy's histories; the rape of the Vestal (Rhea Silvia), issuing the twins, Romulus and Remus, and Rome; the rape, or *abduction*, of the Sabine Women, bringing forth the Roman people; the rape of Lucretia, bringing forth the Republic; the rapes in the Hebrew Bible (Yamada); the Chaste Rape of Mary, ending the Roman Empire and issuing Christ; and the rape of women, as well as of men and children, up to and including yesterday's newspaper, which is taking place everywhere, now. In other words, what is established (as a point of stasis), by way of rape narratives, is *community*.

ease creates its own spin-off cure, becoming an immunology. Such is *the work of the negative* (see Green). Rape in some incipient, pathological way contributes to legitimacy.[7]

---

[7] Cf. Representative Todd Akin (6-term member of Congress) *NYTimes*, August 19, 2002. "Senate Candidate Provokes Ire with 'Legitimate Rape' Comment." <http://www.nytimes.com/2012/08/20/us/politics/todd-akin-provokes-ire-with-legitimate-rape-comment.html>.

Methodos (μέθοδος)

My intention is *to turn* Aristotle's methodology, specifically, Aristotle's tripartite division of *knowing* (theory), *doing* (practice, pedagogy), and *making* (euretics), into *reversible arts*.[8] Polymorphous-perverse arts.[9] I begin again, here and hereafter, therefore, with Vilem Flusser, who states: "Narrative is no longer the model for historical events. That is film. From this point on, one can speed up events, watch them in slow motion, and work them into flashbacks. Most important, however, one can cut the tape of Western history and splice it back together. I propose cutting out the twelve hundred years between...."[10]

Hence, some production notes: I would cut the tape of narrative history founded on rape narratives. Disrupt its chronological flow. Even more so. I would accept *the chronology of water*.[11] Accept *the chronology of chance*.[12] I would work with a temporality of *too early* and *too late*. In doing so, let us recall and apply the rhetoric of Sig-

---

8 That is, unknowing, undoing, and unmaking. For Aristotle, see *Metaphysics*, Bk E (VI, 1025b-). For "reversible arts," see Pavić, "Beginning."

9 Are we having fun yet? Are you getting dizzy yet?

10 (132; cf. 24-25, 133-37, 145-46). In cinema there is nothing but the cut. Cinema is made by way of cuts. Of course. But there is *Cut...The Unseen Cinema*. (A pharmakonic cut.) See Baxter Philips.

11 This is the title of Lidia Yuknavitch's memoir, which is associated with film throughout the short cuts among the memories captured by Yukavitch. Towards the end, as a new beginning, of the memoir, she says: "If this is the story of my life, no wonder it's in fragments. It's got a messed chronology because that's how I feel about life—it's not linear. It moves in fits and starts, doubles back, repeats or extends an image. I thought if my life has a chronology, it's the chronology of water—the way water carved the earth, the way water carries us into the world, the way that we are made of water, the way that water retreats or returns. I had...found my central metaphor" (300).

12 See Michael Haneke's *71 Fragments of a Chronology of Chance*. 1994.

mund Freud's *Nachträglichkeit*. But without a necessity of an originary trauma.[13] I would view and experience the tensions of cinematic long shots with the camera too close and too far, as found in Jean-Marie Straub and Danièle Huillet's *Too Early, Too Late*.[14]

But let us also get real! After all, once the mythic gods and *the* God are found dead, it is rape by other means. By human beings, *as it has always been*. Or by *Ancient Aliens*, as is touted on the History Channel.[15] And yet, our sense of thinking, nonetheless, continues in a connection with the gods and especially the God. If only in terms of nihilism. What has always been narrated is the everydayness (the banality) of rape[16] that informs our canonical pedagogies.

What is known about history and its mistakes is that this, our history, founded on rape narratives is hysterically-obsessively repeated. Let us, therefore, rethink Ockham's razor and the law of parsimony with a perverse razor (Flusser 132). Let us, even more so, contrary to George Santayana, *add* and *insert* the contradictory notion

---

13 Is such even possible? It is a challenge I would take. Cf. LaCapra.

14 For *Nachträglichkeit* (variously translated as deferred action, belatedness, afterwardness), see Freud (*SE* I, 353-54; *SE* XVII, 7-122); cf., Nägele, *Reading* 3-5, 169-201, 215-17. For a discussion of Huillet-Straub's *Too Early, Too Late*, see Rosenbaum's "Intense Materialism."

15 The PBS show *Ancient Aliens* on The History Channel originally ran for three seasons. In popular culture there is the notion that aliens (i.e., *extraterrestrial creatures) rape human beings. As a popular case in point, Daniel Thomas* ("Dan") O'Bannon and Ronald Shusett, who scripted the early storyline of *Alien* (1979), speak of alien rapes. O'Bannon in the documentary *Alien Evolution* (2001) says: "This is a movie about alien interspecies rape." For popular culture discussions, see <http://www.imdb.com/title/tt0078748/faq>.

16 Cf. "The banality of rape," in Sarah J. McCarthy (15). The allusion here, of course, is to Hannah Arendt *(Eichmann in Jerusalem: A Report on the Banality of Evil*, 1963).

of the necessity of having *to forget* a narrative history of rapes so that we do not repeat its mistakes. Remembering is repetition with subtle permutations and recombinations. *And let us realize* that it is time (in an untimely time) to cut, cut, cut, scramble, etc., the rape narratives. To destroy the templates. By any means compossible.[17] And, thereafter, call for George Bataille's (Immanuel Kant's) sovereign laughter.[18]

---

17 This logic of compossibility is initially put forth by Leibniz (allowing for *one* best possible world) and thereafter reconsidered by Borges and Deleuze as a paralogic of compossibility (allowing for countless incompossible, i.e., co-extensive, worlds). Hence, I will *tarry with the negative* on my own terms (see Hegel, *Phenomenology* on "determinate negation" and "absolute negation" (e.g., 50-51, 58-66, 111-19). Cf. Žižek, *Tarrying*.

18 For the linkage between Kant and Bataille (via laughter), see Nancy, *Discourse* (130-39).

A Background Check

In this, my second effort at writing about sexual violence, I am situating myself, as in a standpoint, within Christopher J. Koch's novel (1978) and within Peter Weir's film based on that novel (1982). Yes, I am alluding to *A Year of Living Dangerously*. (Are you still with me? Would you alternately follow a ventriloquist? With a puppet?[19]) I am placing myself in that novel/film, so as to think and to write from both works (or rather, *ways*[20]), which are significantly different. I am placing myself in that mix to think and to write about sexual violence in cinema, though this novel and film only touch on the topic. I am taking as my persona *Guy Hamilton*, who has his *first assignment*, as a foreign correspondent in Indonesia (1965), and who is befriended by the dwarf Billy Kwan.

The theme of *Living Dangerously* pivots on betrayals, in the land of insurrection. Hamilton is played by Mel Gibson. Kwan, played by Linda Hunt. I cannot forget how Kwan is sacrificed for the story. For community. It is near impossible to determine between Hamilton and Kwan who is the puppet (the Western view), who the shadows (the Eastern view), for they are imminently reversible. For me, there is a Bataillean economy and a Kantian syncopation at work in the novel/film (confusing, mixing, repurposing the two into a non-synthetic third). As Kwan recalls: "all is clouded by desire" (Koch 75), which brings to our Western mind, the paradoxical sacred shadow play, the *Wayang Kulit* (see Campbell).

This background check is confronted with even more concerns, given my approach through a string of paradoxes: divinity and filth, sacred and profane. In Koch's

---

19 Cf. Žižek, *A Year of Dreaming Dangerously*.

20 Cf. Heidegger, *Parmenides*, xiii.

novel, there is such a paradoxical scene, virtually one among many. Kwan explains what is another paradox for Westerners—"we worship shadows, we worship foulness"—but Hamilton does not know what to make of the mix (222). My own thoughts, however, as *Hamilton*, focus on a remix. A repurposing. Of shadows and foulness. My own thoughts, specifically, focus on *what we can hope for* in rethinking and rewriting such paradoxes, driven by desire. My own thoughts focus *on coherent contradictions*.[21]

My assignment is to find ways into this subject (of abjection)—namely, unorthodox ways that are at best eccentric. To reintroduce the topic in scattered ways. Each a separate turn. On the wheel of meditations. The writing of this book is, in so many ways, another *Test Drive* (Ronell). And yet, I am attempting all this without a hammer or a tuning fork (Nietzsche, *Twilight* 21-22). I am turning and refolding the problem of rape over and over against itself, by way of unlikely perspectives. In hopes of discovering less the cause (the philosophical precept of negation itself, which is known), but more so remedies (the sophistic exception of denegation itself, which is unknown).

I cannot accomplish this end, for a new beginning, however, by myself. In writing this book—a novelistic book, or rather a shooting script—I am attempting to bring the readers, you, also into the writing and thinking of the book. I provoke and invoke the readers, you, in terms of self-reflective questions as well as assignments in hopes of an eventual life-enhancing assignation. All of this is

---

21 Again, a mix of coherence/contradiction. For Flusser, such is a "sophistic paradox" (143-49). While the precepts of reason must resolve paradoxes and exclude contradictions, desire is driven to include them. My concern is what can we *make* of them (through euretics)? For examples, see Derrida who speaks of a "coherent contradiction," in "Structure, Sign, and Play" (279); Ulmer, "The Euretics of Alice's Valise."

attempted throughout the book but most self-reflexively in the "Excursus: The Assessment-Test Event."

Which is to say: This is not just one more film- or cinema-studies book, but an "extras" book.[22] To supplement films and videos that I refer to in *our* discussions. And those that you, too, I presume, have questions/concerns about.

To add to this impossible stumbling—syncopating—giggling—book, to the broken syntax, causing the leaps, of destabilizing thoughts, I will work from a grounding of *base materialism*—yes, Bataille's materialism—which can bring us again back to the paradox of *Divine Filth*.[23] And ask, namely, *how* is it that rape-abjection (filth, excluded thirds) gets associated with the Divine in film, in a community, *making for a Chaste Cinematics*?

In an improper-proper name, I will begin, again in the background—unworking in the foreground—with Bataille's notions for grounding, or rather ungrounding (*Abgrund*).[24] Why? Because it is Bataille's post-philosoph-

---

22 I am alluding to *extras* in a DVD and in a film itself, along with everything else in between. It is an experiment in establishing personae to think and write from.

23 Stoekl in his introduction to Bataille's *Visions of Excess* describes Bataille's paradox, or un-resolvable tension, as situated "in an impossible neutral space, between absolute knowledge and its implacably hostile double.... Bataille is not simply privileging a new object (excrement, flies, ruptured eyes, the rotten sun, etc.) over the old one (the head, the king, spirit, mind, vision, the sun of reason, etc.)" (xiii). Cf. Nikolopoudou.

24 Lest I give the impression that Bataille originates, so to speak, this whole theme of grounding ungrounding itself, especially as a creeping base materialism, we must keep in mind Immanuel Kant's role in recognizing a *syncopation* at work in unworking an equilibrium as well as a decidability in philosophical thinking. Many others, far too many to list and discuss here, have noted this linkage between Kant and Bataille. But I would at least cite Nancy's *The Discourse of the Syncope* (1976, trans. 2008). Cf. Catherine Clément, *La Syncope*. The *syncopation* in history (time/space) or syncope parallels references to *event (Ereignis), caesura, finitude,*

ical notion of a *base materialism* that destabilizes binaries, fixedness, and brings forth excluded thirds.²⁵ That brings about the syncopation in history. That brings forth wild heterologies.²⁶ The other of the other. Again, base matter. Which I would now refer to as *a scene of writing images*²⁷ that would turn all into potential *ob scenes*. About these, heretofore, excluded thirds (turds). In flesh and blood, in thinking, and in writing. The very topic itself remains forever to haunt. Hence, living dangerously in this *haunt* that can only remain unknowable.²⁸ Hence, *perhaps*—that is, through chance—we will have eventually come to grasp the necessity to study the unknowable, the *haunt*, or as Bataille writes: *The Unfinished System of Nonknowledge*. About sexual violence. As if, capable of ever being finished (see Nikolopoudou).

Perhaps, all that we can accomplish is the question itself: unnamely, *why* is it that a *repressed third, or a third*

---

etc. Therefore, in this preamble, when I am disgusting [Sic] Bataille, I am also discussing Kant. Both bring an irrepressible *laughter* to the table. Under no circumstances, however, is this to think the end of philosophy.

25 My reference to a "post-philosophy" is not, again, the end of philosophy. On the contrary, "post-" is perpetually the beginning of philosophy. (See Nancy, *Discourse* 15-16.) For Bataille's own discussion of *base materialism*, to start with, see *Visions of Excess*, *Encyclopaedia Acephalica*, *Unfinished System*, *Absence of Myth*, and *Divine Filth*. For commentators, see Noys, Hollier and Allred, Grindon, Stoekl's *Politics* as well as Sweedler's *Dismembered Community*. And Gross on Bataille and others. Venture out on your own. In the neighborhood. Bataille is often considered under the rubrics of mysticism, surrealism, and de Sade. See, e.g., for mysticism, Hollywood, "Bataille and Myticism" and *Sensible Ecstasy*; Hussey. For surrealism and de Sade, see Bataille, *Absence of Myth*; Weiss, *Aesthetics of Excess*.

26 See Pefanis, *Heterology* (chaps. 3 and 4).

27 The notion of a *scene of writing images* is best understood by reading and studying D. N. Rodowick's expansive and thorough discussion of the search for *filmic thinking and writing* (*Reading the Figural*, 76-106).

28 See Chamberlain (100), for the haunt as "unknowable."

figure, returns repeatedly, most specifically and strangely as a "product" of rape and torture?[29] Returns as shadows. A product that Jean-Paul Sartre and Page duBois suggest as becoming a new "species."[30] This, too, is our primary concern.

Note: If you, the reader, continue reading, it will take more than your reading. This is a writing for activism. About this matter (base matter), nothing more will be said. This foreground will now become the background. Yet, manifesting itself in the shadows. With their own shadows. Which again bring to mind, "the sacred shadow play."[31]

---

29 I have documented this phenomenon of thirds in *Sexual Violence*. See in the index to that book the term "third figures." Especially important is the beginning of Chapter 2, in which I stress how Kate Millett is most concerned with the question of the "product" being made through rape and torture in *The Basement*. Additionally, see Page duBois and Simone de Beauvoir in the index. These thirds continue in this book, *Chaste Cinematics*.

30 For Sartre, see "Victory" in *The Question* (xxxii, xlii), and for DuBois, *Torture* (153).

31 Leonard, in his dissertation (August 2003) and later in his book, *The Cinematic Mystical Gaze*, points to Ventura's *LA Weekly* discussion of Weir's film *A Year of Living Dangerously*. I quote Leonard's quote and insertions in Ventura's insights in terms of his discussion of *shadows* within his own quotes of Weir. Leonard quotes: "Rarely has a director so clearly stated his aesthetic: 'The shadows are souls and the screen is heaven', and 'You must watch their shadows, not the puppets.' In the West we want answers to everything, but in the Way-Yang no such final answers exist.' Instead, it teaches us that 'the forces of light and dark' are forever in furious 'balance.'... [Weir states], 'I don't care about the pictures, I care about the content'... Billy Kwan is a holy man. He seeks 'the unmet friend.' He believes that you must 'add your light to the sum of light'. 'The unseen is all around us', he says, and then firmly suggests, to the likes of you and I, that 'we must give love to whomever God has placed in our path.' Billy actually lives these things and, as Jesus long ago proved, there is nothing more dangerous. Billy also makes mistakes, and there is absolutely nothing more dangerous than making mistakes on this level of being" (Dissertation, 27; Ventura, 5)

xxvi CHASTE CINEMATICS

A Program without a Program:

The chapters (as *extras*) are presented as an unfolding of Chaste Cinema I? II? III+? But they can be reshuffled, remixed, repurposed, and read in any dis/order. Before all, they are less an argument and more a contestation—each in its own way (wave) a meditation. In no certain order. The *first* that is listed takes an unsettled look at rape with a remix of divinity and filth, sacred and profane, eschatology and scatology. Toward a community without a community. An *inoperative community* (Nancy). Or rather a "Cavalcade of Perversions" (Waters). It is this so-called *first* section that is indebted to Bataille's thinking and unthinking. The *second* takes again an unsettled look and a reading of one documentary film and a scholarly discussion, in a roundtable, concerning the film. The *third+* takes still more of an unsettled look at rape, memory, revenge—a non-linear narrative: one video of rape interrupted by a film of *memento mori*.

The so-called chapters—rather *extras*, read out of this numerical sequence—can bring about an *intensity*. To spur and stir our readings. Thinkings. Meditating. Writings. From desert (sand) to waves (ocean); vice versa. Or from oasis to mirage; mirage to oasis. Perpetually unsettled. To remain open.

A reminder: The *extras* are written for test drives. Each extra has *its own introduction*. Do not buy into any one of the *extras*; rather, continue testing the drives (cf. Lyotard, "Acinema"). Searching and following a path for three+ scents at a time. At kairotic times. As (Abbas) Kiarostami would have it.

Now, forget everything that I have written in the preamble! And begin again, reading the "extras" up and down and transversally.

Dedication to

The Inoperative, Unavowable, Coming Filmic Community/Cavalcade

Acknowledgments

I begin with my colleagues, my mentors: First, Wolfgang Schirmacher, for the Media and Communication Division at the European Graduate School. Then, Giorgio Agamben, Yves-Alain Bois, Victor Burgin, Manuel De Landa, D. Diane Davis, Claire Denis, Atom Egoyan, Barbara Hammer, Friedrich Kittler, Peter Greenaway, Claude Lanzmann, Sylvère Lotringer, Jean-Luc Nancy, Gasper Noé, Avital Ronell, Gregory Ulmer, Agnes Varda, John Waters, Krzysztof Zanussi, and Slovaj Žižek. I thank them all—as well as each of them separately—to varying degrees, for our seminars and conversations on cinema as well as on sexual violence and so much more. Q: An Oasis or a Mirage? A: Both! Our collective opportune moments were made possible for the last fifteen years or so during our summer gatherings, in the Alps, in Saas-Fee, Switzerland.

Additionally, I thank my colleague and mentor Luanne Frank for help with the German language in Helke Sander's works.

I thank the *Goethe Institute* in Chicago for a copy of Helke Sander's *Liberators Take Liberties*; thank *Women Make Movies* for a copy of Margie Strosser's video *Rape Stories*; and thank the *Inter-Library Loan office* at Clemson University for tracking down and providing necessary works. I thank especially Camille Copper.

I would also like to thank Chris Piuma and Eileen Joy with their help making this work into a extraordinary book, that is, a Punctum Book.

Image Permissions

I thank the following for permissions to reprint images:

page xxvi The sacred shadow play: *Wayang kulit performance, Museum Wayang, Jakarta* photograph by Wikipedia user Jpatokal, distributed under a CC BY-SA 3.0 license.

page 99 "Russian Soldier Tries to Buy Bicycle from Woman in Berlin, 1945." Anonymous photo, seen in *BeFreier und Befreite* (1992). © Hulton-Deutsch Collection/CORBIS.

page 190 Divine raped by Lobstora. From *Multiple Maniacs* (1970). Photo by Lawrence Irvine. © Dreamland Productions (1970). Permission granted by John Waters.

page 191 Unused publicity still from *When Dinosaurs Ruled the Earth* (1970), Hammer Films. Believed to be out of copyright.

CHASTE CINEMA I?

> Lord, make me a great composer! Let me celebrate your glory through music—and be celebrated myself! Make me famous through the world, dear God! Make me immortal! After I die let people speak my name forever with love for what I wrote! In return I vow I will give you my chastity.
>
> Old Salieri, *Amadeus* (Scene 19)

> ...chastity is a flux.
>
> Gilles Deleuze, *Dialogues* (90)

To begin again—ever again—I return to the question of Chaste Cinematics to discuss three films from an array of film economies, with all three directed, supposedly, by biological males: *Amadeus* (Miloš Forman, 1984, 2002), *Henry Fool* (Hal Hartley, 1997), and *Multiple Maniacs* (John Waters, 1970). I discuss each film in terms of Chaste Rapes.[1] I variously approach the films by ways of "extras," behind-the-scenes commentaries often found as *supplements* in DVDs—specifically, three such commentaries—one for each film—in the form of imaginary polylogues among people involved in the making of the films, including the directors.[2] In addition, there are commentaries from

---

1   See my *Sexual Violence in Western Thought and Writing: Chaste Rape*.

2   I am avoiding the notion of an *imaginary dialogue* for a word spelled $p+o+l+y+l+o+g+u+e$. The term is claimed by many users. But my own inevitable misuse of the term is from Julia Kristeva's practices. Kristeva,

people whose writings and discussions have shaped my thinking about *Chaste Cinematics*. I call this supplementary para-genre *DVD installations*.[3] But I could as well call them "refrains" (cf. Deleuze, *Dialogues* xiii; Deleuze and Guattari, *Thousand* 310–50). For some readers, these installations would be but another impertinence or at best a trick of metacinema as well as metafiction. Let us suppose, however, that these conversations are fluxes (struggles and play) recombining with other fluxes.[4]

I find that the directors and screenwriters, as well as editors, of the three films progressively merge canonicity (establishing a canonical text of excess) and pedagogy

---

as best as I can tell, originally published her comments on polylogue in *Tel Quel* 57 (Spring 1974): 19–55. Thereafter, reprinted in her *Polylogue* (171–220). Paris: Seuil, 1977. And again reprinted in her *Desire in Language* (159–209). Each iteration is under a different title. Entitlement. Illustrating the point-cum-beside-the-point unravelling of poly-logoi? In each, Kristeva discusses *H*, which is a novel by Phillipe Sollers. Besides the influence of Kristeva on my thinking, I am, in arrangement (*dispositio* or *taxis*), influenced by Robert Altman and his film *Short Cuts* and by Raymond Carver's stories. Carver! I would like to see myself collaborating with their collaboration.

3 There is, here, added footage of the behind-the-scenes making of *Amadeus* (both versions), with interactive menus, production notes, cast/director highlights, theatrical trailers, scene access, languages, subtitles. Hartley and Waters's films, to date, do not have these additional features. I perversely add my installations to the three. Water's film remains legally in VHS format.

4 Simply put, flux for my purposes takes One actuality and turns it to radical multiple actualities. Reel-alities. A Deleuze sampler: "To write has no other function: to be a flux which combines with other fluxes—all the minority-becomings of the world. A flux is something intensive, instantaneous and mutant—between a creation and a destruction. It is only when a flux is deterritorialized that it succeeds in making its conjunction with other fluxes, which deterritorialize it in their turn, and vice versa" (*Dialogues* 50). The fluxes composing chapter 1 continue, intermittently, through the other chapters to the last excursus and beyond. At times, the fluxes manifest themselves as *test drives*. Gone wild.

(teaching a perverse lesson) with acts of Chaste Cinematics of Rape (trafficking in communicative exchanges by way of women, and yet, reaching for a third exchange, by ways of the obtuse, the neutral). I say "progressively," for there is no overt, but implicit act of rape in Miloš Forman's, or Peter Shaffer's, *Amadeus*. I say "obtuse" and "neutral" in the sense given by Roland Barthes ("Third Meaning [Sense]"). This generic work called "Amadeus" itself is exceptionally fruitful to deal with, for it has gone through many revisions as a *play*—with productions in England and the United States—and exists in two versions as a *film*, the theatrical release and the so-called Director's Cut, restoring twenty minutes that had been *cut*.[5] Again, the trans-formations: play, film, cut. *Amadeus*, in its avatars, should remind us—and this is the gift of fluxes—that there is a compossible world of *Amadeus*, with a radical infinite finitude of incompossible (co-extensive) worlds of this much-revised story of master and divine rape.

As we progress (virtually, regress) across the three films, however, the act of rape becomes less implied, more emphatic, until we get to John Waters's film *Multiple Maniacs* in which rape takes three different forms, all represented as *perverse* "Divine" rapes. All three films, however, represent rape in a (bizarre) Chaste Cinematic

---

5 See Shaffer's preface and film introduction to *Amadeus* (the play), for the history of the play (specifically, *Peter Shaffer's Amadeus. With a New Introduction to the Film Edition by the Author*. NY: Signet, New American. 1984). When commenting on *Amadeus*, I designate the citation from this edition of the play and in terms of Act, Scene, and page numbers. See the Works Cited for two other separately published versions. I also intermittently cite passages from the film shooting scripts (by scene number). See the Works Cited for the scripts that I work as well as play with. In all cases, however, I have cross-checked with the film itself, to make sure that the script is as it is in the film. When commenting on the Director's cut, I also refer to the film itself.

manner. All three films, moreover, are informed with a deep concern for the absolute (the Divine)—for immanence, for subjectivity, for immortality, and for a sacrificial and rather perverse-Chaste attitude toward an economy of community fixed, fixated, on rape. All three films recapitulate, in various ways, the very mixed etymology of the word "Chastity" as well as "caste" itself.[6]

As we revisit the films, we will see how the absolute as well as immanence informs a notion of divine rape. Moreover, as we revisit the films with their co-extensive possibilities (i.e., incompossibilities), however, we will also see them as less totalized and more fragmented, or more *powdery*. Yes, *powdery*! With the death of God, the desert, or nihilism, continues to grow. As Zarathustra teaches: "Wilderness grows: woe unto him who harbors wildernesses!" (Nietzsche, *Thus Spake* 417; cf. Heidegger, *What Is* 29–30, 49–51, 55; Nikolopoulou 112–16). Therefore, though perhaps paradoxically, as nihilism moves from *passive* to *active* and then on to *accomplished* nihilism, radical multiplicity also grows (see Vattimo; cf. Steigler's discussion of negentropy in *Technics 1* 54, 61, 68–69). Throughout the

---

6 A reminder: My use of the word "Chaste" and its variations is borrowed and recycled from Stephanie Jed's title *Chaste Thinking*, which deals with rape and the cover-up of rape in especially Humanistic thinking. *A Test Drive* (Ronell). Your first major assignment. A study of etymologies in flux. Including conductive paralogics. I will leave it to you, readers, to conjugate the various proto-meanings of and allusions to "Chastity." Including improper proper names. Keep in mind that when conjugating the paradigm, so much unrealizable is far left over (see Barthes, *Neutral* 6–7). So to repeat: I leave it to you to determine or over-determine: see <http://www.etymonline.com/index.php?search=chastity> along with the associations of cleansing, innocence, integrity, chaste, incest, honesty, honor. And then caste: <http://www.etymonline.com/index.php?term=caste&allowed_in_frame=0>. While you are at it, check out the etymology of *rape* <http://www.etymonline.com/index.php?term=rape>. What is rape's relationship with *turnip*? What is the folk etymo-logic that connects the two? Three?

three films, there is a flux-movement toward an *accomplished third figure*.

In an attempt to balance the overly masculine and eccentric gender-bending of the cinema-shadows[7] to be cast on the discussion in this chapter, I mirror chapter 2 opposite this chapter: Therein I discuss the controversial film *BeFreier und Befreite* (by Helke Sander, a German female director, 1992) that documents the liberation of women in Berlin from fascism, and yet the mass rape of them by the occupation soldiers in 1945; hence, as the title in German suggests in English: the liberators take (took) liberties. (But this mirroring is not a mere contrast in a male versus a female director. The males succeed in over-coming their selves as well as the females, in their own different ways. Just as commentators on the film reach for a third, non-transcendental way to rethink the event.) Along with Sander's documentary, I will in passing *test drive* (Ronell) the equally controversial film *Baise-Moi* (written and directed by Virginie Despentes and Coralie Trinh Thi, 2000, based on Despentes's novel, 1995). *Baise-Moi* is for me the most reactionary film on rape and murder that I could find as an exemplar. And yet, is it a reactionary film? Hence, the call for a *test drive*. The overall mirroring will work in this manner: Forman-Hartley-Waters → || ← Sander-(Despentes). Think of mirroring as a series of beginnings or redoublings. A multiplication of fluxes. In the history of the word "Chastity."

---

7   By way of a shadow, the balance I search for is in terms of Nietzsche's "mid-day; moment of the shortest shadow; end of the longest error; zenith of mankind; INCIPIT ZARATHUSTRA" (*Twilight* 41). Cf. Zupancic, 27. But, apparently and perhaps inevitably, the shortest shadow becomes the error of the longest shadow. Hence, in ch. 2, possibly, the necessity of the inessential *shadow narratives*, which I previously mentioned in the *Preamble* to this point and thereafter beyond: It is shadows casting shadows until the end.

Given all this mirroring, there may be the risk of a "desert of mirrors" (Abé, *Face* 232). My mis/understanding, as I take my lead from Avital Ronell, however, is that the risk of mirrors is no longer a risk, for "we" as a community without a community, are "a community shattered and way past the mirror state of self-recuperation" (*Finitude's Score* 2).[8] And as I follow Jean-Luc Nancy, I think, "Maybe it is still true to say that 'the desert is growing.' However, the curtain has fallen on the luxuriance and fertilities by comparison with which our 'desert' could be measured.... The growing of the desert could indeed unveil for us [as it did for Kobe Abé's man in *Woman*] *an unknown space*, an unknown, excessive aridity of the sources of sense. The end of sources, the beginning of the dry *excess* of sense" (*Sense* 24; emphasis mine. Cf. Nancy, *Experience* 142–47. For Abé, see *Woman* 230–32). There are worlds, not the world. There are senses, not the sense. There are multiple scents. Pulsations. Fluxes. (Of still frames that remain intense.) Let us enter into the excess of compossible-incompossible worlds. Let us search in a polyphony (towards cacophony), in a polytheism (towards struggle, war, play) for the filmic, or third neutral meanings.[9] After all is said and undone, *all that is solid melts in the air*, which is *the experience of modernity*.[10]

---

8 cf. Nancy, *Inoperative Community* 71; Blanchot, *Unavowable Community*; Agamben, *Coming Community*).

9 Again, the *filmic*, along with the *obtuse*, refers to Barthes's third meaning (sense). And additionally refers to Barthes's *neutral* (*The Neutral* 6–7). This third (a turd) should not be confused with the syllogistic third figure. Also, my discussion of mirrors and desert seems to preclude the possibility, incompossibility, of "the desert of the real," which is established by Baudrillard and referred to in the film *Matrix*. See Baudrillard, *Simulacra* 1; Žižek, *Welcome* 15.

10 I am alluding *in italics* to Marshal Berman's book, in which he writes: "Others believe that the really distinctive forms of contemporary art and thought have made a quantum leap beyond all the diverse sensibilities of

modernism, and earned the right to call themselves 'post-modern.' I want to respond to these antithetical but complementary claims by reviewing the vision of modernity with which this book began. To be modern, I said, is to experience personal and social life as a maelstrom, to find one's world and oneself in perpetual disintegration and renewal, trouble and anguish, ambiguity and contradiction: to be part of a universe in which all that is solid melts into air. To be a modernist is to make oneself somehow at home in the maelstrom, to make its rhythms one's own, to move within its currents in search of the forms of reality, of beauty, of freedom, of justice, that its fervid and perilous flow allows" (*All That Is Solid*, 345–46). Berman's understanding of Modernism (Modernity), of course, is at odds with others' understandings but also with others' notions of Postmodernism. This disarray of understandings, therefore, is in flux itself, which requires, at least, some of us to remake ourselves perpetually somehow or other in an uncanny home in flux (cf. Marsh, Caputo, Westphal, *Modernity* 12, 15–17, 24–25; also Vidler, *Uncanny*). Obviously, however, the title of Berman's book is a direct reference to Marx and Engel's *Manifesto of the Communist Party*: They write: "All that is solid melts into air, all that is holy is profaned, and man is at last compelled to face with sober senses, his real conditions of life, and his relations with his kind" (5).

Short Cuts

> I took my "little movie" photographs for years without telling anybody. It all started with my obsession to have *a still* from one of my older films which was never taken on the set. I remembered Divine's face in the one moment [instant] *between* rape and miraculous intervention where he lived up to the spiritual side of his name, but I didn't have the picture to prove it. I took hundreds of shots off the TV monitor, *blundering* my way into photography the same way I *blundered* into films, until I finally produced the still I wanted.
>
> John Waters, *Director's Cut* (283; emphasis added)

> No one could scan the cut....
> Avital Ronell, *Crack Wars* (69)

> [A] finished finitude, infinitely finished ... occurs in an instant ... which means not within an instant, in the present time of an instant, but by a cut in the middle of the instant: the cut of freedom that unexpectedly comes up in this time and fills it.
>
> Jean-Luc Nancy, *The Experience of Freedom* (118)

In the first two films—*Amadeus* and *Henry Fool*—there is a typical bonding, a forming of community, between men at odds or in rivalry, while in the third—*Multiple Maniacs*—there is an atypical diffusion among freaks banding together for mayhem. All three films are located in homosocial space (Sedgwick). Or so I will say at first. But this space *as* homosocial is totalitarian, with the world *as* controlled by the O/one, or the exaggerated masculine itself. It is a world that must become, as Nancy would have it, "always the plurality of worlds: a constellation whose compossibility is identical with its fragmentation, the compactness of a powder of absolute fragments" (*Sense* 155). Or a powder of sand grains. ParaFragments. Crumbs.[11]

---

11 There is absolutely no connection whatsoever between the word "powder" here and the film *Powder* (1995).

Unlike Leibniz's compossible world that is dominated by the monad of God Himself (the divine, transcendental signifier), this world is without an archi-world to direct or limit incompossible (co-extensive) worlds. This world has no stasis point. In such a compossible world, there are not just men, nor just men and women—this is not to say, however, that there is no man or woman as such—but to say that there are singularities of sexual pluralities, or what some might call *a cavalcade of perversions*, or *third sexes* (cf. Nancy, *Corpus* 34–39; Fausto-Sterling).

Cut to One: In *Amadeus*, Antonio Salieri is a mediocre artist, yet the much celebrated court composer, while Mozart is a genius, yet unappreciated by his contemporaries (with the exception of Salieri), but is to be remembered and canonized as the great genius-artist of the court, the world, and heaven (at least, as Salieri recounts). While Amadeus is lucky with women, Salieri is not. (For his part, Salieri as a child promises God to remain Chaste if God would only give him great music to write, but God gives Amadeus both women and angelic music and Salieri nothing, at least, in most of the revisions [versions, incompossibilities] of the story.) As a result, Salieri curses God and promises to frustrate His attempts through "Amadeus" (meaning "love of God" or "beloved by God") or, if necessary, to murder Amadeus (suggested meaning a A mad [d]eus, or mad, perverse "love of God"). In both cases, the men share in a love-hate bond (Salieri-*God*-Amadeus, Salieri-*Music*-Amadeus, Salieri-*Katherina Cavalieri*-Amadeus) and in the success of (the) one. The sharing is emphasized further, when Salieri demands sex from Constanze (film, scene 74; play, Act 2, Scene 1: 79–80) in exchange for recommending Amadeus as the teacher of the Princess Elizabeth. But Salieri rejects Constanze and humiliates her when she returns to accept the bargain, just as he has the Emperor, Joseph II, also reject her husband, Amadeus, as a teacher of the Princess on the grounds that Amadeus "molested" one, if not more, of his piano students (film, scene 81; play, Act 2, Scene 2: 82).

This story line, comparable to *Henry Fool*, is inextricably entwined with sexual, though not always practiced, perversions. In some versions, Salieri gives up his chasteness and, against both God and Amadeus, beds Katherina, who remains, Salieri boasts, his "mistress for many years behind my good wife's back" (play 81). Though Amadeus had seduced Katherina (Act 1, Scene 8: 44, 46–47; Scene 10: 57), Salieri claims, "I soon erased in sweat the sense of his little body, the Creature's, preceding me" (Act 2, Scene 1: 81). But in the exchange between the two men, the traces remain to propel Salieri into acting against Amadeus. (In the first Installation that follows, I examine more fully how a perverse, Divine Rape brings the two composers together along with their women.)

At the end (a beginning), old Salieri is the narrator (when confessing his alleged murder of Mozart) of the grand story of Wolfgang *Amadeus* Mozart. In the very act of *confessing* this musical saint's story—in his hospital room—Old Salieri himself is *immortalized, canonized*, yet strangely *becoming* "the patron saint" of "mediocrities everywhere" (Act 2, Scene 18: 150). In a section that was cut from the script of the film and not re-added in the Director's Cut, Shaffer has Salieri say: "From now on no one will be able to speak of Mozart without thinking of me. Whenever they say Mozart with love, they'll have to say Salieri with loathing. And that's my immortality—at last! Our names will be tied together for eternity—his in fame and mine in infamy. At least it's better than the total oblivion he'd planned for me, your merciful God" (Scene 174). But it is clear from what remains in the text of the play, Salieri is not confessing his sins to Father Vogler; rather, he is putting forth an apologia (for his life): "[He comes downstage and addresses the audience directly.] This is now the very last hour of my life. You must understand me. Not forgive. I do not seek forgiveness. I was a good man, as the world calls good. What use was it to me? Goodness could not make me a good composer!...Was Mozart good? Goodness is nothing in the furnace of art. [Pause] On that dreadful Night... my life acquired a terrible and thrilling purpose. The blocking of God in one of His purest manifestations" (Act 2, Scene 1: 78).

While *Amadeus* in its various metamorphoses (incompossibilities) is this and that way and then altogether otherwise, *Henry Fool* has a stable story line, though there are deviations, as expected, from the shooting script in the film itself (see *HF* xxvi). What is especially interesting, however, by way of comparisons is that the character Henry Fool himself in two sections of the film script begins to speak of Leibnizean compossible and incompossible worlds for the characters of the story (see *HF* 67, 85) and equally interesting is that Hartley himself "think[s] of this story in terms of it having many sequels."[12] Let us turn to the story-film.

---

12 Hartley continues: "At the very beginning, I was thinking of *Henry Fool* being part of an epic series of movies about Henry. So when Fay lets Henry go off to Sweden at the end of the film, it opens up all sorts of possibilities" ("Responding" xviii). In fact, on the table of contents page, the screenplay is referred to as "Henry Fool, I." And as we have come to see Hartley eventually refers to his films, in the credits, as "Possible Films Production." In *Fay Grimm*, the number of incompossible films (or counterfactual possibilities) become countless. Thematically, in this follow-up film, Henry's over-production of stories parallels "the harem fool" or male-Scheherazade seducing the sultan's concubines. As the story continues, the sultan allows the "fool" to confess his sins before death, which Henry Fool engages in. But the confessions themselves, taking forever to tell, are metafictions.

Cut to Two: In *Henry Fool*, Henry walks into town like a Rabelasian man and changes the lives of Simon Grim and his family (his sister, Fay, and mother, Mary, and several other characters, if not the whole world indirectly). He takes a room in the *basement* of the Grim family house. Immediately, Henry boasts of his writings collectively called "my confessions" (which are in several volumes of manuscripts, and which—when eventually read by Simon and Angus James, the book publisher—prove to be unremarkable, mediocre at best, without an audience, and therefore unpublishable [*HF* 118–21]). However, Simon, a trash man at the local dump, whom Henry had encouraged to write, had tutored, and had sent to Angus, is silent about the long, allegedly pornographic, poem he writes (which, after originally published on the Web [*HF* 102–03, 111] and then in print by Angus, wins the Nobel Prize for Literature seven years later. Given the epic proportion of the story, Hartley is able to get away with this kind of exaggeration). Simon becomes so in/famous that a young girl whom Simon had given a note to (*HF* 60) in the local library "warn[s] other girls [on the Internet] about [his being] a potential rapist" (101) and that even the Pope warns against reading him (13). Henry, however, has a real history of statutory rape (a 13 year old girl) for which he spent seven years in prison (*HF* 62). He is driven by his sexual impulses: As a case in point, he "rapes"[13] Simon's mother, Mary (40), who is in a depressed state and on

---

[13] Henry "rapes" Simon's mother. I enclose the word *rape* in quotes, for Hartley in the script and film itself slightly undercuts and makes ambiguous the accusations from within the characters' perspectives. E.g., when Henry in later scenes returns to the Grim house and sees Fay—who says, "Oh, shit! Not you again!"—Mary blurts out, "Beast! Fiend! Rapist!" (*HF* 46). Immediately, however, Fay says to her mother: "Oh, shut up, Mom!" The directions read and the action is "Fay stomps back upstairs. Mary slams her door shut. Simon runs out after Henry." In the next scene, Simon and Henry discuss the situation: Simon, following Henry, says,

sedatives and who suffers from the loss of her husband in Viet Nam and from having no interests in living. Mary's daughter, Fay, is depicted at first as rather angry and promiscuous, bringing men home to have sex with them while her mother and brother are downstairs. And Mary's son, Simon, at the beginning is withdrawn, inarticulate, stammering, and possibly retarded.

Simon's poem, which we never get to read or hear even a part of, has a rather odd influence on those characters who have read the manuscript in part or in whole: Gnoc (Mr. Deng's daughter), who has never spoken in her life, begins singing (*HF* 21–22); Fay says that her period comes early (67); and Mary commits suicide.[14] Simon comes home and finds his mother in the bathroom, having cut her veins and bled to death, during which Henry and Fay are having wild sex in Henry's *basement* apartment. (The two scenes are cut and folded into each other [92–95]. Everyone is im*pli*cated in every scene.) Eventually, Henry marries Fay, for she is pregnant with their son (*HF* 107), Ned, and has to take a position at the local dump (*HF* 100) to support his family. Simon, however, makes so much money from his book advance of $200,000 that he leaves the dump. Both men, like Amadeus and Salieri, thereby exchange positions of prestige and fame. It is a seesaw effect (with

---

"Henry, wait up!" Henry says, "I am not a rapist!" At that moment the two of them are interrupted by Officer Buñuel, Henry's parole officer (46–47). Buñuel! The event of Henry having "raped" Mary is never referred to again. Complicating the incident is a span of possibilities and interpretations of what took place among the various incidences of Henry's having raped Susan (prior to the film) and having gone to prison for seven years, Henry's "rape" of Mary, and Henry's helping Pearl, who is being sexually abused by Warren. Hartley suggests in the film with this span of possibilities (rather, incompossibilities) that Henry is progressing away from his propensity to rape. In any case, rape remains Chaste in the film.

14 The cause and effect for Mary's suicide is set forth by a series of scenes, which I reclaim later in the second Installation. Hartley suggests that Mary's loss of her husband is the source for her desperate act.

only one round, and yet perhaps another and still another in this compossible epic) or it is a scale of justice (again, with only one, and yet with many sub-scenes, balancing) act that drives both films. In any case, both sets of men are immortalized, canonized. If there is any saving *grace* at all in Henry, it takes place one night when Fay is upset with him—Henry has taken Ned to the "Inferno," a strip joint—and tells Henry not to come home. True to his nature, Henry returns home to his potential trouble (but) in the basement apartment to sleep *where* he finds Pearl (14 years old), who has repeatedly been sexually abused by her stepfather, Warren. She offers Henry sex in return for his killing Warren (*HF* 135). He rejects the offer and goes to Pearl's home to see if Warren's wife, Vicky, who has been physically abused by Warren, is okay and to speak with her about the sexual abuse of Pearl. While there, Warren awakes and repeatedly beats Henry, but in a scuffle Henry accidentally causes Warren's death (136–37). There is a sense of justice in this scene.

In a rather unexpected ending—another beginning?—to the film, Simon further bonds with Henry and balances the scales of justice as well as lives up to his ethical promise to Henry (*HF* 116–17; 122–27). Simon knows that Henry has had a great influence on getting him to write his opus. He sees Henry as his *teacher-pedagogue*, but with all of its etymological connections. (Part of their exchange— besides communicating by trafficking in women, both Mary and Fay, Vicky and Pearl—is cemented in Simon's promise to Henry that, as repayment for all that Henry has given him, he will not sign a book contract for his poem without requiring the publisher's having also to publish Simon's "confessions"—which of course the publisher, Angus, flatly refuses to do. Simon—in the famous hospital scene of the birth of Henry's son, Ned—relates to Henry why he has reneged on the deal. They do not part amicably.

Seven years later, Ned brings the two men together, and Simon, out of a sense of his promise to help and acknowledge his mentor and brother-in-law, ends up sending Henry to Sweden in disguise as himself to accept the Nobel Prize in Literature. In this closing scene the ethical bond between the two appears to be in balance.[15]

In both cases—*Amadeus* and *Henry Fool*—a mediocre composer or writer becomes attached to the canonization of the ingenious, great composer-writer. In both cases, the bonding and canonization are linked conductively with the themes of rape and pedagogy, but more so in the second film. (Rape becomes progressively more pronounced, and yet remains Chaste, as we move from film to film.) In John Waters's film, rape and canonization take on major perverse, campy Christian, Catholic, universal, overtones, adding to the theme of Divine Rape and to its being undercut by parody and pastiche (cf. Frappier-Mazur).

Cut to Three: Among the three films, *Multiple Maniacs* (1970)[16] is the most complicated: Quickly put, men (or clear binary-gender distinctions) are less important; third sexes-freaks are more so. There are three rapes: Lady Divine is raped in the streets by a male while being pinned down by a female; Divine is raped anally in a church with a crucifix attached to rosary beads by a female, Mink Stole; and finally Divine, in a crazy state of mind, is raped by a fif-

---

15 It is difficult, however, in the closing shots of the film to tell whether Henry is running toward or away from the plane on the tarmac that is waiting to fly him to Sweden. Hartley says the film has an ending, purposefully left open for the audience ("Responding" xx–xxi). Later in *Fay Grimm*, this same notion of not knowing, or openness in the film is made fun of in the script itself, with the actors-characters in their discussion with authorities. Hartley and others also in the interviews, extras on the DVD, make fun.

16 For the script, see Waters.

teen-foot (mechanical) Lobster, or Lobstora, which can be traced back to an actual postcard that advertises Baltimore.

The thematic of canonization (great art, film, to be immortalized) informs this film in its production, execution, and distribution and in its characters (all outcasts, remainders, multiple maniacs, freaks in "a Calvacade of Perversions," riding on the prior infamy of Russ Meyer and specifically Herschell Gordon Lewis's *Two Thousand Maniacs*, 1964, and Tod Browning's *Freaks*, 1932). *Multiple Maniacs* is an underground film that has been perversely canonized. There is a hilarious scene of Christ feeding the hungry ones with Wonder Bread (a precursor to Holy Communion) and canned tuna (symbolic of Christ himself). Waters is good at recasting our cultural, or Absolut/e, canonized heroes, in commercials that inform our contemporary lives.

Divine is God (though a rather Mad God, a.*ma*Deus [cf. Genet, *Our Lady*]). The theme of Divine Rape permeates the entire film,[17] with Divine becoming obsessively hysterical, until s/he, like a monster (GODzilla in a "B" film within an underground film)—the im*pli*cations of the foldings in this film border on being inexplicable—is shot down in the streets by the National Guard. The divine freak "Lady Divine" is dead! Though she continues to cast *a shadow* in the caves of our memories and in yet other Waters's films such as *Pink Flamingo*.

---

17 As I have pointed out in the Preamble, immortals (gods) raping female mortals is a common theme in mythology, which informs our view of what drives the constitution of the Greeks and Romans and modern-day notions of nation building.

Scanning the Cuts

> He was my idol! I can't remember a time when I didn't know his name! When I was only fourteen he was already famous. Even in Legnago—the tiniest town in Italy—I knew of him.
> Old Salieri, *Amadeus* (film, Scene 15)

> Mozart! Mozart! I cannot bear it any longer! I confess! I confess what I did! I'm guilty! I killed you! Sir I confess! I killed you!
> Old Salieri, *Amadeus* (Scene 2)

> Have you not heard of that madman who lit a lantern in the bright morning hours, ran to the market place, and cried incessantly: "I seek God! I seek God!"..."Whither is God?" he cried; "I will tell you. *We have killed him*—you and I.... Do we smell nothing as yet of the divine decomposition? Gods, too, decompose."
> Friedrich Nietzsche, *The Gay Science*, Book 3, sec. 125. (Nietzsche's emphasis).

Installation, DVD One (Shaffer and Forman, *Amadeus*, Canonization): *Set, In a workroom. Bookshelves, filled with books, photocopies, CDs, videos, and curios. On various tables, three computers with screens lit. Against a wall, a set of old drums covered and nested one over the other. On a wall, a print of Karl Marx and a signed original print of Andy Warhol's Campbell's Tomato Soup shopping bag. The floor is littered with stacks of papers and magazines. V.V. sits at a computer, which has a full screen picture of Old Salieri. To his left are notes and versions of Shaffer's and Forman's scripts. He sits listening to a roundtable of discussants on a DVD of Amadeus—call it Vitanza's Cut—while composing and interjecting his comments:*

PETER SHAFFER: "To me there is something pure about Salieri's pursuit of an eternal Absolute through music, just as there is something irredeemably impure about his simultaneous pursuit of eternal fame" ("Introduction," *Amadeus* xvii).

ANTONIO SALIERI: Yes, "I wanted Fame.... I wanted to blaze like a comet across the firmament of Europe! Yet only in one special way. Music! Absolute music!... A note of music is either right or wrong absolutely! Not even time can alter that: music is God's art" (*Amadeus*, Act 1, Scene 2: 11).

א Shaffer's plays (Miloš's films) interrupt this myth of God's presence—immanence—in music.

JEAN-LUC NANCY: For me, there is something too pure (i.e., too substantially a tantalization refined of remainders) about Salieri's pursuit of an absolute myth of the presence of God in music—in communion, community—just as there is something equally too pure about Salieri's desiring fame for himself. He would be—as the myth of the Eighteenth century would have it—he thinks *he*, not Mozart, should be—the incarnation of God, the magic flute of God, on Earth. But he is apparently frustrated by his God, who favors Mozart. Hence, opting for infamy, he is given to rivalry with God through Mozart. It is the case—in this case—that the thinking of subjectivity, of fame, or even infamy, of canonization, "thwarts" community (*Inoperative* 23). Unless one would insist on sacrifice as the basis for community!

"DOCTOR-BIOGRAPHER" of KARL MARX: "He [Marx] writes with nostalgia and longing for something *thwarted*. For something that didn't happen" (Kipnis, *Ecstasy* 249; emphasis mine). Why did this god communism fail him! Fail in founding a new man and community!

א As Nancy summarizes and argues—and Blanchot picks up on—"the word 'communism' stands as an emblem of the desire to discover or rediscover a place of community" (Nancy, *Inoperative* 1; Blanchot, *Unavowable* 1–3). But "*Community*," as Nancy says, "*has not taken place*" (11; Nancy's emphasis). What has taken this place of communism (or of the canonization of the proletariat) is the idea that man, through his work, produces his own essence, "and furthermore producing precisely this essence *as community*. An absolute immanence of man to man—a humanism—and of community to community—a communism—[but One that] obstinately subtends [delimits]... all forms of oppositional communism [or resistance, seen as counterrevolutionary].... [I]t is precisely the immanence of man to man... that constitutes the stumbling block to a thinking of community.... Essence is set to work in them; through them, it becomes its own work. This is what we have called 'totalitarianism,' but it might be better named 'immanentism'" (2–3; Nancy's emphasis).

א Therefore, it does not matter, man or God, God or man, or for that matter, G/goddess or woman. But it could as easily be, as it has been repeatedly, *the* man's own essence *eman*ating a Stalinist community, which would be the *rapedeath* of community (*Inoperative* 12).

א For Salieri, it is God emanating through Amadeus directly to him. Hence, GOD → (ravishes) → Amadeus but only indirectly Salieri himself. Shaffer describes this indirect ravishment of Salieri, as if he were Judge Daniel Paul Schreber, being raped, impregnated by

God Himself, for the second coming.[18] Shaffer has Salieri reading Amadeus's manuscripts: Salieri recalls, "Here again was the very voice of God!" Then Shaffer gives his stage directions: "The music swells. What we now hear is an amazing collage of great passages from Mozart's music, *ravishing* to Salieri and to us. The Court Composer...walks around and around his salon, reading the pages and dropping them on the floor as if in a rough and tumbling sea; *he experiences the point where beauty and great pain coalesce.* More pages fall than he can read, scattering across the floor in a *white cascade*" (scene 70; emphasis mine).[19]

MILAN KUNDERA: Yes, I have written much about the beloved and music, about the failure of communism, and the trickiness of immortality. I have written a whole novel—*Immortality* itself—that is based on a fictive character named Agnes and her gesture and have used it paradigmatically in association with Bettina née Brentano's confrontation with Goethe's wife, Christiane, and Bettina's subsequent attachment to the Maestro himself, Goethe, which to this day has guaranteed Bettina's own canonization and immortality (45–47, 56–58). The *pièce de résistance*, of course, took place when Bettina jumped into the lap of Goethe, hugged him, and fell asleep, or so she tells us in her writings. It really does not matter if this is

---

18 In *Amadeus* (Act 1, Scene 6: 30), Salieri prays to God to "enter" him, yet He does not. (Cf. Schreber, *Memoirs*.)

19 This scene of *ravishment* is filled with double entendres. E.g., Amadeus boasts to his Majesty Joseph II, about *how long he can keep it up*. In response to the Absolute, elevated themes of gods and legends, in the film, Amadeus responds to Von Swieten: "Elevated? What does that mean? Elevated! The only thing a man should elevate is—oh, excuse me. I'm sorry. I'm stupid" (script, scene 113). In the play, Amadeus says: "Oh, elevated! Elevated!...The only thing a man should elevate is his doodle" (Act 2, Scene 4: 89).

the way it was, for "she is revealing to us how she wants us to see her" (57). She offers us a photograph. An instance. A still. A quick cut! She directs her own cut!

JEAN-LUC NANCY: But how are we to read Shaffer's rendering of Amadeus's deathbed scene and burial. As sacrifice? Or as the beginning of a community without a community, as infinite finitude? As an exposition but simultaneous ex-scription?

AVITAL RONELL: Or *as* the occasion for finitude's score!

> ℵ There is the notion in eighteenth and nineteenth-century literature, as Lawrence Kramer reminds us, that characters die in "the lovedeath," to advance the spectators (who might be another actor or members of the audience, as in the play *Amadeus*). Kramer writes: "Their death absorbs, and turns to bliss, the guilt that the spectator feels for desiring what they do.... Only the spectator can both experience and survive the lovedeath. Only the spectator can both 'have' *jouissance* like a woman (the imaginary experience) and 'know' it like a man (the survival)" (134–35). This is drama, still, as a sacrificial *rapedeath* and *lovedeath* rite.

JEAN-LUC NANCY: What must be thought, instead, is a community without community, a community constantly coming, never arriving and staying fixed in music (*Inoperative* 71). This *community without* is based not on religion and sacrifice (135) nor on any "theologicopolitics" (*Sense* 89, 91–92, 105–06), but on finitude.

AVITAL RONELL: Yes, on finitude's score. Let me elbow back in here and say: "Finitude is not about the end in terms of fulfillment [e.g., *jouissance*] or teleological accomplishment but about a suspension, a hiatus in meaning, reopened each time in the here and now, disappearing as it opens, exposing itself to something so unexpected and possibly *new* that it persistently eludes its own grasp" (*Finitude's Score* 5; Ronell's emphasis).

> ℵ Finitude may be a Heideggerian *Ereignis* (an event, expropriation), or interruption, or caesura. Or as demonstrated in all versions of *Amadeus*, a giggle. A childish giggle. A *becoming* child of a giggle that interrupts an absolution of all who are but mediocrities. In a hospital madhouse. As a voiceover at the end of the film (or as the virtual curtains fall). Seen or experienced as a Wink: As Nancy writes: "This presence of no god could however carry with it the enticement, the call, the *Wink* [nod] of an à-dieu: a going to god, or an adieu to all gods" (*Inoperative* 137; Nancy's emphasis. Cf. 115, 119). As Salieri exposes himself and all those other so-called mediocrities, he also ex-scribes himself as in what Deleuze calls a *conversation* with Amadeus.

JEAN-LUC NANCY: "[O]ne begins to imagine"—having viewed *Amadeus*—"that what has been most genial in Europe, and maybe even its very idea of *genius*, arose above all out of a formidable necessity of putting on stage *the sense of sense* [i.e., to represent the Divine, the very desired community—communion, communism—itself, which can but end in violence (sexual violence, rape) as a founding event of community].... No doubt the cycle of dramatic [violent] representations is closed. It is not by chance that theater today is without any new fable, without *mythos*, having exhausted the total fable... the fable of the end of fables.... The curtain has fallen on the metaphysical scene, on metaphysics as scene of (re)presentation" (*Sense* 23).

> ℵ Nancy makes clear, the fable *in Chaste form*—nonetheless, an immanentism—lives on and on and on. (See Weber, *Theatricality as Medium*.)

JEAN-LUC NANCY: But again, How are we to read Shaffer's rendering of Amadeus's deathbed scene and burial. As sacrifice? Or as the beginning of a community without a community, as infinite finitude?

AVITAL RONELL: Or again, as an occasion for Finitude's Score!

> ℵ Ronell and then D. Diane Davis strongly suggest something about Mozart by way of Deleuze, which can help us in responding to Jean-Luc's enquiry. Ronell's scanners pick up on Deleuze, whose "example for becoming with regard to Conversation calls in the birds [that] signal *the uncanny space that travels between us* when we converse."[20] Ronell quotes Deleuze: "It is like Mozart's birds: in this music there is a bird-becoming, but caught in a music-becoming of the bird, the two forming a single becoming, a single bloc, an a-parallel evolution—not an exchange, but 'a confidence with no possible interlocutor,' as a commentator on Mozart says; in short, a conversation" (xvi; Deleuze, *Dialogues* 3). But what is alluded to in terms of a "conversation"?

---

20 *Dictations* xv–xvi; emphasis mine; cf. Davis, "Finitude's Clamor" 136. About becoming, see Deleuze, *Dialogues* 2–3; cf. 29–31; Deleuze and Guattari, *Thousand* 232–309; cf. Bergson, *Creative Evolution* 272–370.

א Ronell, in *Dictation*, answers: "For his part, Deleuze develops an understanding of Conversation that conditions a commonality in which the 'we' does not work *together* but between the two. Writing between themselves they are writing *à deux*, each witnessing the other in his solitude.... The evolution of a between zone, with which this work tries to negotiate in the cases of [Amadeus and Salieri], makes it necessary to consider not only what happens between two proper names but also to read the place which emerges between [Shaffer] and his mutating text. This place, which is a place of testimony, remains essentially atopical, however, as it does not take place in one or two of the terms but tries to articulate what there is between, in the dynamic between that sets relations into provisional positions" (xiv–xv; Ronell's emphasis and bracketed interpolations mine).

JEAN-LUC NANCY: Then, what you are getting at, Victor, with your interpolations (interruptions, finitudes) is that "we" should read Shaffer's rendering of the final death-bed-writing scene of Amadeus's writing "his" *Requiem* and Salieri's copying it *as* what Deleuze calls a *conversation* and what Ronell calls *dictation*, or a *writing à deux*, a writing *in between*.

AVITAL RONELL: So then, Victor, the *conversation between* the two composers, with the stand-in of it as the *Requiem*, is *Finitude's Score*. In fact, all the music referred to in the film—not just the mass—is part of that Score. And yet, as I say in *Dictations*, none of the conversation between the two is *in* the film, for what is *in between* is "the noncanonic excess of [Mozart's] signature" (ix). It's not about the subject Mozart and the signature "Mozart," or "Amadeus," just as it is not about the so-called successful and unsuccessful composer but what lies *in between*—in some third figure—as noncanonic excess. Which, yes, the versions of the play and the film are filled with!

> א Yes and Yes. It is, as Jean-Luc might say, not only in terms of *immanence* a story necessarily to be read or seen, hermeneutically, in *the realm of being*, but also in paraterms of *finitude* a parastory to be anticipated-ly listened to—in *the realm of relations*. (I say "para"story, for it is a radical finitude of stories that lies alongside, or in between, the so-called stories of Amadeus-Mozart *and* Salieri, the ones that would be canonized.) One would have to be hysterical to proffer them. One would have to hear....

PETER SHAFFER: "...a high-pitched giggle, which is going to characterize Mozart throughout the film" (film, scene 25; cf. play 24).

> א Yes, the giggle, or Wink (the nod), as Jean-Luc discusses it, an *à-dieu*, to an absent god.... The parastory, as you might say, Avital, "points to the *thirdness* that they [Amadeus and Salieri] conceived between themselves and subjected to consistent morphing" (*Dictations* xii; emphasis and interpolation added). We can hermeneutically-communicatively say that the music is Mozart's and the frame of the story is Salieri's (or Shaffer's) rendering. But the parastories between them are not in any *realm of being*, or immanence. We cannot say that they are theirs. They belong to no subject (they are not substantial). As a caseless in pointless, Amadeus cannot control t/his giggle. When he attempts to be serious, inevitably, contrary to his intentions, he but giggles, or butt f/arts, which is how Shaffer introduces Amadeus to Salieri and to us.

Causing consternation around him and for himself. Mouths open agape. Out of the mouth of the adult, but obscene childish beast (*infans*), comes giggles. Out of the mouths of Amadeus's fictive contemporaries comes... (silence that assaults our eardrums). The entire framing device that Shaffer constructs for Salieri's apology is undercut—cut!—cut!—cut!—by the final Amadeusian giggle before all goes finally black on the stage or screen.

א I must greatly emphasize what I have not yet said enough, for this parastory of finitude's mis-take on *Amadeus*'s in betweens, his potential tweenings, is not one that can be easily told or read, given what counts for telling and reading, in terms of *being* and *difference*. Hence, the reasons for my referring in the introduction to this chapter to the men sharing a *homosocial space of trafficking in women*, which they *do* share in society. No doubt about it. This point, we, indeed, can immediately understand! For the parastory to be heard and listened to and read, however, would require, as Diane Davis might explain, that the story of Mozart, "Amadeus," and Salieri—their in be tweens—"would have to be radically redefined: not according to immanence's registers of being and difference [not that kind of discourse] but according to finitude's resisters of becoming and *différance*" ("Finitude's Clamor" 135). And not just the between of the men, but the tweening of Amadeus and Constanze in their perverse fugue-(flux-neutral)-like scatological ex-change (play, Act 1, Scene 5; film, Scene: 29),[21] which Salieri cannot even begin to understand once

---

21 I am referring to the scene in which Amadeus is talking to Constanze in perverse-reverse strings of phrases and sentences. Salieri remains in hiding, listening with mouth agape at this person. *Amadeus*, in reverse

he sees that this obscene childish twenty-six year old man *is* Wolfgang *Amadeus* Mozart. (Is it not also wonderful that Amadeus is the middle, the in between proper, but Oh, so improper, name!) WAM is driven to lose his (proper) names: Wolfgang and Wolfie. Amadeus and beloved by God. Mozart and belittled by Father. WAM tweens. Which is precisely what "Divine" (in *Multiple Maniacs*) attempts.

א And yet, we can hear finitude's clamor of the parastory—the nondialectical tweening back and forth, zigzagging—if we but retune our ears. One possibility would be to listen not deductively, inductively, or abductively, but *conductively*.

DIANE DAVIS: Yes, Victor, "Though finitude is, strictly speaking, *un*speakable, it's not incommunicable: It communicates itself constantly, irrepressibly, as inscription's exscriptions. The saying continuously haunts the said, coming through in textual disturbances, interruptions in the manifestation of meaning and being" ("Finitude's Clamor" 133; cf. Nancy, "Exscription," *Birth* 319–40). My gods, have we not ex-perienced enough of these kinds of hauntings and interruptions in y/our own earlier book, *Sexual Violence in Western Thought and Writing: Chaste Rape*! You make demands of y/our readers' having to shift, to zigzag, between academic-immanence's registers of being and difference and finitude's registers of *becoming* and *différance*!

DIANE DAVIS: "Levinas says it comes through [to us] as 'a blinking of meaning' (*Otherwise* 152). Thanks in part to

---

word order, tells Constanze to *Eat my shit*. Cf. Divine, in Waters's *Pink Flamingos* (cf. Laporte, "Of Divine Shit," *History* 109–12).

the purely performative [theatrical] dimension of language, to what Paul de Man calls the 'text machine'—which is responsible, Ronell writes, 'for effects of meaning generated by sheer contingency, elements of uncontrol and improvisation' (*Stupidity* 170)—the exscribed does leave a(n inassimilable) trace. That is, thanks in part to language's finitude... the exscribed does manage to crash inscription's party, intruding on the festivities by making some ssstatic-y noise, gesturing to us from the door (from the outside)" (134).

> ℵ Yes, Mozart *speaks*, but also, as you might say, Diane, "disruptive bursts of the unintelligible" *speak* Mozart (134; cf. Davis, *Breaking Up*).

DIANE DAVIS: Yes, "This *we*-who writes [and giggles, winks, nods] doesn't work 'together' (in the typical sense of collaboration) but *between* the two, at the limit, where the encounter with the Other necessarily takes 'you' out: You are written, or as Ronell says, you are 'overwritten' (*Stupidity* 45) by it" (137; interpolations mine).

> ℵ It may very well be that the giggles are channeled through Amadeus by *a mad* god (*deus*)—and yet, an hysterically mad and obsessively made God—but the giggles are still more than enough excess to ever be canonized![22] Or Is this—after all has been possibly undone and redone by Capital—the case? (I will take up the issue, the replaying of, the Divine by Nancy in my discussion of *Multiple Maniacs*, in which the newest Divine is excess itself [ever-] confronting possible ap/propriation, canonization.)

---

22 About a mad God (Deus) and the crucifixion, See Foucault, *Madness* 78–84.

א But for now, let us say that the two—Amadeus and Salieri—minus God—minus immanence—form "a bloc," as Deleuze would say, "of becoming" (*Dialogues* 7). Overwriting Finitude's Score. A singular bloc of birds-cum-wasp and orchid. De-volving in a-parallel mannerisms (2–3).

> If a teacher puts her mind to it, none of her students will succeed.
> Elfriede Jelinek, *The Piano Teacher* (9)

> At the center of...pedagogy is the fuck.
> Andrea Dworkin, *Intercourse* (180)

> Let us take an example as simple as: *x* starts practicing piano again. Is it an Oedipal return to childhood? Is it a way of dying.... Is it a new borderline, an active line that will bring other becomings entirely different from becoming or rebecoming a pianist, that will induce a transformation of all of the preceding assemblages to which *x* was prisoner?... Schizoanalysis, or pragmatics, has no other meaning: Make a rhizome...a becoming, people your desert. So experiment.
> Gilles Deleuze and Félix Guattari,
> *A Thousand Plateaus* (250–51).

Installation, DVD Two (Hal Hartley, *Henry Fool*, Pedagogy): *Set simultaneously at "The World of Donuts" (a setting in* Henry Fool) *and in a piano classroom (a setting in* The Piano Teacher)!

א Pedagogy is everything in *Henry Fool*. Piano pedagogy! In a quasi-confessional scene, after Henry has "raped" Mary and told Simon that he has made "love" with Mary, Simon Grim talks alone in church with Father Hawkes about Henry:

SIMON: "...do you think Henry is...dangerous?"

FATHER HAWKES: "He needs help. Our help. Yours especially."

SIMON: "But what can I do?"

FATHER HAWKES: "The best parts of himself come to the surface when he's helping someone learn: I've seen this. Let yourself be taught. Show your appreciation for his guidance. In this way, you know, perhaps. Well. There's hope for everyone. Even. Even Henry" (*HF* 65).

> א Simon willingly thereafter becomes Henry's student, which raises the question of whether or not Simon is calling Henry's attention away from Mary, his mother, and toward himself...

HAL HARTLEY (*interrupting*): I don't think that in writing and shooting that section, I would have Simon drawing attention away from Mary. After all, Simon must know, given what Father Hawkes tells him, that Mary is only one possible student or person that Henry would give attention to, if a student at all. What constitutes a "student" here? And what constitutes a "lesson" in this film! There is that contrastive parallel between Mary and Pearl. Let us not forget that Henry gives attention to Pearl as well and attempts to teach Vicky to leave Warren and then attempts, though fails, to teach Warren, who may be uneducable, unchangeable except by the Owen Feers of the world, with their right-wing politics. Henry does change in the film just as Simon and Fay change...

> א ...Good enough! But there is a huge leap away from the direction I thought this installation was drifting toward. So okay. The conductive links are among Henry-Mary-Simon. Henry is a naturally born teacher (pedagogue) *and* molester (pedophile) while Mary fails as a student and Simon succeeds. (Later, however, the pedagogical relationship between Henry and Simon is reversed as circumstances change every-

thing. When Simon's poem becomes noticed and there is a chance it will be published, Simon has the authority and voice to tell Henry that he must marry his sister, Fay, who is pregnant.)

HAL HARTLEY: "Most of my films have had that kind of *bildungsroman* quality" ("Responding" xiii). Henry perhaps changes the most. "One handy phrase I used a lot during the writing was, 'What happens if the most untrustworthy man in town were the best person in town?' Henry is a completely unreliable, polymorphously perverse egomaniac, but he's a good man—the most selfless, the most honest, the most truthful, the strongest. I love telling stories like that, when people just don't fit into the box correctly" (xx)....

HAL HARTLEY: But I still think that one of the central scenes in the film is when Henry comes home and enters his *basement apartment* and Pearl is there waiting for him. "I wanted that scene in the basement between Pearl—who's aged thirteen—and Henry to be really harsh, and I wanted us to at least fear that Henry is capable of doing something stupid and horrible again" ("Responding" xix; emphasis mine).

> א Prior to this scene with Father Hawkes, Hal, you write the scene of Henry giving Simon a piano-spelling lesson. What motivates this pedagogical scene is the previous one with Henry's tearing a page from Simon's manuscript and Gnoc's displaying it for all to see in The World of Donuts. Vicky reads and denounces this page as pornographic.

HAL HARTLEY: Yes, people in the film respond to the poem in different ways. While it makes Gnoc sing (speak) for the first time in her life, it annoys others ("Responding" xvii). We don't see the poem; and yet, we see it by way of a variety of effects and affects it has on people.

> א Then after Vicky's response, you introduce a quick cut to the piano-spelling scene with Henry at a piano, hitting one note for each possible spelling of the homophones there-their-they're. (This thematic punctum of the one staccato note is prevalent in the film at strategic moments.)

HENRY FOOL: "See, Simon, there are three kinds of there. There's 'There.' T-H-E-R-E. There are the donuts. Then there's T-H-E-I-R; which is the possessive. It is their donut. Then, finally, there's 'they're.' T-H-E-Y-'-R-E. A contraction, meaning they are. They're the donut people. Get it?" (31).

> א I don't know about Simon, but I get the DONUT progressively (or regressively as an ex-scription) to mean Do Not. (The transformation is part of the problem of spelling the various homophones for *there*, which is philosophically *there is*, *es gibt*, *il y a*. Get it?) There are the *do-not* people and their *do-nots*. People are what they do. Or do not do. Thou shalt not. Therefore, they *do not*, except to add to the do-not Decalogue. By telling others to do-not. Hence, there are and they're the do-not people, making up—composing—the World of Do Nots. These are the people who obsessively engage in the hortatory negative. Against people like Henry, Simon, and Fay. Who act; suffer; learn.[23] And yet, there is Henry who acts against the Decalogue; in fact, he thinks it is his vocation to do so.

---

23 But these are the major characters. What is remarkable—though a dramatic convention—is how much Amy changes in respect to Simon. (Cf. Hartley, "Responding" xiv–xv.)

The world of donuts and *do nots* is not an easy one to determine, anymore than anything that is happening in *Henry Fool*. Which is a film not about interpretation but about experimentation.[24]

א On this piano in the Grim house there is a picture of a man dressed in a uniform, perhaps a U.S. Army uniform. Prior to the spelling-piano lesson, Henry is speaking briefly with Mary. The film directions read: "He stops and lifts a small framed photo of a soldier off the piano" (*HF* 22).

HENRY FOOL: "This your husband?" (22).

א The film directions then read: "Violated somehow, she gets up and snatches it out of his hands. She puts it in a drawer and cringes as Henry plays one note on the piano." Punctum!

MARY GRIM: "Stop that" (22).

א This scene thematically links with the other piano lesson scene of Mary's sitting at the piano and playing when Simon walks in on her and they exchange a similarly laconic exchange. But we are left with the question Who is in the photo?

HAL HARTLEY: It is most likely Mary's husband. I've surmised, as a method actor might, that "the father probably died in the Vietnam War. I thought a lot about how different Mom could have been and I worked it out that she had once shown some promise as a pianist. I wanted her to be

---

24 Cf. Deleuze, *Dialogues* 48–49; Lyotard's *"pagus"* and *"pagani"* in *Differend* 151–81; and *Just Gaming* 9–10, 12, 14, 34, 49; Kittler, *Discourse Networks*.

creative because I thought it was very important to get her and Simon into that scene when she's playing the piano, and he says, 'That's nice,' and she makes the distinction between 'nice' and 'unremarkable,' which is a harsh reality. [See *HF* 77.] I imagined she got knocked up in high school while she was waiting to get into music school, and then her boyfriend was drafted and got killed so she got stuck with these kids" ("Responding" xvi).

> א So Mary stops playing when Simon sees her because her playing is "not remarkable"! In the next scene Simon takes his manuscript to the publisher Angus, hoping that it will be remarkable and, therefore, publishable. But while he takes this risk of showing his poem, Mary takes her life by cutting her wrists. Though in the unfolding events of the film, Simon's poem is rejected by the publisher, Simon's poem becomes remarkable and the publisher changes his mind! Simon has a future. Mary thought she did not. She becomes a *do not*. It is the case, however, that she is totally overwhelmed by her situation—her life is as her name says, grim—she comes to being a do not.

HAL HARTLEY: Mary "is a total life-negating person" ("Responding" xvii).

> א I am tempted to say that Henry also is a do not. Because of his getting Fay pregnant, he has to give up, as he says, his "vocation" (*HF* 32, 48). But as Salieri is linked to Mozart, Henry is linked to Simon, who is the Nobel Prize winner.... Like Salieri and Amadeus, Henry and Simon are in a "conversation" together. That is what is between them.... Salieri does something. He's constantly trying.... But the whole issue of whether or not Henry himself is a great writer is

indeterminable. In terms of Salieri and Henry, this is not the issue we should be concerned with.

HAL HARTLEY: Yes, "I didn't...want us to be able to see either Henry's confession or Simon's poem, because I didn't want us to get involved with judging them. That wasn't really the issue. It could be that Henry's confession is a great piece of writing even though Simon and the publisher guy dismiss it. I was much more interested in showing how the value of creative activity is often measured by the particular kind of reaction it elicits" ("Responding" xii).

HAL HARTLEY: Let me slightly modify what you have said in your comparisons between Salieri-Amadeus and Henry-Simon. Perhaps it is a different case with Salieri and Mozart. These are real people with real music. But our attitudes toward them could turn on a dime, contrary to the principle of canonization. Shaffer-Forman's telling of Salieri's telling brings Salieri to the forefront now. Our ears and eyes are taught to be obsessive, but they are given to *becoming* hysterical. Shaffer and Forman's film *Amadeus* has taught us of Salieri himself and in a contrary way. If we could all be but patron saints of mediocrity! This apparently is an option. Simply recall Blake's reading of Satan as the hero of Genesis. God-Satan-Blake form an assemblage, a bloc. There is something Satanic in both Salieri and Henry. They are angels but devils. And it's the same with Fay and Mary! They enter the discursive scene and change how we hear and see the incompossible world of that scene, creating new incompossibilities. And we should not think of Amadeus and Simon as simply angels (cf. "Responding" xiv). Nor should we think that Mary must succumb to her end, for she does not in other incompossible worlds.

א Yes. And yet, as we have said, we must be careful of recognition, immanence, the Absolute, immortality, subjectivity, verticality. Perhaps we can say again that the two sets of men are in the between zone. Your picking up on the change in the conditions for incompossibilities is what can help us avoid the myth of immanence.... And yes, yes, yes Mary.

א As Avital said, finitude is "a suspension, a hiatus in meaning, reopened each time in the here and now, disappearing as it opens, exposing itself to something so unexpected and possibly new that it persistently eludes its own grasp." I am thinking of the open mouth that runs throughout *Amadeus*. Who spouts out whatever does not come to mind. People cannot believe what Amadeus is saying as he moves from being serious to becoming vulgar and consequently their own mouths become agape. And, I would remind us, the open mouth runs throughout Jean-Luc's writings.[25]

א Ah, and let us not also forget that this giggling, this pouring forth, "gushing" forth, from the open Amadeus (a Mad Deus) mouth of the jug, as Wolfgang points to and further develops from Holderlin and Heidegger (see "The Thing" in *Poetry*; 172–73), in terms of *Geviert* (the fourfold), is the gift. But what Wolfgang is pointing to is ...

---

25 For the image-theme of the open mouth as an expression of finitude, see Nancy, *Experience* (90, 114, 145). Also, see *Shaffer's Amadeus* (play, 90, 140, 144.); Fynsk, *Infant* (11, 17–20). But also, see Bataille, "Mouth" in *Visions* (59–60).

WOLFGANG SCHIRMACHER: ...Homo Generator who has the capability, the nature, of originating new life forms. S/he (whatever sex, if sexed) can pour forth not just thirds, as Victor suggests, but four folds of life, bringing together what, heretofore, was never thought acceptable to combine. I worry when Victor talks about threes, for they do have a tendency to fall back into a Hegelian thinking and result in a synthesis. But I am well aware that Victor is willing to take that risk. And I applaud him; after all, I think: "Homo generator has no fear of his or her mistakes, for they are inseparable from his or her succeeding—as body politics teaches us" ("Homo Generator" 71). Homo Generator, like Amadeus himself, with all of Victor's puns on the name, "is rebellious, takes no prisoners, interrupts quite violently the daily routine. But all that with a smile [perhaps a giggle!], please" (73).

> א Yes, Wolfgang, I think that you put it well, this whole notion of the interruption and on the basis of our daily lives. *Wolfgang Mozart* irrepressibly interrupts. For me what you say in terms of your fourth law of media—"mediation is the flow [the flux] of media"—captures well what we are wrestling with, and on the basis or baselessness of our lived lives. You write: "Mediation is no longer a deal between partners or a communication following established rules, but an innovative process of media to which we belong. In such a mediation there is not even the goal of mutual understanding, because the flow [the flux] needs breaks. Dissent is the salt of mediation and designed to eliminate anthropocentric arrangements, the mafia practices of humankind. Mediation floods any content, fills the artificial lifeworld, evokes the 'fourfold' (*Geviert*), and allows us to be life's on artist" (79). What Amadeus stands for at court, with all those who

would flatter the Emperor Joseph II, is to evoke, in his communications with them, both in the play and the film, the pouring forth of lives upon lives.

א I want now to slightly return to the spelling-piano lesson. There is something there that wants to be explored further in the light of what you just said, Wolfgang. Specifically, the complexity of and the implications within *there. Da*. When linked to the verb To Be. That is, There is. *Da-sein*. There is this wonderful habit that inhabits many of the scenes with Joseph II in *Amadeus*. He has the habit of saying "There it is." Recall the scene that goes like this:

VON STRACK: "Your majesty, Herr Mozart."

JOSEPH: "Yes, what about him?"

VON STRACK: "He's here."

JOSEPH: "Ah-ha. Well. There it is. Good." (film, scene 45)[26]

א This is Joseph's typical expression of a conclusion to something that is to begin. An event (perhaps *Ereignis*, but only Gregor Samsa would be sensitive to such an event). As I read this expression earlier, it is *es gebt*. It gives (itself)! It is...what Jean-Luc refers to as "the generosity of being" (*Experience* 147). This is what Amadeus listens to—this generosity—and its forever remainderless becoming. This is *the conversation*. Between Amadeus and Salieri in the deathbed scene. If we but listen. To. The caesura. The enjambment.

---

26 The lines are different in the play version (see Act 1, Scene 7: 33).

Interrupting and jamming the pull toward the immanent-transcendental signal. This gift is finitude's score.

ROLAND BARTHES: I have wanted to interrupt this thought for some time. I recall having written, "I am increasingly convinced, both in writing [composition] and in teaching [pedagogy], that the fundamental operation of [is] fragmentation, and, if one teaches, digression, or, to put it in a preciously ambiguous word, excursions. I should therefore like the speaking and the listening that will be interwoven here to resemble the comings and going of a child playing beside his mother, leaving her, returning to bring her a pebble, a piece of string, and thereby tracing around a calm center a whole locus of play within which the pebble, the string come to matter less than the enthusiastic giving of them" ("Inaugural Lecture" 476–77).

GIORGIO AGAMBEN: Let us not forget that Vittorio discusses the child in great depth in his book *Sexual Violence in Western Thought and Writing: Chaste Rape*. He specifically discusses Freud and the child and Kristeva's view of the centralization of the child in psychoanalysis as an error, and then goes on to discuss Derrida's and my own views of the child in relation to infancy and history. He gives time to a rethinking of Heraclitus's melancholy child playing a game of dice.

א *Becoming-children* can best play the game.

MILAN KUNDERA: Yes, and your saying such reminds me of Bettina (Brentano) and Goethe and the whole issue of immortality and attachment and the game. I have written: "In 1807, on the day of their first meeting, [Bettina] sat herself on [Goethe's] lap, if we can trust her own description.... She said, 'I am interested in nothing but you.' Goethe smiled and said the following fateful words to the young woman: 'You are a charming child.'... She felt so good snuggled up against him that soon she fell asleep. [...] Nothing is more useful than to adopt the status of a child: a child can do whatever it likes" (*Immortality* 57–58; see 59–74).[27]

Joseph II: Ah, yes, this, too, reminds me of Mozart and Antoinette. When I introduced Mozart to my court, I recounted the time when Mozart "was only six years old. He was giving the most brilliant little concert here. As he got off the stool, he slipped and fell. My sister Antoinette helped him up herself, and do you know what he did? Jumped straight into her arms and said, 'Will you marry me, yes or no?'" (film, scene 47).

> א But are these exemplars not the reverse of Salieri-Amadeus! Is not Salieri attaching himself to Amadeus, and is not Amadeus the child while Salieri is the surrogate, super-ego father! But perhaps, you two, are suggesting that it is Amadeus, the child, who

---

27 The relationship between Bettina Brentano and Goethe is rather infamous. The letters that Bettina wrote to Goethe and that he encouraged are hysterical discourse. The letters are, as Kittler suggests, mere chatter or hysterical discourse becoming-literature. Goethe edited, polished, and saved the letters each day that he received them. Kittler writes, "Bettina published *Goethe's Correspondence with a Child*, and she did it to finance a monument to her god that she herself had designed. Goethe sits on a throne, cloak buttoned around his neck, his gaze directed toward the clouds. Next to him Bettina, a graceful childlike menad standing on her little head, and the inscription: 'Turn your tiny feet toward heaven only without care!' She who once threw her dress over her head so as not to be recognized by the people of Frankfort, or so as to be recognized by the spirits, remains Bettina in marble, too; a menad with no shame in the presence of shame" ("Writing" 62; *Discourse Networks* 127–34). Bettina becomes the child of the father. For Betinna-Goethe's letter writing and the postal system, see Siegert, *Relays* 62–73.

is attaching himself to Salieri, instead of the other way around that I have pointed to in the play and film. Hence, the child, again, would be father of the man. It is, after all, what Salieri himself announces when, as a child, he idolizes Amadeus-the-child (film, scene 15). Who remains for the most part a child throughout the story-confession. These positions, too, are imminently reversible: Salieri-Amadeus and Amadeus-Salieri. Referring directly to Deleuze again, I can say that the bloc of the wasp and the orchid can change positions, refolding into different assemblages. It is, as Deleuze says, a "double capture since 'what' each becomes changes no less than 'that which' becomes" (*Dialogues* 2). Salieri becomes part of Amadeus's creative apparatus (a mad deus) at the same time as Amadeus becomes the creativity of Salieri (a patron saint of mediocrities).[28]

HENRY MILLER: If I might be impertinent, "I remember sitting at the piano in my nightshirt, working away at the pedals with bare feet.... I was on the piano stool and doing a velocity exercise. I always began with Czerny.... Long before I read Wittgenstein's *Tractatus Logico-Philosophicus* I was composing the music to it, in the key of sassafras.... This vomit of learned truck was stewing in my guts the whole week long, waiting for it to come Sunday to be set to music.... I would get my inspiration, which was to destroy all the existent forms of harmony and create my own cacophony.... One Sunday... I composed one of the loveliest scherzos imaginable—to a louse.... Sunday came like

---

28 I use a slot and substitution approach in regards Deleuze's sentence in *Dialogues*.

a thaw, the birds driven so crazy by the sudden heat that they flew in and out of the window, immune to the music. One of the German relatives had just arrived from Hamburg, or Bremen.... She used to pat me on the head and tell me I would be another Mozart. I hated Mozart, and I hate him still and so to get even with her I would play badly, play all the sour notes I knew.... One of the reasons why I never got anywhere with the bloody music is that it was always mixed up with sex.... Lola was my first piano teacher. Lola Niessen..." (*Tropic* 248–50)....

> ✡ Hal, there is something very anarchistic in Henry Fool's thoughts and actions.

HAL HARTLEY: Yes, as I say, "he symbolizes anarchy and he brings the blood into our interactions with each other" ("Responding" xiv). Recall what Henry says to Father Hawkes and Simon.

HENRY FOOL: "Listen, father, as I was about to tell my friend Simon here, I am, without doubt, the biggest sinner within a hundred miles of this parish. But still, I've gotta stay up late at night to outdo the unending parades of mundane little atrocities I see committed everyday right out in the open spaces of this loud and sunlit culture we call home" (*HF* 48).

> ✡ Henry says, "outdo." This is so ambiguous here. Henry reminds me of Professor Avenarius, a character in Kundera's *Immortality*. Avenarius is an anarchist of sorts, but it is too simple to call him such, just as it is to call Henry an anarchist. What Avenarius does is to play a game, a sort of childish game of introducing prankish, chance interventions into people's lives. Marx speaks of no longer interpreting the

world but changing it. Avenarius sets out to do just this! But he does primarily one thing. At night while jogging, he travels through the streets of Paris on foot with a hidden knife in a sheath in his long coat and, spontaneously, selects an automobile and stabs at its tires. Flattening them (245). The act is best thought of, according to Avenarius, as totally irrational episodes, being introduced into the world.[29] The Narrative of the world. Avenarius says, "I dreamed of writing a big book: *The Theory of Chance*" (225).

א In a metafictional manner during a pause in story-time, Avenarius discusses a character in the novel with Kundera, arguing over whether the character is symbolic (heuristic) or something else such as chance (*touché*, aleatory). Avenarius explains to Kundera "how to perform a perfect subversive act, effective and yet safe from discovery by the police" (245). What motivates Avenarius is that he believes he is fighting Diabolum. He has no faith in Marx or others in their attempts to fight evil or as Henry Fool says, "mundane little atrocities." Banal atrocities. For Avenarius it is his subversive acts that change the world.[30]

HAL HARTLEY: So Avenarius would rather rely on chance

---

[29] Kundera discusses Aristotle's rejection of *episodes* in the *Poetics*. Kundera's aim is to rehabilitate the concept and figure of *episode*, which informs *Immortality* (305). Episodics.

[30] The paradigm that informs the narrative fluxes of *Immortality* is that of Heraclitus's child playing a game. Throwing the dice. Or playing on or running into the street. In the fluxes of Kundera's *Immortality* a child for some unknown reason sits in the middle of the road, causing cars to crash and people to die. The child is not hurt. Cf. Robert Altman's *Short Cuts*: Begin with "Logos" and "Opening Credits" and then jump to "Casey's Accident." Thereafter. Stop. Return to "Logos." View until the end. My neighbor.

than some socially-dialectically engineered way of attacking Diabolum.

> א Yes, apparently.... Well, one night while Avenarius is out for a jog and a tire slashing, he is mistaken by a woman as someone who is charging toward her with a knife in hand. She tells the police: "He threatened me with a knife! He wanted to rape me!" (263). Before being taken away by the police, a man who is a lawyer walks up and gives Avenarius his business card. The man is Paul, a major, connected character in the story. After handing the card, Paul returns to his car to see that the tires have been cut (264).
>
> In the closing pages of *Immortality*, Kundera and Avenarius talk about Paul, who gets Avenarius acquitted. What we know going into this episode by way of the unfolding narrative is that Avenarius was the lover of Paul's wife. (The coincidences thicken.) Avenarius explains to Kundera that he does not tell Paul that he is innocent of attempted rape.

AVENARIUS: "[N]o man will suspect someone known to rape women at knifepoint to be the lover of his wife. Those two images don't go together."

MILAN KUNDERA: "Wait a minute," I said. "He *really* thinks that you wanted to rape women?"

AVENARIUS: "I told you about that."

MILAN KUNDERA: "I thought you were joking."

AVENARIUS: "Surely I wouldn't reveal my secret!" And he added, "Anyway, even if I had told him the truth he wouldn't have believed me. And even if he had believed me, he would have immediately lost interest in my case. I was valuable to him only as a rapist."

MILAN KUNDERA: I was strangely moved. "You were ready to go to jail as a rapist, in order not to betray the game...." And at that moment I understood him at last. If we cannot accept the importance of the world, which considers itself important, if in the midst of that world our laughter finds no echo, we have but one choice: to take the world as a whole and make it the object of our game; to turn it into a toy. Avenarius is playing a game, and for him the game is the only thing of importance in a world without importance. But he knows that his game will not make anyone laugh.... I said, "You play with the world like a melancholy child who has no little brother."

AVENARIUS: I smiled like a melancholy child. Then I said, "I don't have a little brother, but I have you" (344). Avenarius-Kundera, Kundera-Avenarius. The metacharacter is the father of the author. And vice versa

> א Kundera and Avenarius part never to see each other again. Kundera writes: "Avenarius was going to the basement, where he had parked his Mercedes" (345).

CHASTE CINEMA I?

Mat Hinlin: Do you believe in God?
Babs (Divine): I am God.
> John Waters, *Pink Flamingo* in *Trash Trio* 84–85

Only a [Divine] can *still save us*.
> Martin Heidegger, "*Der Spiegel* Interview"
> (57; emphasis mine)

Installation, DVD Three (John Waters, *Multiple Maniacs*, Chaste Rape in Divine Places): *Set in John Waters's parents front yard in Baltimore, Maryland.*

- א To discuss *Multiple Maniacs*, we need to begin again with Jean-Luc Nancy's "Divine Places" in *The Inoperative Community*. Jean-Luc thinks of God, or gods, not as being, but as place (114). The onto-theological question What is God? leads but to a deflected transcendence in the name of immanence. This obsessive desire for an object called God/gods that would be *the* subject, this thinking of the object relation to subject, is what thwarts community. Such thinking is insidious and invidious. In dealing even with the possibilities of God as place, Jean-Luc sees that he must be forever suspicious of falling back into "a discourse *de Deo*, of whatever sort" (114). Hence, he chooses "to fragment [his] argument" (114). And eventually to singularize it.

- א But it is important to note that this place is not the traditional *topos* of philosophical-ethical or rhetorical-political thinking. Rather, it is a place in relation to, adjacent to, any traditional *topos*. It is what Jean-

Luc refers to as "the tying of the (k)not" (*Sense* 111–12). It is the other place—that is not traditionally other— of contestation and tests.³¹ It is an*other* place of third figures.³²

א In asking the question, "What does 'my God' mean?," Jean-Luc reflects on the nature of the question and sees it as "interpellative: you, here, now, are entering into a singular relationship with me. This does not ensure the relationship, nor in any way provide the measure of it. But it proclaims it, and gives it its chance" (*Inoperative* 117).

א Jean-Luc turns to a pertinent discussion by Jean-Marie Pontevia on "the cult of the Virgin." Pontevia sees this "major event" (i.e., the advent of the cult) as "the last example in the West of the birth of a divinity" (*Inoperative* 114; qtd from *La peinture* 69). Jean-Luc chooses to read "last example" as saying "that a divine birth is always possible, and that it is therefore *still possible*. But at the same time it means that such a birth bears no relation to a 'return,' a restoration, or a reinvention of the divine—quite the opposite.... The divinity born in the figure of the Virgin was in no way the return or the reincarnation

---

31 Acts of *contestation* and *testing*, both of which reopen and keep open (guard) a question, avoid reactionary processes of thought (see Derrida, *Of Spirit* 7–13; Foucault, *Language* 36). Testing is an act of reading that I take from Ronell (*Test Drive*). Both Foucault and Bataille point to Blanchot as the thinker of contestation. (See Bataille, *Inner Experience* 10–12, and 101–57.)

32 Nancy is aware of the missing third possibility: "Perhaps neither affirmation nor negation may be substituted for the question. It could be a question of another disposition, one that has no logical name" (*Experience* 165). Cf. Foucault's "nonpositive affirmation" (*Language* 36).

of a former divinity. It was the divinity of a new age: of a new age of painting and of woman, as well as of the age in which God himself would vanish into the Concept. It was a divine sign opposed to God" (114–15; emphasis mine. Cf. Kristeva, *Tales of Love*).

JEAN-LUC NANCY: Yes, I guess the important thing here—for I am beginning to see the indirection you are going in—is that this god that is coming, this new Divine place, among places, is a third figure (not to be confused with the trinity of spirit).

GIORGIO AGAMBEN: Ah, yes. This will be the coming community?

AVITAL RONELL: The community without a community? One that keeps coming, never arriving. Always deferred.

א Yes, if there is something like a *topos*, it is *différance*, not the old philosophical-rhetorical *topos* of difference. To cut to the chase and to risk being chastised, I would venture that this new Divine place is something that gets replayed by John Waters in the old forms as a *parody* but more so as a series of *pastiches*—so *as if* to critique the myth of immanence itself—but then, this new Divine place is also something entirely new.[33] As John Waters tells us: "Being Catholic always makes you more theatrical" (*Shock Value* 65). Yes, I remember High Mass! And the Stations of the Cross! But what Waters is talking about and enacting in his Divine films, similarly to Jean-Luc's take, is a

---

33 For a discussion of *parody* and *pastiche*, begin with Jameson, "Postmodernism" and Hutcheon, *Poetics*.

theatricality (a theater model of a third place) without foundations, without substantiality.[34]

א But, I must insist, *this theatrical moment*—and all that there is here, in this space—is a series of moments—*is of the chorus*. Expropriating the stage. The traditional academic actors (agents), after all, have left the stage. Call this moment the *parabasis* (see de Man, *Blindness* 187–228). It's an interruption of self-consciousness, a series of moments, kairotic moments, best called finitude. Para-acts of finitude. It is us! In this non-traditional polylogue. Here. Now.

א So our thoughts about a Divine place. First, there is the God, then the cult of the Virgin—both an expression of immanence and infinity. But then there is what is new in terms of Divine (places)—an ex-position of imminence and finitude, a radically infinite finitude. So as I see Water's film, there's a movement towards a third that is not a 1, 2, and then 3, etc.

JEAN-LUC NANCY: This third Divine "is precisely what manifests itself and is recognizable outside of all knowledge

---

34 About theater, Nancy writes: "One would thus demand a politics without dénouement—which perhaps also implies a politics without theatrical model, or a theater that would be neither tragic nor comic nor a dramatization of foundation—a politics of the incessant tying up of singularities with each other, over each other, and through each other, without any end other than the enchainment of (k)nots, without any structure other than their interconnection or interdependence, and without any possibility of calling any single (k)not or the totality of (k)nots self-sufficient (for there would be 'totality' only in the enchainment itself). Such a politics consists, first of all, in testifying that there is singularity only where a singularity ties itself up with other singularities, but that there is no tie except where the tie is taken up again, recast, and retied without end, nowhere purely tied or untied. Nowhere founded and nowhere destined, always older than the law and the younger than sense" (*Sense* 111–12).

about its 'being.' God does not propose himself as a new type of being—or of absence of being—for us to know. He proposes himself, that is all" (*Inoperative* 115–16).

> א His proposal is a singular one. Not One, but a singular one that is not part of a set of numbers. There is no knowledge of such a singularity, for it establishes a relationship only momentarily. With ex-position comes ex-scription.

JEAN-LUC NANCY: Yes, for to know (under the terms of identity, non-contradiction, and excluded middle); for to expect a permanence would only take us back to the myth of immanence and a "theologicopolitics," which is the source of a "sacrificial politics" (*Sense* 89; cf. 91–92, 105–06). God *proposes* himself, and yet there is no "he" or "she." Rather, *there is* the nothing…that remains of gods" (*Inoperative* 116). After the death of God. But this nothing is not negative. Nor is it something positive. Rather again, it is what "remains"—call it the remainders—for which there is no proper-improper vocabulary in the language of reason. Or call it singular. Or call it crumbs. God has crumbled. Or still, call it, as I offer a list in *The Sense of the World*, the "fallen pieces, waste, wreckage, jagged bits, remains, inner organs of slaughtered beasts, shreds, filth, and excrement, on which contemporary art—*trash art*—gorges itself" (132). All that has been ex-scribed.

> א Yes, we are referring perhaps to the excluded middle here—all that has no proper name for itself, other than a traveling freak show, a "Cavalcade of Perversion" (*Multiple Maniacs*). Therefore, we are referring—deferring—to what remains as third Divine places. We can casuistically twist and stretch the language in such a mannerism, as Michel Foucault has, and refer

to this third Divine as a "nonpositive affirmation" (*Language* 36).

א In terms of sex, it is a third, neutral figure of sex. Which gets us to Divine in *Multiple Maniacs* as well as *Pink Flamingoes* and *Pink Flamingoes Forever*—all, as you might say, are "trash" art, "shock" art (*Sense*, 132, 133). Divine, after awe, in *Pink Flamingos*, eats dog (god) faeces. Making Peace.

א We can perhaps say now that Divine is a transgression in the form of a wicked parody of Christianity. But we can also say—more so—that Divine is a wicked pastiche of Christianity. Of a God caught up in being on its way to becoming. In a space. And yet, Divine is something new in opposition to both God and the cult of the Virgin. Divine is constantly interrupting and con/testing.[35] On her w*ayves* with others, becoming, devolving, into yet something else. For example, in the intended sequel to *Pink Flamingos*, Divine says:

> DIVINE: There is only one man in my life— my husband, Crackers II, who you may remember is also my son.

---

35 For the literalists, Waters says: "Underneath all this cockeyed glamour lives a serious actor [Harris Glenn Milstead] who wants nothing more than to work every day.... Divine is certainly no transvestite. He says he sometimes dreads getting in drag but realizes these flamboyant outfits are his 'work clothes.' The only time he goes through the drag ordeal is for a play, movie, or personal appearance. Thank God, he is also not a female impersonator—I can hardly imagine him making people suffer through Judy Garland or Carol Channing imitations. Divine is simply an actor who usually is cast as a woman. He seems comfortable living his 'interpretation of a man' and says he is quite satisfied with his natural 'plumbing'" (*Shock* 145; cf. Mueller, "Divine" in *Ask* 220–22).

UPI (*appalled*): You're talking about incest?

DIVINE: I cannot begin to describe to you the genealogical miracle of producing a grandchild in my own little oven.

UPI: Is the kid retarded?

DIVINE: Another bourgeois myth handed down by generations of charlatans in the American Medical Association. My child is living proof of a new strain of heterosexuality.
(*Flamingoes Forever*, in *Trash Trio* 189)

א Divine, as you might say, Jean-Luc, "does not behave like a sign. Perhaps ["her"] nature is that of a [Divine] Wink, of a gesture that invites or calls" (*Inoperative* 119; cf. *Dis-Enclosure* 104–20). That calls us not home but to thinking. To uncanny thinking. Recall, Barthes' use of the *twink*, or *twinkling*, as of a star. A flash of considerations in an instant (*Neutral* xxi, xxiii, xxv, 10, 30, 47; cf. Nancy, *Sense* 42–45).

JOHN WATERS: I just can't believe, Victor, what you are saying about Divine!

א John, I am not interpreting; I'm, as Deleuze says, experimenting. I'm calling on Divine in mixed ways. My wa*yves*.

א Heidegger intuited that only Divine (spaces) could still save us. But Divine (spaces) remains veiled from the beginning. "In fact, the history of Western thought begins, not by thinking what is most thought-provoking," Heidegger says, "but by letting it remain forgotten. Western thought thus begins with an omission, perhaps even a failure. So it seems, as long as we regard oblivion only as a deficiency, something negative.... The beginning of Western thought is not the same as its origin. The beginning is, rather, the veil that conceals the origin—indeed an unavoidable veil" (*What is Called Thinking* 152). In other words, all has been kept Chaste. It is not a matter of our raising the veil to chastise. It is rather a matter of what still remains unthought. Heidegger amusingly gives us this exemplar: "The sentence 'The triangle is laughing' cannot be said. It can be said, of course, in the sense that it can be pronounced as a mere string of words. But it can not be said really, in terms of what it says. The things that are evoked by 'triangle' and 'laughing' introduce something contradictory into their relation.... To be possible, the proposition must from the start avoid self-contradiction. This is why the law, that contradiction must be avoided, is considered a basic tenet of the proposition. Only because thinking is defined as [*logos*], as an utterance, can the statement about contradiction perform its role as a law of thought" (155). But you see, John, *the triangle of* « God—Cult of Virgin—Divine (places) » *here is laughing*. And not only the triangle is laughing, but also the reader. It is a laughing matter. Even if a laughter in dis/belief. But this is a laughter, perverse as *it is*, that will shatter the law of what has gone for thinking, just as the generosity of thinking has shattered love (see Nancy, *Inoperative* 82–109; cf. Davis, *Breaking*). All triangles are not necessarily Euclidean; many have attributes, in other compossible geometric worlds, of varying degrees in relation to angles such as hyperbolic and elliptical geometries. These geometric worlds are imminent.

CHASTE CINEMA I? 55

JOHN WATERS: So you are saying that at the basis of thinking is rape, but there is a way around this basis and that is parabasis, interruptions, to non-traditional other spaces.

> א Yes, actually and figuratively.... So let's begin again: John, you have written about Jean-Luc Godard's *Hail Mary*.[36] You have disclosed the divinity of rape itself not only in your own films, but also in Godard's.

JOHN WATERS: Yes, I remember, Victor. I said, "Although the cinematography [in *Hail Mary*] is incredible, the acting first-rate and the script guaranteed to bring a smile to anyone with a sense of humor who was raised a Catholic, it is also very confusing.... The film is reverent in its own ironic way.... As an ex-Catholic, *Hail Mary* actually made me think fondly of religion for the first time in decades. Who knows what effect Hail Mary will have on my own spirituality? Of all people, I never thought *Godard* might tempt me back to the Church. Now, at least, I have a new respect for the outrageousness and originality of the concept Immaculate Conception. Maybe I won't be as angry as I used to be when I hear childhood Catholic trauma stories, such as the one a friend named Mary (her real name) told me recently; All through the year in grade school the nuns showed the class a mysterious hole in the wall at the end of the hall. One by one, each girl was taken to peer in but forbidden to reveal what they saw. When Mary's time finally came, she apprehensively approached, stuck her head through, and saw herself reflected in a mirror across from her, framed in a nun's habit. She finally got to see herself

---

36 *Hail Mary* was received in Europe and the U.S. as blasphemous. Waters says: "Pope John Paul II... denounced the film and led a special prayer ceremony 'to repair the outrage inflicted on the Holy Virgin'" (*Crackpot* 134–35).

as a nun. Did the good sister accompanying her whisper in her ear, 'Hail Mary'? I wonder" (*Crackpot* 138–39).

> ℵ Ah, sounds like a second attempt at the mirror stage. In any case, Divine and the Mary of *Hail Mary* and all the other Marys, in questioning and adding to the Cult of the Virgin, prepare the waYvES for Divine (places). By ways of irony.... I want to turn to the scene we might call *Divine* rape of *Divine* by Lobstora. (The double articulation of Divine, as adjective and noun, is awkward, but will become more unclearly clear as we proceed.) I find this whole scene confusing.

JOHN WATERS: Oh, there you go again!

> ℵ I'm just echoing what you said about Godard!

> ℵ This scene, toward the end of the film, is supposed to be a projection of the crazed Divine, who is foaming at the mouth after having killed several of the characters.[37] At best, we might argue—given the in-joke of the giant, mechanical lobster—that this is Caca-pitalism appropriating the crazed Divine and, thus, your film, John, like so many, if not all, studio films, is always already appropriated. Which of course *it is* in/appropriated *as* canonized filth. Yet something—an excess—still remains. As an exscription. And how shall we approach that remainder? Let's consider the context.

> ℵ The third, the lobster-Divine rape scene, has other possibilities in terms of the two previous rape scenes.

---

37 The scene is captured on YouTube: <http://www.youtube.com/watch?v=tm2PPPKlX8Y>.

The first rape is perpetrated by two members of Divine's Cavalcade of Perversion. A male and female drag her into an alley and, while the female holds her down, the male rapes her. (It is in this scene that you searched for the *still frame* of "Divine's face in the one moment *between* rape and miraculous intervention where he lived up to the spiritual side of his name" [*Director's Cut* 283; emphasis mine].) The second rape is perpetrated by Mink Stole, the *religious whore* in church, who stalks, sits next to, and gives Divine a "rosary job" during the stations of the cross. Popular episodes from the life of Christ (from the feeding of the multitudes to His crucifixion) are enfolded into scenes of Mink anally raping Divine with the prosthetic crucifix of the rosary. Rosy Crucifixion! You cannot get more perverse than this, John. But at the levels of parody and pastiche you are referring to the sadomasochism embedded in the founding narratives of Catholicism, which are played out analogically in the assemblages not only of the crucifixion but also of the stations-of-the-cross and the Divine-Mink "rosary job."[38] Which gets us to the point of seeing this assemblage of entities forming a single becoming, a single bloc, an a-parallel evolution (or devolution), a double capture, a *conversation* (between the stations of the cross and scenes in *Multiple Maniacs*). Herewith, the single bloc of Chaste CruciFictions: Christ being crucified, celebrated in the stations of the cross/

---

38 The question of whether Waters is constructing a *parody* or a *pastiche* of the crucifixion is one that I provisionally answer by saying that Waters's constructions are both a parody and a pastiche and yet something new, which will become unclearly clear eventually. Cf. Francis Bacon's paintings of the crucifixion and Fynsk's discussion of them (*Infant* 15). for Serrano's "Piss Christ," see Serrano. But keep in mind that the "rosary job" in *Multiple Maniacs* comes from de Sade (see Zoe Gross, 21, n19 on 35).

Divine being "crucified" by Mink, re-celebrated in *Multiple Maniacs*.

א Deleuze and Guattari discuss the lobster in *A Thousand Plateaus* and in such *wayves* that it might cast some light or darkness on the *third* rape in *Multiple Maniacs*. They write: "God is a Lobster, or a double pincer, a double bind" (40). Yet another double articulation! The classic double bind places the female in the position of being both revered and raped (see Haskell; cf. Russell). Divine is both revered and raped repeatedly.

א But more on the third rape, with Lobstora "doing" Divine: Deleuze and Guattari are in part talking about "the geology of morals" (39-74). If previously by way of Heidegger we introduced the paralogy of "triangle is laughing," and how the correct thinking of philosophy could not allow for such an utterance, now we introduce the paralogy of *Lobster (God) is raping Divine (God),* and how a proper protocol of reading could never allow for such a linkage.[39] But then it is not simply a matter of my idiosyncratic linking; it is a matter, John, of your linking three rapes with the third one by way of not just any lobster but Lobstora, which greatly complicates matters! Lobstora is the sign of CacaPitalism? It is not that

---

39 I allude to Lyotard's notion of *it is necessary to link but not how to link* (in *Differend*), and call on Ulmer's principles of conduction in making these paralogic linkages (*Heuretics*). Besides the paralogies constructed by Waters, we have in my insertion of Deleuze and Guattari's statement that *God is a Lobster*, the paralogy of *geology of morals* (echoing Nietzsche's *Genealogy of Morals*). Cf. Bataille, et al., "Crustaceans," in *Encyclopaedia* 38-40.

I want to interpret this sequence and this strange (attractor) of Lobstora. (John, you are not merely critiquing capitalism, if it can be said that you are "critiquing" anything or anybody!)[40] It is that I want to experiment—or otherwise put, I want to contest in a non-traditional manner and to go on test drives— with these already experimental constructions across different semiotic as well as symbiotic systems.

א In a logical and justifiable sense, as Deleuze and Guattari might say, God raping God (A is A, A raptures A) is quite appropriate, as a primordial, self-reflexive, kairotic moment, yet still tautological if not paradoxical. And exuberantly laughable! If you, John, are devout—but of course you are not—you might laugh nervously. Or explode in anger against such a sacrilegious act. But how would you explain, otherwise, this God on God, or Dog on Dog, to someone else? Is it your intention that the scene is to be explained? Or is the scene for affect? At best, about this sacrilegious-blasphemous move in *Multiple Maniacs*, or antics, I can say, John, that you mock what you see to be the sacrificial economy. And you do so without mincing a word or image. You question anyone's participation in the ritual of the *Stations of the Cross* (cf. Žižek, "Divine Violence" in *Violence* 178–205).

JOHN WATERS: Really?!

---

40 The scene of Lobstora's raping Divine was not Waters's original intention. He had planned that Divine would be charged with the death of Sharon Tate and others. But when Charles Manson and his group were captured and charged with the crimes, Waters had to rethink the ending. Hence, a giant lobster, Lobstora. (Cf. Cookie Mueller, "Abduction and Rape" in *Ask*, 102–13.)

א And yet, John, it is not possible to miss the fact that in having Mink "crucify" Divine, you may be trafficking in a sacrificial economy yourself. As Georges Bataille says, "The crucifixion...is a wound by which believers communicate with God" (*Guilty* 31). But perhaps *Multiple Maniacs* is not a critique, not a visual utterance of a festering wound that leads but to acts of *ressentiment*, but an exchange or communication of another kind. Let's take, from Bataille again, the possibility of two forms of an exchange: First, "communication linking up two beings (laughter of a child to its mothers, tickling)," and second, "communication, through death, with our beyond (essentially in sacrifice)—not with nothingness, still less with a supernatural being, but with an indefinite reality (which I sometimes call *the impossible*, that is: what can't be grasped (*begreift*) in any way, what we can't reach without dissolving ourselves, what's slavishly called God)" (139; cf. 140–43).

The former, I will eventually elaborate on; the latter can but lead to pure immanence. Someone is going to be sacrificed. And yet, Bataille further explains that if we do not opt for immanence, "the sacred, God," we "can remain in an undefined state (in ordinary laughter, infinite laughter, or ecstasy in which the divine form melts like sugar in water)" (*Guilty* 139).[41]

My experiment, my experience with re-viewings of *Multiple Maniacs*, is that you, John, are dis/engaging less with a parody of sacrifice and more with pastiche. You are not interested in correcting the scene but in

---

41 The manner in which Bataille draws out this distinction applies well to what I am experiencing in my experimental relation with *Multiple Maniacs*. I would recommend now that the readers study the section on "The Divinity of Laughter" in *Guilty*. I would rather leave to the readers the task of thinking through the connections.

enjoying the obscene. And at times, vice versa. After all, you want to have your scene and eat it too, but you experienced two rival scents. (I fully understand, for I cannot get out of my mind the story of Gérard de Nerval putting a leash on his lobster and strolling down the gardens of the Palais-Royal in Paris. I can no longer eat lobsters!)

Hence, *you are laughing as a child would* at the so-called adult view of life-death-heaven/or/hell story of Catholicism, or any Protestantism.[42] You can be read as moving toward a third possibility of contestation. Through laughter, corrupted or otherwise....

MILAN KUNDERA: Ah, let me interrupt and jump in here, for I discuss through Rubens how classical and traditional painters avoid the open mouth in laughter, for they see it as either the sign of evil or of a human being's inability to think, to reason, or to rule himself. For Rubens, "Faces lost their immobility, mouths became open, only when the painter wished to express evil. Either the evil of pain: the faces of women bent over the body of Jesus; the open mouth of the mother in Poussin's *Slaughter of the Innocents*. Or the evil of vice: Holbein's *Adam and Eve*. Eve has

---

42 Here is a slight modification by addition (paralogy) and placement (adjacency): Let us recall Tiresias, becoming the middle term between two sets of copulating snakes, between two sets of being both female and male, and between two gods. As mythical versions have it, s/he was blinded by both Hera and Athena (see Loraux, *Experiences* 10–11). By Hera, for Tiresias sides with Zeus that men have more pleasure in sex than women; in a completely different version, by Athena, for Tiresias looks upon her body. If we initially think of the Lobstora rape scene in terms of Divine's being like—or rather becoming—Tiresias, we might come to see "Divine"-the-character caught *between* two gods (or double pincers) and, hence, mis/appropriately "Divine," like Tiresias, is both male *and* female. Having a *conversation* in between. Deleuze writes: "A thing is sometimes this, sometimes that, sometimes something more complicated—depending on the forces (the gods) which take possession of it" (*Nietzsche* 4).

a bland face and a half-open mouth revealing teeth that have just bitten into the apple. Alongside, Adam is a man still before sin: he is beautiful, his face is calm, and his mouth is closed. In Correggio's *Allegories of Sin* everyone is smiling! In order to express vice, the painter must move the innocent calm of the face, to spread the mouth, to deform the features with a smile. There is only one laughing figure in the picture: a child! But it is not a laugh of happiness, the way children are portrayed in advertisements for diapers or chocolate! The child is laughing because it's been corrupted!" (*Immortality* 322–23)...

א Milan, that is an interruption that builds on what I was about to remind us. Namely, that Bataille writes: "I wouldn't give up *laughing* for anything!" (*Guilty* 54)...[43] There are adults. Who will laugh at anything! But let us not forget the child, which takes us to my final experiment in thinking about *Multiple Maniacs* (or radical singularities).

א First, however, let me continue writing-the-pastiche and let us recall how Bataille complicates for us, as you do John, the question of laughter: "[T]he suddenness of...change (the fall of the adult system—that of grown-ups—into an infantile one) is always found in laughter. Laughter is reducible, in general, to the laugh of recognition in the child—which the following line from Vergil calls to mind: *incipe, parve puer, risu cognoscere matrem*." ["Begin, young child, to recognize your mother by your laughter" also as "by *her* laughter."] (*Guilty* 140; Bataille's emphasis).

---

[43] There is also Cixous's *the laugh of the medusa*, which can topple phallocratic discourse. For a further discussion of mine on laughter and its limits, see *Sexual Violence* (178–81).

א This exemplar of the child *recognizing its place* in its own or its mother's laughter works well for the Cult of the Virgin. With child.

א But will it work or play well for the Cavalcade of Perversions, for the *lumpenproletariat*, that follows not recognition of its place, but Divine (places) where *there is* laughter and giggling? The *lumpen/proletariat*, which was, as Marx could have said: "the whole indefinite, disintegrated mass [absolute negation]... *la bohème*...this scum, offal, refuse of all classes."[44] But which Mr. David, the barker in the very beginning of *Multiple Maniacs*, does clearly stipulate: The "real actual filth...assorted sluts, fags, dykes, and pimps."

א Suffer the *infans*. The interruptions, corruptions, eruptions.

---

44 Marx says precisely what I quote (see *Eighteenth* 75). But in alluding to Marx, I change the context and the meaning of his notion of the *lumpenproletariat*, which I see as third figures. I have my disagreements with Eagleton on how to read the figure, though I agree with Mehlman. I add the slash in *lumpen/proletariat* to signify my difference with Marx and Eagleton. Eagleton writes: "Jeffrey Mehlman sees the elegant dialectical schemas of Marx's *Eighteenth Brumaire* as fissured by an uncouth, irreducible cackle of farce: the farce of Bonaparte himself, the non-representative, Bonaparte pries a crack in that conceptual architecture through which floods a heterogeneous swarm of lumpenproletarians, a flood that threatens to swamp Marx's own orderly text under the semiotic excess it lends to his language. The upshot, Mehlman comments '[is] a Marx more profoundly anarchical than Anarchism ever dreamed'" (in *Walter Benjamin* 162). See Mehlman, *Revolution*. I have previously and in greater depth argued for Mehlman's position and have extended it in *Negation* (391). Also, see my "Hermeneutics of Abandonment." Hence, I am arguing that the giggles-laughter that I identify in *Amadeus*, *Henry Fool*, and now *Multiple Maniacs* is the non-canonical excess, a third figure, or Divine (places).

א In keeping with this discussion, what is most intriguing, in terms of laughter, in *Multiple Maniacs* is the transitional scene between the first and second rape of Divine. I am referring to the appearance (in[ter]vention) of the *Infant of Prague*, taking Divine by the hand *from* having been raped by the male and female in the streets *to* the church of St. Cecilia, where Devine will be anally raped-"crucified" by Mink. How are we to read this! Divine says, "Had God sent him [the infant] as some sort of sign?" She concludes: "I put my future in this little saint's hands [who said] 'The more you honor me, the more I will bless you'." Honor me! Bless you! There are a number of double entendres in these promises.

א Should we call on Father Freud to rethink the *relation* of child to Divine and rape! I doubt it! In any case, whereas initially we have here the *Virgin* as mother, or father, of the son, we now have the *infans* as father, or mother, of Divine (places). And throughout we have John, the Divine! Exiled in Baltimore. Filming his apocalyptic view of the Divine.

If you remember, John, we started this conversation on your film with a reference to Jean-Luc's "Divine Places" in *The Inoperative Community*. Then, the cult of the virgin, to *Hail Mary*, to the Lobstora-Divine rape scene, and then God as a lobster—all of which converge in Baltimore, Maryland. I want to add now that I spent some time searching through dictionaries of etymologies for the name "Baltimore." I finally found in the *New York Times*, way back to c. December 17, 1880, the following report of a paper entitled "Celtic Baltimore, its Etymology" that was read by General Charles E. Phelps at a meeting of the Maryland Historical Society, in Baltimore. The reporter writes: "General [Charles E.] Phelps said 'Bal' was Celtic for 'place.' Ti-mor means the Supreme Being. Now, add the common Celtic prefix meaning place, and you have Bal-Ti-mor, which, being literally translated, with nothing but the usual inversion to make idiomatic English, reads 'God-Place'." Mary Land. Conductively, my case rests. But you knew this as some pop culture level, right? ☺

(To be continued.)

> [A] change metaphorically comparable to that which made Euclid's geometry into that of Riemann. (Valery once confided to a mathematician that he was planning to write—to speak—on 'a Riemann surface.') A change such that to speak (to write) is to cease thinking solely with a view to unity, and to make the relations of words an essentially dissymmetrical field governed by discontinuity.
>
> Maurice Blanchot, "Interruption: As on a Riemann surface" in *The Infinite Conversation* (77).

Cut To Paste: Writing flux aside flux in countless flows on "a Riemann surface": In this re-opening chapter, I have conversed with the characters and commentators. At times, my approach has been conventional in terms of a montage or collage.[45] Cutting and pasting passages together. Other times, however, I have attempted to write by wa*yves* ~~~ of a relation of a third kind, a third interval, a third relation, as Blanchot says, that "inaugurates a relation that would not be one of subject to subject or of subject to object" (*Infinite* 69). I am a writer—in dis/respect to my imagined interlocutors—without any horizon. I have no being or presence in my interlocutors' imaginary lives. Speaking to or with them (*Infans* in themselves) is like speaking in "a relation of impossibility and strangeness" (71).... *Infans* to *infans*.... *Infans* should be heard and not seen.... This

---

45 Cutting-and-pasting, as a method without method: See, of course, the unwork of Brion Gysin and W. S. Burroughs along with Paul Miller (Dj Spooky). But there are also the paintings of Simon Hantaï, who cuts, knots, and folds. For a further explanation, see Nancy, *Ground* (118–25); Hayes, "Body."

is... has been... not a dialogue but a polylogue... perhaps a cacophony... a relation of the third kind. Situated in between. A place that "we" could abandon ourselves to in dis/order to listen and think. The limit.[46]

---

[46] Flux within flux unworks the limit, as *ex-stasis* (*ecstasies*) unworks *stasis*. John Sallis writes: "Let it be said, then, that Dionysian ecstasy is an exceeding of the limit that would delimit the self, and exceeding in the dual sense of transgression and disruption. Thus is expressed in the logic of the Dionysian the dual nature of the god: reunion and dismemberment as transgression and disruption. *The logic of being outside oneself*, the logical dynamics of the figure of ecstasy, is such that, as transgression, *it cannot but disrupt the very limit by which it would be defined;* hence, in turn, there can be transgressive disruption of the limit only if the limit is also redrawn reinstated, as the very limit to be transgressed. The logic of the figure is such as to generate an unending round of transgression, disruption, and reinstatement.

Such is, then, ecstatic logic: a logic of reiterated duality, of the duality of transgression and disruption and of disruption and reinstatement. It is a logic to be written only by way of a certain duality, which has already been in play without my having, up to this point, marked it, a duality of effacement and (re)inscription, a crossing of what is said with an unsaying—in short, a double writing" (*Crossings* 55; emphasis added).

CHASTE CINEMA II?

> The most celebrated of [interpreters of the play *Penthesilea*] was Hans Neuenfels, whose *Penthesilea* at the Schiller-Theater in Berlin in 1981 was both a multimedia extravaganza and a sociohistorical exegesis. The men were variously costumed as Prussians, Greeks, and naked savages. Achilles was a jovial, compliant, middle-aged beau. The women skipped about by candle-light in flouncy white gowns, wielding dainty bows and arrows, reminding one reviewer of the 'obscene chastity' of Nazi kitsch. A hysterical Penthesilea burst from this pallid sorority like a hyena, crawled around on all fours before charging off to demolish Achilles, then came back lugging three bloody suitcases presumably filled with his remains. During the breaks, while the sets were changed, a silent film of the love-that-might-have-been was projected onto a screen, complete with a wedding feast blessed by the Amazon High Priestess.
>
> Joel Agee, Forward, *Penthesilea* (xxvi–xxvii)

The title of Helke Sander's controversial three-and-a-half-hour documentary film *BeFreier und Befreite: Krieg, Vergewaltigungen, Kinder* ("Liberators Take Liberties: War, Rapes, Children") itself never stops speaking and on multiple registers, filling the silence, articulating the unspoken, with a multimodal exposition of what has taken place and what it takes to reclaim, in perpetuity, that place.[1] Sander's book version, with the same title, is

---

1   The title is filled with puns. Levin writes: "The word '*Befreier*' designates a liberator (or liberators), but the film's title spells "Befreier" with a

in German—and edited—with Barbara Johr. In my discussions, I will refer to the film, however, which displays the multiple radicals of presentation that I am most concerned with, and will, when available, cite the discussions by way of the book. Because the film at this writing is still not easily available except through the Goethe Institute or through an out-of-print DVD (PAL version), I will provide a more full account of the film than would be usually expected.

Both the film and book (1992) deal with the mass rapes perpetrated by the Allied forces in Berlin as well as other occupied towns and villages in Germany between March and May of 1945. The forces included mostly Russian soldiers but also United States, British, and French soldiers. Sander speaks extensively with women raped and with their children born of rape. She also speaks with Russian men and women who fought in the Battle of Berlin. For some viewers, the film, however, is not solely documentary in style. For some, Sander becomes overly performative and theatrical in her presentations of discussions in scenes. Consequently, the film has many critics. I am limiting my discussion of the reception of this film (Facts, Statistics, Testimony), however, to those critics participating in the special issue "Berlin 1945: War and Rape" of the journal *October* 72 (Spring 1995), which includes an introduction to the film and its issues, criticisms of the film (resistance to it), Sander's response (counter-resistance), and a poly-

---

capital "f," thus drawing attention to the word '*Freier*' contained within it. In antiquated German, '*Freier*' designates a suitor (or suitors), one who would seek the hand of a maiden; in modern German it designates a john or johns (in the sense of a prostitute's customer).... [H]ere then, sexual relations and sexual exploitation are manifestly inscribed within liberation.... [T]he title can be understood to mean 'Liberators and Liberated,' 'Liberators and Wooed,' 'Wooers and Liberated,' 'Johns and Liberated,' 'Johns and Wooed,' and so on. The film sets out to explore the terrain opened up by these rather disparate meanings" (65).

logue of critics (meditations). We will get to the critics in due time.

First, I will take up the issue of whether or not the event had been discussed publicly before Sander's film. (This issue arises about mid-way through the film. It at times appears to be *the* main claim, or the one that appears to be most crucial, in the discussions!) Thereafter, I want to suggest with "lists,"[2] which in the opening of the film become an extended montage, the kind and amount of research that Sander gives to the discovery process. I will relate a few of the anecdotal accounts—rearranging each out of the order of the film in a rhetoric of oscillation—and will examine the "facts"[3] as Sander gathers and infers from statistics, for example, the numbers of German women raped. But it is not just German women raped, any more than it was not just Jews who died in the camps. We must respect and acknowledge the many threads that go into the making of this event of mass rape, murder, and genocide. Sander respects and acknowledges the threads through a *thinking discourse*. She is concerned with what is

---

2 There is nothing objective in Sander's list or sequencing of interlocutors. Montage in film, or juxtaposition, is highly rhetorical and suggestive of meaning. (For Sander's use of montage, see Levin 71.) And yet, anything "objective" would still be highly rhetorical and suggestive!

3 My purpose in rearranging-remixing-repurposing the sequences in an oscillation, that is, of the very facts of the film itself, is to achieve *a different rhetorical affect* in print as well as to encourage the reader to view the film itself for maximum comparison. Additionally, I place the word *facts* in quotations to emphasize the danger of taking facts as in themselves true. Like many, I take facts—the "hard facts" (see the book *BeFreier* 11)—as discursive constructions owing to the rules and regimens of verifiability. A fact is true or false and provable as such through these rules. In reference to Sander's pursuit of facts, Grossmann finds Sander "naïve" and Dr. Richling as equally naïve at the blackboard explaining the facts to Sander. Grossmann sees this scene as "border[ing] on parody" (44). On reporting facts and experiences as truthful, Grossmann cites Joan Scott, "The Evidence of Experience." Cf. Nancy and Kiarostami, *The Evidence of Film*.

called thinking? in regard to rape,[4] which, as I read critical responses to her work, misfires more often than not. But it is this inevitable misfiring that makes for a community of discussants for this film. On this event.

---

4   For Sander, thinking, as she would engage, is open and complex. Her book *The Three Women K* is one of the most remarkable discourses on thinking about human relations in terms of being a German female in post–WW II Germany and a patriarchal world, being with men and women.

Sander's *Liberators take Liberties*

> The Rape of Nanking should be remembered not only for the number of people slaughtered but for the cruel manner in which many met their deaths. Chinese men were used for bayonet practice and in decapitation contests. An estimated 20,000–80,000 Chinese women were raped. Many soldiers went beyond rape to disembowel women, slice off their breasts, nail them alive to walls. Fathers were forced to rape their daughters, and sons their mothers, as other family members watched. Not only did live burials, castration, the carving of organs, and the roasting of people become routine, but more diabolical tortures were practiced, such as hanging people by their tongues on iron hooks or burying people to their waists and watching them get torn apart by German shepherds. So sickening was the spectacle that even the Nazis in the city were horrified, one proclaiming the massacre to be the work of "bestial machinery." Yet the Rape of Nanking remains an obscure incident.
>
> Iris Chang, *The Rape of Nanking* (6)

Research (Facts, Statistics, Testimony): We begin with a statement of fact—according to a discursive construction—that the event of mass rape in Berlin, 1945, was kept a Chaste Rape (cf. Kleist, "*Marquise of O*"). While some historians write of the mass rapes in Berlin in books,[5] Sander claims the public did not discuss the rapes before *BeFreier und Befreite*. There had been, however, in the Seventies private discussions between mothers and their children born of rape. In the second reel of the film German women talk about not having discussed *the event*. Sander prompts them: "With whom did you talk about it later?"[6] Their

---

5 See James Burke, *Big Rape* (Frankfurt a. M.: Friedrich Rudl Verlegr Union, 1951) and Cornelius Ryan, *Last Battle* (London: Collins, 1966). I take these references from Grossman 62.n43. Additionally, Lilly, *Taken By Force* (NY: Palgrave Macmillan, 2007).

6 The film is in German, with sections in Russian. I am taking initially the translations from the subtitles, which are *notoriously imprecise*. Then,

responses: "With no one." Sander: "Nobody wanted to listen?" Response: "Nobody could listen.... You couldn't say anything against the Red Army." Sander: "And public opinion?" Response: "No, public opinion didn't exist in that sense. One could not express one's thoughts." Sander: "Had it anything to do with the fact that the liberators from Hitler fascism [*sic*] couldn't be rapists at the same time?" Response: "In the Nazi period we already had to climb down a peg. We just had to shut up. And later it was just the same." Response: "First one dictator and then...the next one. Always with the word 'psst.' That was our word in Germany." But the event manifested itself in sublimated ways. Sander tells of "the favorite game of a friend of [hers] who...together with male and female cousins, was 'playing at rape.' The girls would run screaming into the woods nearby or roll down the embankments while the boys ran after them, finally catching and throwing themselves on top of them" ("Remembering" 22).

In responding in print to these anecdotes, some critics, however, challenge Sander on being *the first* to bring the event to the attention of the world. Sander, however, claims the film first brought the issue to the public sphere. In the above exchange, the women say, "public opinion didn't exist." (It is difficult for me to begin without interruptions discussing Sander's discourse of facts, as she constructs

---

when in doubt about the translation, consulted a Germanist for advice. Since there are two languages being spoken, there are translations within translations, which often are not rendered in direct speech but in indirect speech, e.g., by the translator to Sander herself who apparently does not know Russian. (When the translator translates by way of indirect discourse, I state this fact.) Additionally part of the problem is that the exchange between Sander and her interlocutors is often simultaneous speech, that is, speech over speech. I have called on colleagues who translate German to English to help me through especially difficult, noisy sections of the film and with comparing German in the film with German in the book version. But the additional problem, across cultures, is that viewers need to be cautious also in reading the body language.

them, for there is much contestation about her film and book as there was about Susan Brownmiller's *Against Our Will*.) More important, however, than Who was on first? is that *the event* of mass rape not remain Chaste! The children playing the game of rape become, so to speak, the fathers of the man-Russian soldiers who raped their mothers. (The child is the father of the rapist!) And yet, the stories remain Chaste. Remembering can be forgetting. In fact, Sander's full title for the translated version of the first chapter of *BeFreier und Befreite* is "Remembering/Forgetting." *Remembering* can be read as *mourning* so as to forget. But remembering/forgetting can be a *self-exoneration* that some critics find at work in this documentary. The title of the film "liberators take liberties" echoes as a charge and counter-charge among the critics who would presume, in this instance, special status (*stasis*) for one group over another.

In this introductory chapter of the book *BeFreier und Befreite*—included in the journal *October*—Sander relates a story that she says was "the catalyst" for researching *the event*.[7] Sander writes of an old woman, Frau G., who lived in the same building in Berlin and who accused her and others of publishing communist papers and holding meetings. Confronting the woman, Sander discovered that Frau G. "had been raped by Russians and that all the other women living in this building in 1945 had the same experience" ("Remembering" 15). At the heart of this anecdote is revenge (15). The larger narrative of this anecdote, however, raises a question of whether or not the rapes of German women by Russians were a payback for all the rapes committed by the German army in the east against Russian

---

7 Liebman and Michelson write that for Sander the event was a "'*Zeitereignis*,' an event whose enormity makes it almost unique in history.... We know of no rapes of comparable scale in all of recorded history" ("After the Fall" 12). Sander says that the rape of Nanking is comparable.

women. Though this possibility is plausible, Sander does not accept it so easily as *the* case or the *only* case. We will return to this issue as we examine other anecdotal evidence,[8] in search of an appropriately inclusive *representative anecdote* (see Burke, *Grammar*). That search must include, as Sander insists, various forces at work on a community's discussions in the public sphere. The community (as inoperative as it can become) would have to take into consideration nascent forces at work. As a case in point, Sander explains that the mothers telling their stories to their children coincided with the growth of new women's movements in the late sixties and the seventies, during which "women in large numbers were...informed [by the women's movement] of the silence surrounding violence against women; although their mothers had encountered it on a far greater scale, [the young women] had still kept it a secret.... Since then, discussion has not ceased. This context was important for my work on this film" (15–16).[9]

Sander in 1987–88 formulated her questions for research. She wanted to move from anecdotes such as the one by Frau G., to "real information for the film" (17); wanted to know what the phrase "many rapes" might mean; wanted to know if the rapes were the result of a "general collapse following the victory over Germany" or whether "rumors of massive numbers of rapes [had been] merely... whipped up for propaganda purposes" or were owing "to the common brutality of war" (17); and "wanted to clarify some of the consequences for the women affected" (22).

---

8 See Brownmiller's discussion of revenge rapes during WWII (*Against* 48–78).

9 I emphasize "context," for it becomes an issue raised by Sander's later critics. During the Eighties and Nineties there were, as Liebman and Michelson remind us, the "historical scandals and media spectacles provoked" by "'Bitburg,' 'Historikerstreit,' the 'Jenninger Affair'" ("After" 6–8). See Liebman and Michelson's references to these events that establish a context for the reception of Sander's film. Cf. Lyotard, *Differend* (3).

Finally, she says: "The results of our research made it clear that we were dealing with a singular event, comparable, perhaps, to the entry of the Japanese into the Chinese city of Nanking in 1937" (17).[10] While documenting and representing her findings, Sander compares the mass rapes to contemporary mass rapes reported in 1992. She moves from a reductive to a wider scope. She begins the film with this comparison: "This is a film about rape in wartime. Because I know the circumstances in Berlin best, the film will treat what happened here. Everyone knew about them, though no one spoke of them, just as in Kuwait and in Yugoslavia today" (*BeFreier* 108).[11]

I will proceed with the opening interviews and anecdotes[12] that critics comment on as well as ignore. After the opening scene of rape in wartime, Sander turns to "Mrs. Prof. Dr. Ballowilz" in the archives and asks about data that would indicate children born of rape. There are rows of thick files on metal library shelves. There is much *archive fever* (Derrida) in the scene. Ballowilz begins opening file after file for the camera to record the singular events that become *the* singular event of mass rape. Sander asks Ballowilz about children born in 1946. Children "fathered by rapists," again, are the index. Ballowilz answers: "The reports state details about the parents and the identity of the father is recorded. In 1946 3.7% of the fathers were Russian, 1.2% American, 0.7% British and 0.4% French, and in many of the cases it was added that they were rape cases." In the data there is a distinction

---

10 See Chang; also, for a film about Nanking, see Lu's film *City of Life and Death*.

11 For rape during the wars in Yugoslavia, see Catherine MacKinnon, "Turning Rape."

12 The version of the film that I studied from the Goethe Institute was printed in two cassettes, or reels. I refer to the scenes as being in one or the other, or attempt to locate them in the book version.

made among women who were raped, or raped repeatedly, or engaged in consensual sex with the enemy for favors or survival,[13] or who had a venereal disease. Ballowilz reads from individual files: "Father Russian, rape. Russian, rape. American. Russian father. Unknown American. Russian, raped repeatedly. English, gonorrhea. In the year 1945 the number of Russian fathers was even somewhat higher," Ballowilz continues, "so we can assume that some of the women were refugees, who were raped while on their way to Berlin" (*BeFreier* 108–09). Sander asks Ballowilz: "Could you agree that we could take these figures as a prognosis applicable to the total births in Berlin at that particular time?" Ballowilz answers: "With some reservation, these figures are based on the total of children born and admitted here in those years. More or less they may be taken as representative for Berlin" (109).

In the second reel of the film, Sander dramatically introduces a mathematician—Barbara Johr, her co-author—with music in the background. Sander asks: "How many [births owing to rape] were there? Barbara Johr, our arithmetician, reaches the following results," which Sander and Johr include in the book version as a list:

1. Official statistics for the period between September 1945 and August 1946 show a total of 23,124 births (both live and stillborn). Of these, approximately 5% were "Russian children": 1,156 children.

---

13 The possibility of "consensual" sex in the event is ridiculous. Any women who did engage in the exchange of sexual favors for whatever they needed to survive were branded as collaborators. The film in the second reel shows photos of French women being paraded or marched through the streets who had their heads shaved and clothes marked with the Nazi swastika. There are scenes in the second reel of the war brides, women with children by–I can only infer—Americans. A whole ship of them is shown arriving in the United States.

2. Some 10% of the pregnant women had abortions, of which 90% were successful. Therefore, ten times as many women had actually been impregnated: 11, 560.

3. About 20% of the raped women became pregnant. Therefore among those of childbearing age, five times as many were raped: 57,800.

4. In 1945, 600,000 women of childbearing age (18 to 45 years) lived in Berlin. 57,800 of them were raped. That represents 9.5% of this age group.

5. In 1945, 800,000 girls between the ages of 14 and 18 and women over 45 lived in Berlin. If one assumes that 9.5% of those in this age group were raped, that would mean that 73,300 of those younger and older women were affected. (If a 4.75% figure is used, then the number is 36,650.)

6. Conclusions: Of the 1.4 million women and girls in Berlin, between 94,450 and 131,100—and average of more than 110,000—were raped between early summer and fall of 1945. ("Remembering" 21; *BeFreier* 54)[14]

While the music continues, the film cuts from Johr's statistical figures to two women walking in a forest. Sander tells the woman, "I only know of one case where a woman after having been raped demanded to be recognized as a war casualty. You were the first to work on these rapes. What can you tell us?" (The shift from one scene to the next is exceptionally strategic, moving from numbers of women

---

14 In the film, when the statistics are given, Johr refers to Dr. Reichling who is supportive of the numbers and inferences drawn from them. (Reichling appears with Sander toward the middle of the second reel.)

in mass rape, pregnancy, and death to the one brave woman who demanded to be recognized as a casualty of war and, by implication, to receive all the benefits that men in the war have been receiving.) The other woman: "It's very significant that so far you have only found this one case. For contrary to the men, whose imprisonment and wounds have been socially accepted and who receive an allowance this is not the case for women. Moreover, men can do something about their traumas that has been organized for them by society.... Women don't have that possibility. I also see the problem that for women this desire to hush up the whole thing and pretend it didn't happen was welcome in as much as in this way it was easier to get on with relatives and men." Then in a voice over, we are told: "Many committed suicide. About 4,000 in April alone, although there is no division between men and women." The irony here among ironies is that there is a division between men and women categorically in terms of who can be a casualty of war, but none in terms of having committed suicide as the result of the trauma of war.

The most telling scene in a long sequence of scenes on categorical exclusion is of a woman who had been raped by a Russian soldier. When she tells a "former [German] officer Dreiha" of being raped, he in turn tells her: "If that had happened to my wife, I would shoot her." In recollecting she says: "I wanted to live, not be killed."[15]

---

15 Cf. Wolf's "third alternative": To kill or To Die. No, To Live! (*Casandra* 106–07). (Per my discussion in note 3, stating that I have rearranged-remixed-repurposed the sequences for a rhetorical affect, see the test-drive question in the Excursus. This is the last prompt for using the Excursus.)

> You can't count the dead. There's absolutely no sense in it. Mathematics stops there. Woman or man, it's the individual that is destroyed. That's why it makes sense to take a personal interest in at least one individual man or woman. Many may experience death simultaneously but it's always each person's own individual terror.... It made no sense whatsoever to the dead to speculate about what was ghastlier, to be drawn and quartered by the Church, to be tortured first and then burnt at the stake, to be gassed by the Nazis, or to be shot by the Stalinists while doing forced labour. People who refuse to acknowledge that this kind of horror must start somewhere, that it has to be tried out on a small scale before it can be carried out on a large scale, only confirm Eichmann's thesis that a thousand corpses are statistics. They only see the past in terms of statistics.
>
> Helke Sander, *The Three Women K* (126–27)

Further Testimony (German and Russian): After Sander opens the first reel with an archivist reading accounts of births resulting from rapes, she turns exclusively to oral testimony: There is a shot of a long conference table, with empty green chairs lined on both sides, creating a vanishing point of two women. One is Sander, who says: "Mrs. Hoffmann, I'd like to see an official body dealing with this [event], to find out the personal and political effects of these rapes, and especially how many women were affected." She asks the first questions of the film:

> Sander: In April and May '45 it was much worse you said. What did you go through?
>
> Hoffmann (*begins*): Well, I witnessed the Red Army's march into Königsberg, and also the way soldiers and officers behaved there. There was mass raping, they queued up.

Sander: You mean every day?

Hoffmann: Yes, at first every day, we were not safe anywhere. There wasn't anybody to protect us. Anyone protecting us would have been killed himself. And then they got the people out of their houses... me, my mother, other women and girls. Well, and then they threw themselves on us, you know.

Sander: What did you mean by queuing?

Hoffmann: Well, one would grab another chap's belt and say: Hurray up, I want to have her too. There were sometimes 5 or 6 of them standing in line, so there wasn't any privacy...you just get numb. Somehow you let it engulf you.

Sander: How long did this go on?

Hoffmann: It lasted for about 2 weeks with varying intensity.
(*BeFreier* 109–10)

After this exchange, Sander turns to Mrs. Ursula Ludwig. The scene begins with feet going down steps that lead to a cellar. Many German women hid in cellars. The scene, which is a reenactment, is dark, except for the flashlight that leads us down to and through the cellar. Finally, as if the flashlight is searching for someone, the beam finds a woman clutching jars of preserved food. Once we see her, there is a quick cut to military film of Russians launching rockets from a truck into what we might infer is Berlin. The editing brings to mind stock cuts that substitute for actual scenes of sexual acts (figuration for actuality, but in a *shadow narrative*).[16] While the rockets are launched, there is a voice over:

---

16 Reising and Skoller write of shadows—narrative shadows—as interrupting the flow of the narrative toward progress, as if the unconscious of the film *thwarts* the melodramatic consciousness of living happily thereafter. The shadow narratives, as Reising (12–13; 16, 17, 333–34) and Skoller (39–42) specifically suggest, are driven by political unconscious forces against the ideology of melodrama itself. Moreover, the shadow narratives are driven to complicate the storyline, so to speak by *forelining*, *backlining*, and *sidelining* traditional linear progression. I am suggesting here, therefore, in my further discussions of shadow narratives that this phenomenon of shadows interrupting an expected linear movement can occur not only within a single film but across films themselves. In addition to the work put forth by Reising and Skoller, I have also been influenced by Jean-Luc Nancy (*Inoperative* 23; cf. *Evidence of Film*) and by Jacques Rancière, in his expansion of Jean Epstein's declaration "Cinema is true. A story is a lie." Specifically, Rancière's discussion, while it does not refer to shadows, but to the camera itself casting its own shadow, nonetheless, addresses *the fable of linear progress*. Rancière writes: "Life is not about stories, about actions oriented towards an end, but about situations open in every direction. Life has nothing to do with dramatic progression, but is instead a long and continuous movement made up of an infinity of micro-movements. This truth about life has finally found an art capable of doing it justice [i.e., the camera and cinema], an art in which the intelligence that creates the reversals of fortune and the dramatic conflicts is subject to another intelligence, the intelligence of the machine that wants nothing, that does not construct any stories, but simply records the infinity of movements that gives rise to drama a hundred times more intense than all dramatic reversals of fortune.... Cinematographic automatism settles the quarrel between art and technique by changing the very status of the 'real.' It does not reproduce things as they offer themselves to the gaze. It records them as the human eye cannot see them, as they come into being, in a state of waves and vibrations, before they can be qualified as intelligible objects, people, or events due to their descriptive and narrative properties. This is why the art of moving images can overthrow the old Aristotelian hierarchy that privileged *muthos*—the coherence of the plot—and devalued *opsis*—the spectacle's sensible effect," etc. (*Film Fables* 1–2; cf. Nancy and Kiarostami, *Evidence*).

While I find Nancy and Rancière's takes on potential and impotential shadows and spectacles for the most part promising, I must in my writing-thinking here also turn to Lyotard's understanding of "the nihilism of

I was in the cellar on a sort of camp bed to get a bit of shut-eye and I had blackened my face. But suddenly three Russian soldiers came in. By the look of them they were Mongolians. They had their firearms and yelled: 'Woman out.'.... [T]hey pushed me into a room somewhere upstairs.... They threw me down on the sofa and raped me, all three of them. They took me downstairs again and brought me to a cellar of a house further down the street. There an officer appeared, quite a young chap.

He was very polite, spoke good German. [He asked] if I would like to go with him to the adjoining room. It was a sort of potato cellar and he apologized that he too had to rape me. Nothing I could do. Fair enough. And it happened very quickly. Now it was all over, so I said: But I can't go home now. It's night and I will be shot in the street.... Then he ordered one of his

---

convened, conventional movements" in cinema that he would oppositionally rethink with "pyrotechnics." It is not just a matter of the machine, the camera, or of "looks" or "spectators" (Mulvey, "Visual Pleasure") but even more so of a matter with the experimental paralogic of the cut that allows for "a writing of movements: thus, extreme immobilization and excessive mobilization" ("Acinema" 177). I take Lyotard, as Philip Rosen takes him, as "starkly [posing] a critical question for any oppositional cinema—its relation to totality and pleasure" (*Narrative* 284–85; cf. Martin Jay, 543–86). But the question that remains is just how does someone critique sexual violence without trafficking in it! In other words, how do shadow narrative not themselves traffic in what they purport to disclose? Perhaps, critique has failed us again and again and enough!

There is more, always some more: See on YouTube and elsewhere sequences from the television show *LEXX, His Divine Shadow Narrative*, which is all about the last insect, after the insect wars! <http://www.youtube.com/watch?v=apjMFCm4mbo>. And let us not forget John Cassavetes's *Shadows* (1959), which further complicates this discussion and which we will take up yet another day. Cf. footnote 17, on the *film* and the *filmic* and thereafter as I bring Deleuze, rightfully so, into this discussion.

soldiers to take me home and I accepted gratefully. He took me to my front door. (*BeFreier* 110–12)

In the next scene an unnamed woman, reading from her diary, tells of the joy of being liberated from fascism. She invites a Russian soldier to rejoice with her. He takes her by the arm and says, "Come woman, come." (This expression is reported by many of the German women.) But as the soldier commands her, she hears other women crying for help. She escapes by running to her mother, who says: "So it's true after all. We must show them our Jewish identity cards," which the two women hid in the goat pen. "They will understand." However, the woman says, "They understood nothing. They couldn't even read the identity cards" (*BeFreier* 111–12).

A fourth testimony is given of a woman (Hildegard Knef) who dressed like a boy and "hired herself out as a guard." Eventually discovered to be a female, she becomes a prisoner of the Russians and is questioned by the NKWD (or NKVD, People's Commissariat for Internal Affairs, which becomes the KGB). She is asked why she is dressed in men's clothing and responds, "I didn't want to be raped." Then they hit her and repeat the question. Each time she is told: "German pigs rape, Russian heroes don't" (*BeFreier* 112–13).

Sander thereafter speaks with Valentina Fjodorowna, who served in a women-only regiment. On May 13th she was in Berlin and put her signature on the column of the Reichstag. Sander asks Fjodorowna if she had heard at that time that many women were raped. Fjodorowna shrugs her shoulders and replies: "I can't say anything about such cases." The translator paraphrases: "It is hard for Mrs. Fjodorowna to understand all of this. She believes it is not a matter of love if violence is used. Personally she has not seen such acts of violence." Sander: "She doesn't know either? Did she never discuss it with anyone? Neither with women or with men?" Fjodorowna: "No, never." Then there is a turn in Fjodorowna's responses: "Maybe one should know more about it and maybe one should know about it much earlier. Now it's too late." Sander: "Why do women not hear about it when other women are violated?" The translator paraphrases: "Mrs. Fjodorowna would keep silent and not say anything." Sander: "Why?" The translator reports: "She would keep silent. It might make her unhappy for the rest of her life but she wouldn't talk about it." Fjodorowna: "It can't be undone. What happened, happened. Everybody bears his own cross" (*BeFreier* 114–16). Privately. Silently. End of discussion.

Next is Claudia Gregoriewna, a sharpshooter during the war, who, the translator paraphrases saying, "Gregoriewna thinks that if women had known that Russian men raped German women the relationship between women and men would naturally change. It was war, but even in war a man must control himself. What happened, happened: it can't be undone" (*BeFreier* 116–17).

Finally, a Russian man, Fjodor Swerew (or Feodor Sverev). The translator paraphrases: "He believes that to Western women this rape problem is something different. It wasn't much of a disgrace to them, being deflowered. They don't see that as something terrible. The relationship between men and women has changed since then." Sander: "Since violence is always used by man against woman and never the reverse, I ask what purpose does he see in male power being expressed sexually against women?" Swerew: "It can't be explained in that biologically men are more sexual than women. [There is a long pause while Sander objects.] We can point to examples in the animal world. There, males are always more active than females. Although occasionally females are sexually stronger." Sander: "This has been scientifically refuted. In fact women are more potent than men." Swerew: "If you speak of sexuality only. But when you talk of the origins of the beginning, men play the bigger part." The translator paraphrases: "Mr. Swerew believes that even a woman with a strong sexuality tries to keep up with the appearance that a man is more active than she. He says he can't say that cases [of Russian soldiers raping German women] was widespread. When a soldier saw a woman who could have been his mother, he would not do her any harm. But when a man saw a young woman, he may have had the urge to rape her" (*BeFreier* 117–18).

A Russian solider with his wife sitting next to him, Gleb and Anna Dubrowo. Sander interviews only the man (aka, Fjodorowilsch), but the camera shot is on Anna as much if not more than on Gleb. Anna is stone faced throughout the brief interview. In addition, there is a camera shot of German women and men observing the interview on four monitors. The translator paraphrases: "Fjodorowilsch says that soldiers who raped German women did so because of sexual need [the camera pans to Anna] certainly not for revenge [then to the audience of German women and men]. It would be dishonest if he would say that acts of violence against German women didn't take place. He can understand young men who spent a long time in the field but they were men after all. [Then there is a shot of a photograph of Russian solders saluting to the camera while standing next to a framed picture of Stalin]" (*BeFreier* 118–19). Sander is editorializing with these juxtapositions of receptions.

The intensity of these interviews with Russians grows as they pass sequentially from *women* to a *man* and then to a *man and woman*. The intensity only continues to grow as Sander next moves to a man, Ivan Stasewitsch, who was just a "young man" in the war and yet fought. The scene is his artist studio. (I am going to quote this interview at length, for it illustrates best Sander's techniques of interviewing and it brings to the surface a number of commonplace stories of what took place.)

> Sander: I have a photo here of you as a young man. You went to the front when you were fourteen, and in this photo that shows the train coming from Berlin, you were sixteen. So you were a child when you went to war and you were a man when you returned [*the two pictures along with others are shown*].

> The Translator (*paraphrasing*): He says he was not a man when the war ended but still a boy. He knew that the Red Army was warned against intimate relations with German women, whereas, as he expresses it, there were patriotic German women who infected the Russians with venereal diseases. The German women considered it their duty. He says that the German women were not raped, but did it because of their own needs. Several times he witnessed such situations when he came to German houses with other soldiers. He stayed at the door with a gun. He believes that they were intimate with the German women.

> Sander: Did you discuss this afterwards with the men?

> Slasewitsch: They didn't tell me anything but discussed it among themselves.

> Sander: I simply think that a young man like you were then, that is, curious as well, and also part of the victorious army, would really know more about it and besides you are an artist and probably noticed a lot more than the other people.

The Translator (*paraphrasing*): He only knows of that one time when he was standing guard. The soldiers were punished for ignoring the orders and so the soldiers tried to be secretive about it.

The Translator (*reading from an earlier transcript*): Iwan Stasewitsch said earlier that the soldiers had looked for such relationships on purpose and entered into them in order not to have to go to the front and to stay alive. They went into the hospital for medical treatment and so survived the war.

Sander: Did I get that right? That Russian soldiers slept with German women for that purpose to get infected so that they wouldn't be sent to the eastern front to the war and could survive? That sexual intercourse was a sort of sabotage?

Slasewitsch: Of course, it was a sort of sabotage. [*There is a look of disbelief on Sander's face.*] But the German women also did it out of patriotism and they sought out the Russian soldiers themselves. One German woman put 15 Red Army men out of action.

Sander: So they told the soldiers there are so many women here, they want to infect you and one woman can knock out 15 Red Army men.

Slasewitsch: If she did it out of patriotism she couldn't say she was raped.

Sander: I think that a woman who's sick...after all it hurts. To my mind it's not a good way to conquer the enemy.

> Slasewitsch: This information was read out to the soldiers by political clerks, regularly. That's how they warned the men. (*BeFreier* 119–21)

The child at war, before and after, is the father of the rapists.

There is a quick cut to a U.S. Army film prepared for servicemen, telling them to "get to the nearest venereal prophylaxis station for a treatment." (There is a voice over while a man holds his penis during treatment: "This is my rifle, this is my gun; one is for killing, one is for fun.") In the film there are instructions for the complete use of prophylactics. Women, in mug shots, are blamed in every way for venereal disease (*BeFreier* 122).

Sander returns to Fjodor, the former Russian Officer.

> Sander: You told us that in many German houses you visited you saw photos of atrocities committed by Germans in Russia. Can you describe that in detail?
>
> Swerew, voice over: As an officer I regularly went into houses of Germans and I saw many photo albums with photos that had been taken in Russia in earlier days. What struck me in these photos was that indiscriminately whoever was photographed, officer or soldier, they had themselves taken as Roman legionaries, barbarian murderers. [*A photo is shown of a German man with a pistol being aimed at a nude dead woman on her back. Then pictures of men hanging and of a German soldier cutting off the head of a man with a buzz saw.*]
>
> Sander, voice over: How often did you see that? [*More pictures.*]

Swerew: Very often. I stayed in several parts of Germany. In Pommern, Prussia, and I saw such photos everywhere.

Sander: Is that 10 times, 20 times, 50 times?

Swerew: More than a 100 times. [*Film footage of a Russian soldier taking such photographs out of a dead German soldier's pocket.*]

Sander: You must have guessed that these photos and the appeals from Ilja Ehrenburg had something to do with the atrocities that were committed by the Russian troops. [*Film footage of Russian soldiers looking through photographs of atrocities.*]

Translator (*paraphrasing*): He says that many Russians had an envelope in their pockets and [on occasion] these envelopes showed [one] picture [of] a small Russian child exhorting its father who is at the front. "Daddy, kill a German." When our undisciplined Soviet soldiers were caught, they showed these envelopes and maxims and tried to justify themselves with them. "If you do not kill the German, he will kill you." "If you let the German live, the German will hang a Russian and rape a Russian woman." (*BeFreier* 123–25)

The issue is one of propaganda and revenge and whether or not the Soviet Army attempted to stop soldiers from reprisals against the Germans. Dubrowo testifies that Ilja Ehrenburg[17] stopped writing propaganda when the

---

17 The Russian officer Fjodor Swerew tells Sander that Ilya Ehrenburg wrote articles for the newspaper, "which were to arouse feelings of hatred

Russians invaded Germany (*BeFreier* 125); testifies that every attempt was made to punish Russian soldiers who raped (for revenge or not) or who even took a German woman into his quarters (125). A German man, Herr Schneck, testifies that this is the case (125–26). Mrs. Von Werner speaks of calm and order where she lived, which was close to the command post. She testifies that German soldiers were shot when caught raping (126). A German man, Herr Eisermann, recalls: "After two, three weeks Marshall Schukow issued very severe orders and whoever was caught or reported, they only had to utter a threat, would be executed with a machine gun and that was done in a bunker on the corner of the Karlstreet. We heard the machine gun day and night" (*BeFreier* 126).

The testimony continues, but I will stop with the man who says, dramatically with his body rhythmically moving, his hands gesturing wildly, and his head and eyes thrust up to the ceiling: "How I laughed when the Germans told this story in hospital: A chap named Fritz, a German, hid his girl in the cellar and he didn't let her out so no one would do any harm. After a month she escaped and she rode her *bicycle* to her neighbor. That's where we caught her and of course the entire male choir raped her. I shrieked. The whole sick bay roared with laughter and I, Juri Alexejwitsch Dodelew, who sit here before you also laughed. So much for the theme of hatred. Hatred was the result of this story. Didn't the Germans rape our women? Of course, they did, we read it in the papers.... So an eye for an eye. If they did it, so will we do the same" (*BeFreier* 128–29; emphasis mine).

The interviews in the first reel begin with two

---

against the enemy" and which were to inform Russian troops of what could happen to them or to their women if they did not kill Germans. Other writers were Simonow, Wanda Wassilievskaja, Alexej Tolstoi. (About Ehrenburg's articles, see Grossmann 50–53.)

women at the end of a long table. The women were at the distance in the vanishing point. As Sander moves from one interlocutor to another, from German to German woman at first and then from Russian to Russian combatant, both women and men, all the interlocutors figuratively but materially fill the empty seats *at that* table. These interlocutors—German and Russian, Russian and German—become alike in the very distance of the vanishing point. The tableau forms a community. A public investigation.

> The cinema does not just present images, it surrounds them with a world. This is why, very early on, it looked for bigger and bigger circuits which would unite an actual image with recollection images, dream-images and world-images.
>
> Gilles Deleuze, *Cinema 2* (68)

> When there are photos of these events, the women are usually dead. In these photos they are violated once more as proof of the bestiality of whatever adversary there was. We see Russian women raped by Germans. German women raped by Russians. Russian women, German women. Russian women, German, Russian and so on.
>
> Helke Sander, *BeFreier und Befreite* (a voice over, while photos are shown, reel one)

The Master Narrative (A Pre-meditation): I ended the previous section (further testimony) with a vanishing point and opened this one (master narrative) with a summarizing statement and an orienting quotation—all of which can be read as my underwriting the film in its entirety as a master narrative of women as victims and men as rapists. I could bolster this view by pointing to the opening statement of the film, which includes the rapes in "Kuwait and Yogoslavia," and the closing statement of the film, which includes a scene from Kleist's *Penthesilea* with passages that call for women to wage war against men until women are free as they were in the primal times. I could call this a framing device that contextualizes and informs all the scenes of testimony, all the editing-montage, all the music and drama and special lenses used into one transhistorical, master narrative. My sense, however, is that Sander is not given to making this possible master narrative into one *that is to stand*. She experiments with possibilities in everything she does, in film or fiction. She sets images in motion that incipiently invite viewers (readers) to add or subtract (but by extra-ordinary means to link, through a variety of conductive circuits) from them in unpredictable ways. I am suggesting that to follow the various catastrophes put out by her film is to follow them until being hit by a singular image, a moment, among movement-image but more so time-image (every 24 frames per second) and finding oneself being taken from the *interval* (narration as cause and effect) into the *interstices* (the gap, void), at the limits, the total exhaustion, of reason.[18]

As much as Sander's title, *BeFreier und Befreite*, with its orthographic changes and puns, suggests multiple readings of an event, I would then invite us to read the film across the many registers that the film *ex-hibits*. In every frame the film impresses me with its inscribing by exscribing. (Or with its in-hibiting by ex-hibiting. Not only do the critics resist and Sander counter-resist, but the text-film itself also resists.) But in a few extra-ordinarily peculiar frames, the exscriptions ex-hibit—as Deleuze refers to, by way of Beckett—a beginning of a "third language," one that is singular and finds itself at a threshold, in

---

18 See Deleuze, *Cinema 2* 179–80; Bogue, *Deleuze* 170–77. Conley in "The Film Event" makes a distinction between "interval" and "interstice." Kundera, in his novel *Immortality*, criticizes Aristotle's refusal to accept the "episode" (which is without apparent cause and effect) and Kundera's revalorization of it, which I am attempting to accomplish as well in terms of Sander's film. The *interstice* and the *episode* are *the excluded middles*. What this discussion of mine should lead to is that in the *film* (or any expression of human production) there is a community, communion (founded on brutality and inhumanity) but in the *filmic* there is (*es gibt*) incipiently a communitarianism as espoused by Barthes, Deleuze, Nancy, Blanchot, Agamben, Ronell, *and Waters*. Respectively, there is both the *film* and the *filmic*, the latter becoming the sight of a new politics of the future as Barthes says in "Third Meaning" (62–63). For additional discussions of a single frame in a film, see Adair, *Flickers*; Sherman, *Complete Untitled Film Stills* and *Film Stills*; Ray, *Avant-Garde*; Krauss, *Sherman*; Krauss, with Bois, "Destiny of the *Informe*" 235–52. Cf. Shaviro's discussion of Warhol's "film portraits" in *Cinematic* (210–12).

any-space-whatever.[19] Hence, though Sander might begin and end with a classic framing device, Sander cannot maintain it as the force of singularities begin to disperse the unifying structure until it is always already on the verge of falling into a thirdness (see Deleuze, *Cinema 1* 102–22, 197–15; *Cinema 2* 1–24). Or on the verge of dispersing out of this thirdness. Put more simply, the various interstices (gaps, voids) turn outside inside, threatening any thinking of what the documentary film purports to report. But this threatening of involution, as Deleuze might say, is a threat of novelty, "something new," something coming out of 1 and 2 in the form of a third (*Cinema 2* 180).

The film becomes, strangely, a creation—perhaps a decreation—a potentiality—perhaps an impotentiality—of a third space of *singularities*.[20] The very subject matter of a singular event (mass rape, *Zeitereignis*) makes a film of singularities, which form no classic set, but become dispersed. Become incompossibilities. Perhaps it is intended, perhaps not; it does not matter. Once the film reaches a thirdness, it has a pure im/potentiality of *its own*, driving it to become any-space-whatever. The place might be Berlin turned into a desert of the real, but it might also

---

19 In this section on *a third language*, I am guided by Conley's discussion in "The Film Event" and by Deleuze's "*L'épuisé*"; trans., "The Exhausted." The film event is the *filmic*. (For the phrase "any-space-whatever," see Deleuze, *Cinema 1* 102–22.) I am purposefully drawing implications between, on the one hand, Pascal Augé's or Marc Augé's *Non-Places* (there is confusion about who Augé is; the former, Pascal, was possibly a student in Deleuze's class!) and, on the other, Deleuze's varied notion of "any-space-whatever" and Agamben's "whatever being" and space (*Coming*). Both spaces and beings are thirds. Cf. Barthes, in *Roland Barthes* on "a third language" (68–69, 84, 118, 132, 138, 142).

20 For Lyotard the petit narrative can be a singular event. But I wish to avoid the newer currency of the petit narrative as simply a smaller, more local rendition of a grand narrative. My third term emphasizes a singular event.

be Kuwait, Yugoslavia, or in any neighborhood (Sade, our neighbor) near us. It is any-space-*where*ver but any-space-*what*ever. Actual and virtual. It is not just in basements or cellars, in living rooms and bedrooms, in prison cells and showers, but also in streets with rapists lined up, queuing up, waiting their turn. At least that is how I have come to read and experience *BeFreier und Befreite* through repetitive viewings. How I have come not to interpret the film, but to follow it *as* an unfolding, increasing, experiment at the limits. Moving toward the filmic, or a third sense. (The issue here as throughout is mediality.) As an experiment, this moving, or movement-imaging, toward the filmic, however, is being conducted not by human beings, but by disfigures, or deformatives, of post-humanity.[21]

More specifically, however, it is not the film, but a *film still* among stills in the film that becomes a experimental "conversation" in a third language that invites me and perhaps "us" to attempt to rethink the thinking of rape in terms of the bloc that is formed between the wasp and the orchid. (I am fully aware that this suggestion is jarRinggg. Noisy.) This conversation of contestations is going on *in between* what the interlocutors are saying in a film still.

---

21 The notion of a post-humanity is in terms of cinema, but I speak broadly in terms of a post-Humanism, with human beings as no longer the measure of all things. In the Deleuze's discussions of the shift from the movement-image to the time-image, there is a collapsing into "indiscernibility which will endow the camera with a rich array of functions, and entail a new conception of the frame and reframings" (*Cinema 2*, 23). But these logical connections, though used—this is the difference between classical and modern cinema—are not always used "logically" but paralogically, conductively (213–14). As I say, *I am thinking through mediality*. (This is an ambiguous statement.) For me, as Kittler in *Discourse Networks* argues, the media undetermine, determine, or over-determine subjectivity itself, i.e., a subject that means what "it" says, and says what "it" means. I am at the moment less concerned with hermeneutics (information and its interpretation) and more with a post-hermeneutics (misfiring-information, noise, third senses). And how it can shape a post(e)-pedagogy (see Ulmer, *Applied*).

(I am fully aware that the instability of the wasp and orchid, this assemblage, given the possible analogy with rapist and victim, misfires and can lead to some rather ridiculous discussions if used to deflect the notion of a *conversation*—which is a word, rather, an assemblage, itself that leads to the eighteenth-century double entendre of sexual intercourse. Beings not only must live with their unconscious but also with the dictionary's.)

(As an exemplary event, I see a single frame, among others, in—but taken out of—the film—a still—of a Russian soldier grabbing and pulling up the front wheel of a bicycle being held onto at the handlebars—or wings—by a German woman. What is between them, in this tug-of-war, is *the bicycle*, which in its spatially redistributed form begins to look like a unicycle falling in order to ascend. There is something "machinic" about it, functioning immanently and imminently.[22] The *soldier* and the *woman* stare eye-to-eye. What is the soldier saying to the woman? Come, woman, come? The woman saying to the soldier? Become, soldier, become? What are those Germans in the background seeing and saying? And What is the bicycle itself seeing and saying? It is a haunting image. The single frame requires, as Deleuze would say, "a point of view of variation" [*Fold* 19–20]. But as Deleuze explains, "the point of view is not what varies with the subject, at least in the first instance; it is, to the contrary, the condition in which an eventual subject apprehends a variation (metamorphosis)." Deleuze continues: "For Leibniz, for Nietzsche, for

---

22 I intend "machinic" as Deleuze discusses it (*Anti-Oedipus* 283–96; *Thousand Plateaus* 88–91). The bicycle in the image is *becoming* a unicycle, something molar becoming molecular, deterritorialized. It is a *man-bicycle-woman* refolding and *becoming* a "machinic assemblage" (*Thousand* 88). Becoming molecular, or an assemblage, however, often leads back, in a double articulation, to a reterritorialization. And yet, this molecular-deterritorialization-becoming is the rebeginning-impotentiality of something new and vital. (See Johnston, "Machinic")

Image 1. "Russian Soldier Tries to Buy Bicycle from Woman in Berlin, 1945." © Hulton-Deutsch Collection/CORBIS.

William and Henry James, and for Whitehead as well," point of view "is not a variation of truth according to the subject, but the condition [i.e., mediality] in which the truth of a variation appears to the ["superject"]. This is the very idea of Baroque perspective" [20].[23] Not subject in

---

23 Again, I think in terms of post-hermeneutics (see Kittler, *Discourse Networks*). Cf. Deleuze's discussion of Francis Bacon's paintings, in which he speaks of Bacon's painting (aesthetic) hysteria and how the eye is not a "fixed organ" but "indeterminate" bringing about full presence (*Francis Bacon* 45); and Deleuze's discussion of a Bergsonian view of matter and brain being one, "a flowing-matter in which no point of anchorage nor center of reference [for seeing] would be assignable" (*Cinema 1* 57–58) or the point of view of "the eye of matter" or "in things" (81). Deleuze takes "superject" from Whitehead. As Deleuze argues, both objects and subjects are undergoing a change, metamorphosis, into thirds figures. And yet, again, these thirds or threes are not a dialectical synthesis. (See Bois, "Dialectic" in *Formless* 67–73; cf. Vitanza, "Threes.") In my discussion of Deleuze's "point of view on variation" I am indebted to Johnston's "Machinic Vision" and to Conley's article "Conspiracy Crisis."

accordance or correspondence to variation, but variation in discordance to subject from object or in accordance to superject.

I am not referring to any film still, or frame, printed in an article [see *October* 72 ([Spring 1995] 42) or a book [*BeFreier* 147]; rather, I am referring to a peculiar frame in the film itself, while the camera pans over the photographs and hovers over the *bicycle*, between the two: Russian soldier and German woman [toward the end of reel one]. But understand that the image that I am using in this book (Image 1) is the actual photograph that was trimmed down to fit the scene.

When 2 does not become 1 [I refuse to read the image in terms of the myth of immanence, a movement from bicycle to unicycle], but when 1 + 1 becomes 3, or 2 becomes 3 [in terms of imminence, pure impotentiality, a bloc of becoming tricycle].

But there are other exemplary frames that move while staying still pointless at the limit in *BeFreier und Befreite*, and they are, e.g., shown as photographs in the film while there is a testimonial voice over. I am referring to the photographs of German combatants as Roman legionaries, standing over their prey or cutting the heads off their prey. Irrational, yet rational photographic (crop) cuts. Placed in the film. For a collusion-collision. At the limit. These are the photographs that the Russian combatants pick up from the dead and place in their pockets; these are the photographs that Russian combatants find in the homes of German men and women, find as trophies becoming trophies in any-space-whatever. These are the photographs turn film stills that tear open the film, and freeze the frames. These are the photographs turn film stills that fall from the film, in motion, and lie on the floor, still, at the limits, before the screen. These are the photographs turn film stills that are irrational cuts (irrational-points, cut-points) that are in and yet are not in the film, but in between, and that Roland Barthes would invite us to see as the singular image experienced as the "punctum" [*Camera Lucida* 27]. Or rather, now as the "filmic" ["Third Meaning" 64–65].[24] ... These films stills resist the diegetic horizon of the film and the court records and the archives and begin to display, reveal, the core of excess that lies in the interstices. ... End of parenthesis!)

But I am also aware that the instability of the image of the wasp and of the orchid would manifest itself, in terms of Sander's film, in such questions as Who is the wasp? and Who the orchid? (If a reader-viewer approaches the film *as* a conversation, it is often difficult to tell the difference between victim and perpetrator. They do become in significant [and yet apparently insignificant] instances imminently reversible. Any-instants-whatever. Which is disconcerting. Theirs is, as Deleuze might say, a "false continuity" [*Cinema 2* 179]. Which is Obscene. Scandalous. And yet, it all may be even more disconcerting. A false continuity would only prefigure, as Deleuze says, a modernist cinema [179], in which it is no longer an issue of the traditional logic or politics "of the association or attraction of images" [179], but an issue of a proper paralogically politics that "will be productive of a third or of something new" [180].) ... I cannot forget that men are raping men in wars waged yesterday and *now*. Yes, these men, raped, are being "feminized," turned into a "woman," undergoing a reversal. Male-on-male rape has seldom been discussed in

---

24 The inclusion of the photographs into the film and the potential impact that they have, turning the film into the filmic, reminds me of Marker's film *La Jetée*, which is, of course, virtually all photographs in film (cinema), except for the scene of the woman's eyes animated. This film, then, would be the purest form of filmic films, which for the sake of discernibility to uncover indiscernibility, Marker has to include the eyes (of all human things in cinema) moving. The eyes are preceded and followed by and are surrounded by the world gone filmic.

the public sphere. It deserves the status of a singular event. But this, too, is a false continuity. Perhaps male-on-male rape is not as worse as a woman's fate. Who suffers more? But Who could say? What third party? To determine so, Would *we*, like the pagan gods, have to engage in a forgetive act of decreating a new Tiresias? with its own consequences![25] I do not think so, except as an anthropological experiment of sorts, for we are being dis/engaged, becoming other than human, becoming post-human, becoming thirds! (cf. Agamben, *Remnants* 54–55, 82–83). The image of wasp and orchid becomes some other. Something new. Dreadfully, something arrives that exceeds thinking (juridico-political).

---

25 One counter-argument is that men on both sides are raping. That men get raped is beside the point, for it is men in war who rape men, not women who rape men. Chesler has made this very counter-argument: "Yes, fascist/nationalist Croat and Moslem male soldiers raped women too, with as much ferocity, although on a smaller scale. Some people say: 'You see, both sides did it.' No, 'both sides' did not do it. Only men raped women, women did not rape men; only men, not women, did the killing." I will return to this counter-argument, for it has grave implications in another register when discussing Sander's film. The point is not that male-male rape is worse than male-female rape; the point is that it leads to an endless cycle of revenge that never ends and only escalates to mass rape as a permanent way of dying. Dworkin writes: "Nothing in Madrid or Oslo or in the Rose Garden of the White House will repair a male-on-male military rape. Nor will raped men join with raped women of any description—wife, mother, sister, Jew, feminist. The revenge rape of male Israeli soldiers in captivity is part of the fear, part of the hate that drives the Israeli fear of annihilation. Rape takes everything away" (*Scapegoat* 58).

> The question that I kept on asking myself while watching this film was, what is actually being worked through here? Well, there are various kinds of resistances being worked through.
> Round Table, Eric Santner, "Further Thoughts" (110)

Resistance: The above is an interruption with interruptions. One caesura after another. But it will spill over, as an enjambment does—which is against gridlock in thinking—into this section on resistance, that is, on criticisms of Sander and her film. From here on, I will give expositions of the relevant major criticisms and then report Sander's counter-criticisms. All in terms of a sophistic *dissoi-logoi*. After which we will move on to meditations, or what I would also call *conversations*. These make up a polylogue of commentators about the film and its reception. (The exchange is remarkable, for it is possible to see in it an attempt to deal with the complexity of the film with its many registers and to see in it various rebeginnings of a new zone of *betweens*. Interstices. Which recapitulate my prior experiences viewing this film.) Again, all of these texts are in the special issue "Berlin 1945: War and Rape" of the journal *October*.

The criticisms offered by Gertrud Koch, Atina Grossmann, and David J. Levin at no time attempt to set aside the fact of the mass rapes. Rather, these critics point to implications that are not seen or realized, they argue, in the documentary film itself, implications that contribute to the Chaste thinking that informs the film. (There are those readers, however, who would see only the side of the one over the other and, hence, avoid a point of view of variation.)[26] The criticisms build on Koch's concerns about

---

26 The most pathetic reading is Rosenzweig's "Some Very Personal Thoughts." Rosenzweig deals only in an expressionist form of *ad feminem*.

two main themes in the film that drive the film and appear to move "in two directions": Those of "primal fertility" (or vitalism) and of "the 'genocide of love'" (29). The themes are articulated by two people Sander interviews. The former, Koch says, is put forth by Fjodor Swerew (Feodor Sverev), who speaks of the sexual urges—the desire to procreate—of the Russian combatants who raped. The latter is put forth by Frau Reshevskaya, who speaks of a strange coupling of genocide and love.

Koch finds the theme of primal fertility displayed widely in scope throughout the dialogue on the gathering of statistics and not only in the reflections on quantity (i.e., the precise numbers of women raped) but also on the subsequent quality of life, or lack thereof, for these women and their children born of rape. The primal fertility argument, used to explain rape as a phenomenon, is that the biological urge for procreation is so great that men un/just do what men do. Boys will be boys! Koch points to Fjodor Swerew, who "advocates the customary stereotypical legitimizing thesis for rape as the sexual urges." Swerew explains: "It is so, I suppose: The man can be killed [in war] every moment. And he wants to make a new life. For him it was all the same: Russian girls, Polish, Checkish [sic]. This is, perhaps, a philosophical aspect about man and woman in that Man is man and he wants to give a new life, I suppose, so it happens" (*BeFreier* 136; qtd. by

---

She fails to see that Koch, indeed, takes part—I will use Rosenzweig's own words—in "a new debate about the delayed social consequences and political effects of these mass rapes" (80). All involved need not ingratiate themselves, as Rosenzweig does, with Sander at the exclusion of any possible critique that would lead to a "conversation." Rosenzweig does, however, fill out the spectrum of a point of view of variation. But not until the "Round Table" does the conversation open up with Andreas Huyssen's going "out on a limb" (106), saying that Sander places herself *in between two* discourses. For other promising readings, published elsewhere, see Gesa Zinn; Sheila Johnson.

Koch 31. In English in the film and book). This is a rather telling explanation in the film; it does once again show the reader-viewer the kinds of clichéd rationalizations that are brought to bear on the event. Fear of death causes men in war to rape in dis/order to reproduce quantities of themselves. Along with this rationalization are other rationalized arguments equally based on a discourse of biology, Koch points out, that smacks of "a curious jargon, as if ["principal witnesses"] were still working for the anti-Bolshevik propaganda department or the Institute for Racial and Biological Hygiene" (30). This arguments based on biology attempts to explain *Why men should not shun women who have been raped as possible, future quality "breeders."* Men rape women and then men shun (i.e., rape once again) these women. One witness, Dr. Lutz, Koch explains, "mounts her argument as a defense of women against the masculine notion that, as a consequence of rape, the woman as the 'vessel for the child' undergoes irreparable harm and for that reason must be cast out. In fact, however, she does not abandon the argument's orientation toward racial hygiene" (30). Dr. Lutz argues: "It went so far, for example, that during my student years it was said that when a dog was incorrectly mated it was ruined forever as a breeder. Of course, that is ridiculous. The first pups, naturally, are nothing. But the dog, when newly impregnated by the right partner, is fine once again. And this is naturally the same for human beings. This is a thing which plays itself out and is done with, and when newly inseminated can be vouched for again" (*BeFreier* 176; qtd. by Koch 30). Lutz is responding to the German men who would do away with their wives or daughters, because raped. First, rape; then, murder. (Recall the woman who is told by a former German officer that if she had been his wife, he would have shot her.) But Lutz is saying a great deal more in her pedagogy and not-so-hidden curriculum. Lutz is, by analogy with dog breeding, saying that the children resulting from rape "are nothing" (many of these children, now adults, are interviewed in the film) and that the raped women as breeders, when "impregnated by the right partner," perhaps non-Russian?, but definitely German, are "fine again" and "can be vouched for again." Now, it is first, rape; then, *proper vouchers*. It is rape all the way down! Again, caught in the middle are the children who survived, now adults, and in the film recall openly their fantasies about their *pedigree*. One believed his father was an American only to be disappointed that he was Russian, while another was proud that her father was not an American but a Russian. At all levels *breeding* (out) is the topic! Sander herself writes: "It is one of the ironies of history that a war waged for racial purity laid the groundwork for interbreeding on a gigantic scale, and that contemporary Europe in fact appears different than it did fifty years ago" ("Remembering/Forgetting" 20; *BeFreier* 14).

What Koch makes explicit is the constant zigzagging in the film—from background to foreground—from the rape and victimage of women to "a hidden [Chaste] vitalistic celebration of men's procreative capabilities" (31–32). Or from *genocide* (gynocide) to *procreation* (in terms of quantity and quality). There is never a moment when this Gestalt is not at work, unworking. In viewing the film, we should ask, Why is it that these two forces—perhaps better labeled as *thanatos* and *eros*—are imminently reversible in as much as they are more categorically similar than different? They are not opposites, though we have been acculturated to see them as opposites.[27] Perhaps it has much to do with the implied proper name *Eros*, which we will return to in the section on pagan meditations.

---

27 I allude to Freud's *Beyond the Pleasure Principle* (*SE*: XVIII), but also to Bataille's *The Tears of Eros*.

Opposite to, or complementing, the theme of rape and procreation is, Koch says, "the metaphor of the 'genocide of love'" (32). Frau Reshevskaya speaks in Russian and Warwara Petrowa translates into German: "Sie verurteilten deutsche Frauen zu diesen Leiden, die sie über sich ergehen lassen mussten. Trotzdem glaube ich nicht, dass es sexuelle Aspekte des Krieges waren. Es war ein sexueller Genozid, *ein Genozid der Liebe*" (*BeFreier* 137; emphasis mine). Koch explains: "Frau Reshevskaya, who coins this poetic metaphor, means that Russian soldiers raped German women out of revenge for German acts of cruelty and not for sexual reasons" (32). Koch argues that because Sander does not "pursue the manner in which the metaphor is to be understood," the metaphor begins to take on a "dynamic" of its own and to signify "that the massive rapes annihilated the women as 'people of lovers,' thereby strengthening the impression that German women as a whole took no part in the political events of the Nazi period and that they would have been able to survive unhurt if, at the war's end, they had not become the innocent victims of a horrible conqueror" (32). Koch is very pointed in her accusations of a metaphoric cover up and so I want to call on her own words still further. She continues: "The metaphor of a 'genocide of love' takes over the film as a whole to become an interpretive hypothesis. This phrase is used in such an approving way that it cannot—or is not meant to—allow reflection upon the claim that the Nazi system did not shape women's subjectivity. In May 1945, although they could not or did not want to reflect on their own role in stabilizing the system, German women may have had to ask themselves how 'worthy of love' the soldiers returning from the front were" (32). There are two things that Koch is pointing to that bear emphasis: Namely, that these German women, as victims with their own stories of being raped, are exonerating themselves from their participation in the Nazi system (hiding that fact, making it Chaste), and that these German women are fooling themselves into thinking that their husbands-"lovers" returning from the front were both capable and "worthy of love." Fooling themselves into thinking that they were not at all like the Russian men who had raped them. What comes out in the interviews with the children of rape is that, in fact, in many cases their mothers for the most part were incapable of loving or caring, and they themselves were incapable. The legacy of rape informs life while incapacitating it. Hence, another way of seeing *the genocide of love* (cf. Oates, *Rape: A Love Story*).

Koch's pointing to the "dynamic" of the metaphor itself, with its noisy clamoring, is courageous, for Koch leaves herself—she is aware—open to a charge of *blaming the victims*, that some how or other, the German women deserved being raped—which is a charge that would but again exonerate, to a degree, the former perpetrators of fascism and the latter victims of revenge rapes. Those Russians who spoke openly of the rapes characterized them as "an eye for an eye." Once the dynamic of give-and-take on rape begins, it is impossible to control the spillover effects. But Koch is not saying that the German women deserved what they got, though Both Koch and Sander find themselves obsessively having to repeat this point. Koch is saying rather that the German women's stories also function as alibis in their testimonies, their biographies, that help make Chaste their role in Nazi Germany, and that the metaphor of "The Genocide of Love" in the film with its implications could and did also help make Chaste what Sander was attempting to open up.[28]

For Koch, the cover up continues in terms of the *master narrative* that she and others see as informing the film:

---

[28] Koch is most forthright on these issues (see "Blood" 36).

"Through the narrative's concentration on the rapes at the end of the war the film conceals the speakers' divergent positions. The women's sex assumes transhistorical importance, whether the woman be a Jewess living in hiding or a German interviewed by the Nazi *Wochenschau*; all women now seem to be in the same boat. In biographical research one calls such stories that structure meaning 'master narratives'—and in a certain sense the film itself offers such a master narrative: of women as the central victims of a masculine war in which they participated altogether passively" (35; cf. Grossmann 47–48; Levin 72–73). Master (or grand) narratives, provisional or otherwise, cover up and make Chaste. But there is always something in their inscription that is an exscription, something "filmic" (Barthes) that deterritorializes them into their opposite or into something that resists being narrated, or resists interpretation or indictment and brings on, with its failure, experiments in What is called Thinking?[29]

Koch's last concern is a brief examination of the closing scene of the film, which has Hildegard Knef reading from Heinrich von Kleist's *Penthesilea*: "Vexoris,/the Ethiopian king, appeared" and, after slaughtering the women's men, "took our love/from us by force—they dragged the women from/their husbands' graves to their disgusting beds" (39; qtd. from Martin Greenberg's translation with slight modifications, 226–27. Cf. Agee trans., 92–93). The concluding quote of the film, a few lines following those above, is

> And then they held a council
> where it was decreed as follows: Women
> capable of acting so heroically

---

[29] I am not only talking in terms of the critics' resistance of Sander's film and not only of Sander's counter-resistance of her critics, but also of a third resistances to be found in this exchange as well as others and in the film itself.

> needs must be unfettered as the wind
> that blows across the open steppes and shall submit
> to men no longer....
>   (39; cf. Agee trans., 93–94. *BeFreier* 213.)

If Sander and Knef had kept on reading in this closing scene through to the end of the play, the film's ending would be rather tragically solemn. As anyone knows who has read or seen the play, nothing goes right for Penthesilea after she slays Achilles. Which should remind us of Christa Wolf's "third alternative" of living and not killing and dying (*Cassandra* 106–07, 118–19). In both Kleist and Wolf, Penthesilea kills or attempts to kill and dies.[30] There really is no difference among the accounts in Homer or in Kleist or Wolf, except for the narrative fact that Achilles is killed in Kleist before Penthesilea turns on herself. It is a horrifying end *with no promise of a rebeginning*. Unless we are to view Kleist's version as a pedagogical play of the failure of *too much pride and spirit*, as Prothoë announces in the closing lines. It is Artemis, not just the god Mars, who, as has been surmised in the play itself, that pushes Penthesilea to Thanatos.[31] Ginette Paris reminds us that

---

30 Deleuze (*Essays Critical* 79) offers a rather different reading of Penthesilea's actions in the context of a discussion of Bartleby. Deleuze writes: "Choosing is the Promethean sin par excellence. This was the case with Kleist's Penthesilea, an Ahab-woman who, like her indiscernible double Achilles, had chosen her enemy, in defiance of the law of the Amazons forbidding the preference of one enemy over another. The priestess and the Amazons consider this a betrayal that madness sanctions in a cannibal identification." Along these same lines of flight, Deleuze again speaks of Penthesilea's "demonic element" that "leads her into a dog-becoming." After all, it is her dogs, her dog-becoming, that tears Achilles into shreds and pieces of meat to be cannibalized (Dialogues 42; cf. *Thousand* 268).

31 Agee writes: "Penthesilea's frenzy and subsequent exhausted trance betrays all the symbolic signs of possession by her nation's goddess, Artemis. The murder of Achilles is a sacrifice that consummates, before the eyes of all the Amazons, the *raison d'état* on which their nation is

Artemis "has a liking for bloody holocausts. It is not only animal sacrifice that is attributed to Artemis. In the most distant times of Greek religious history, she was associated with the practice of human sacrifice" (120). But let that not matter, for Sander and Koch toss that event and other possibilities aside for whatever feminine-militant symbolic value they might get out of Kleist's play. Koch reads the unfortunate use of the passages as another means of deflecting, forgetting, the overall context of prewar Germany and the rise of the fascists. She says of Sander's use of the passages and the analog that Sander establishes with them in the film:

> In the beginning there was a paradisiacal primal state. Then the Scythian people were brutally attacked; all the men, both old and young, were killed, and the women raped. As a result, the women organized an armed struggle against the invaders and established their own state. This narrative, a myth from antiquity reinvented by Kleist, can be read in an entirely different way. As the narrative end to a historical documentary, the respective comparison lies close at hand: Everything was peaceful, even the sexes lived in harmony [in Germany], until external enemies [such as the Allies] forced their way in. In fact, that is the very account produced by repression in the 1950s which had already come into existence at the time of the liberation, that is, by the end of the war. The 'golden' prehistory of the Nazi system

---

founded. That nation is neither a feminist heaven nor a culturally inferior, degenerate society, as some would have it, but, for all its revolutionary uniqueness, a state, and as such, just like the Greek state, and just like Kleist's Prussia or France, an embodiment of the unnatural, alienated, impersonal existence, opposed to freedom and ignorant of love" (xxviii). Agee is following Wichmann's analysis in *Henrich von Kleist* (Stuttgart, 1988): 127–40.

which led to the Second World War is excluded from the narrative. (40).

For Koch, the inclusion of *Penthesilea* can also be read precisely for the spin its story puts on the mutual submission to procreative desires. To reproduce their state, the Amazons send out

> 'brides of Mars' to
> 'burst into the forest where
> there men are camped and blow the ripest ones,
> who fall, like seeds, when tops of trees are wildly
> pitching to and fro, back home to our fields.'
> [Cf. Agee, trans., 97]

And for his part, Achilles wants to have a child with Penthesilea:

> 'You'll mother me the new god of our Earth!'
> (40; cf. Agee trans., 103)

Here again, according to Koch, Sander obsessively links "rape and procreation," which Koch has tried "to designate as [being expressed in the film in] an ambivalence between vitalistic procreative and aggressive fantasies" (40). Or possibly through Eros and Thanatos. Koch asks rhetorically, "[D]oes the film not embrace the repressive and self-exonerating scenarios of German history from which it wanted to free itself through the mythic exorcism of a feminist-essentialist master narrative characterized by repression and self-exoneration?" She continues asking rhetorically: "And, in order better to understand the obsessions of the harmless Dr. Lutz, should we not read the film itself as a document linked to major aspects of women's socialization history under the Nazis?" (40).

> But what other kinds of resistances are ostensibly being worked through? A crucial one for Sander is the resistance to acknowledging the special status of violence against women even in the context of a war so clearly dominated, on the German side, by racial anxieties and racial genocide.
>
> Round Table, Eric Santner, "Further Thoughts" (110)

Counter-Resistance: Sander's responds to her critics in an uncomplicated, straight-forward manner. She argues, "my topic was...What really happened at the time? Did massive numbers of rapes occur, or was the belief that they did based on rumors?" (81). She responds at length against two of the five major accusations: Namely, that she "ripped the history of the rapes out of the context of the history of Nazism" and that she "used feminist commonplaces, for example, that all men are rapists instead of embarking on an analysis of the historical circumstances" (81–82). She says that she began with the assumption that the mass rapes were "representative acts of revenge for the cruelties committed by Germans in the lands they occupied" (82). This is important, for if proved true, then, the *context* for the rapes would be primarily the history of Nazism. She says that she no longer believes in the revenge thesis, for combatants other than the Red Army also raped German women. Moreover, it was not just German women who were raped, but also "Jewish women in hiding and female forced laborers, nuns, and little girls" (82). Sander says, "the question about context...always implies the view that rapes of Nazi women would in some way be justified. The idea that they might also affect 'innocents' is then removed by a proverb: they reaped what they sowed" (82). She says categorically, while "some women were also Nazis...in general they did not carry out the German atrocities.

(Female concentration camp guards are the known exceptions)" (82). Hence, for Sander, the context shifts from the history of Nazism to the history of men (of a variety of nations) raping women (of a variety of nations as well as classes and ages).[32]

Still examining context, but taking up the issue of vitalism and procreation as cause of rape, she stresses that White Russian men set aside the notion of the rapes being tied to revenge. "They introduced other grounds: fear of death (e.g., women were connected to 'life' and 'peace,' although both were only to be had through this brutal act)" (82). Sander continues: "'Sexual desire' was another reason often named. The men made no distinction between German or Polish women.... The men express themselves in terms that often sound strange to Western European

---

32 I find *this particular argument* about context and its relation to German women exonerating themselves from German-Nazi history not compelling at all. Sander is trying to confuse degree of rapes (numbers) with kinds of rapes (precisely who was doing the raping). Her own film testifies to the massive numbers of Russian combatants raping the massive number of German women. That other combatants "raped"— both German and other women—is factually verifiable. That there were different notions of what constituted rape by the various members of the Allies is in passing a subject of discussion in the film, but a subject that is not developed between Sander and her critics. (If "we" agree with Catherine MacKinnon on coercion and consent, then the discussion in the film about what constitutes rape is specious. [See *Toward* 171–83.]) The argument, however, that Sander in part wants to make is that of "mass rape," a *Zeitereignis*. It has two contexts in terms of scope and reduction. There is the general context of military and civil rape the world over; and there is the specific context of military rape in Berlin in 1945. But the numbers are not at all there in terms of the Allies as a whole, i.e., *men as a whole*, to set aside the context of the history of Nazism and the history of revenge. That, however, anyone in any context—just one person, no matter whom—is raped is obviously not acceptable. Sander makes this clear in her story "Telephone Conversation" in *Three Women K* 126–27. The game of numbers is double-edged as Sander understands. The context and issue between Sander and her critics, however, is strictly not about numbers but is more political in terms of *how* this story of the mass rapes is going to be told and in terms of whom it will accuse and will exonerate.

and North American ears. In my opinion, this is because no women's movement existed in the old Soviet Union, and hardly any knowledge of psychoanalysis or behavior roles; a discourse on sex was unavailable. Thus they compare, with a complete naivete, male sexual potency with that of animals" (82). In her defense, she says that she did not respond to such loaded statements or "did not go into them more exhaustively because I presupposed an understanding of the context on the part of the film's spectators" (82–83). While any rhetor (Sander or others) can assume that an audience will be able to supply multiple contexts and to fill in the missing part of enthymemes, no rhetor can do so with the topic of rape. The plea for special status of violence against women, as Sander suggests, can misfire. Even among women of different races and classes. While it is understandable that Sander wants the viewer to see the problems as "multifaceted" (84), there are those who would politically focus on a single facet, aspect, at the expense of others. It is important to keep as many of the facets in presence. And yet, even the thickest description of special interests can misfire. (Rape undoes everything in terms of a rhetorical hermeneutics and a material rhetoric.)

Still under the general rubric of context but taking up the issue of a "genocide of love," Sander stresses in response: "On the basis of this phrase, Gertrud Koch makes the absurd accusation that by not commenting on this phrase I stylize the Germans into 'people of lovers'" (83). In her defense, Sander writes:

> women report very drily about what they experienced at the time. They do not even cry... (which is part of the problem).... That I did not correct but instead let stand certain remarks made by my interviewees plays a prominent role in the list of accusations. I did not agree with the content of all that was said to me.... I

wanted to portray an event and in so doing to refer to the multifaceted problems involved [to let it unfold processually]. In order to do so, I had to know what was thought, what images were constructed. I did not have to emphasize to those better informed that many of the arguments presented are 'dubious.'... Irefer to the fact that German soldiers also raped, not massively, though there were always gang rapes.... Many people seem to have difficulty accepting the fact that compared to the known crimes and the Holocaust the Germans relatively seldom committed the crime of rape (as if this in any way lessened their guilt!). In this instance, 'seldom' means acknowledging that the term 'mass rape' acquired a new quantitative dimension following the events in Germany after the war.

If German women did not constitute the majority of those raped one might be able to speak more rationally about the difference between the concepts of 'pogram' and 'Holocaust.' A pogram is something horrible, but it is limited. The Holocaust was planned extermination. After the events in Berlin, mass rape is not an occurrence that may be said to have happened only to a few hundred women. Today, mass rape is to be understood as an occurrence involving several hundred thousand women simultaneously. The Germans were not involved in this sort of crime. It is not all as simple as many would like to think.

The film's contribution lies in its outlining of the extent of the rapes. The 'obsessiveness' with numbers of which I have been accused in New York is correct. It is, however, false to say that I used these figures, these raped 'millions,' to distract attention from the issue of German guilt. Although I can understand the

> distrust on the part of relatives of Holocaust survivors, it is not justified. (84)

Taking on the complete list of charges against her, Sander states: "The rapes were hushed up, and this silence, which had consequences, extended to the social discourse about the events. It was my astonishment at this silence that motivated me.... [W]hy had there been no public discussion of this? Why must this mean to those struggling bitterly to learn to remember the consequences of the Hitler regime they had established but who were not permitted any memory of other events?" (84–85). About the master narrative of *all men are potential rapists*, Sander writes: "At no time do I say, 'Every man is a potential rapist'" (85).[33] About the Nazi *Wochenschau* material (newsreels), Sander says that surely everyone knows that all the footage is propaganda on both sides. (Sander's critics may be expecting too little from the commonplace. Sander may be expecting too much from the varied audiences with their varied predispositions and common ignorance of the *Wochenschau*.) About Sander's claim of breaking the taboo, Sanders affirms there were many books on the Russians raping German women, but the discussions were "considered Cold War literature" and "the Left ignored the book[s]." She continues: "When the rapes stopped, they were an open secret" (86). About the title with its play on words, Sander writes: "There are many different kinds of interpretations of the war's ending among different sorts of Germans" (87).

---

33 It is difficult for me to take Sander's statement as naïve. I can only assume that she is being strategically rhetorical when she makes statements such as this one.

> A film works with images and sounds. Images relate to sounds and vice versa. I do not work with footnotes. For me it is important and wonderful to watch a woman who after the first rapes—and in front of a line of waiting men—looked at the Red Army soldier asleep on her breast and realized that she had developed maternal feelings toward him. She sees that he is still a child, 'a homesick, war weary child.' I am amazed at the woman who is now looking for her father among the millions of old Soviet men. I try to comprehend how it is that a woman whose mother was raped by two French men can imagine her father as a Hollywood hero. I try to comprehend what it means for a young Jewish girl who, having hidden for two years waiting for the liberation, then had to hide again.
>
> Helke Sander, "A Response to My Critics" (87–88)

Meditations: We have rehearsed the discussions of critics (resistance) and counter-critic (counter-resistance). We now turn to *meditations* not on, but within, a passage or two, yet three, that become a zone of *in betweens*, in the transcript of the Round Table, published in the journal *October*. The meditations form a strange assemblage, a "conversation ... an outline of a becoming" (Deleuze, *Dialogues* 1–35; Ronell, *Dictations* ix-xix). At a singular moment of a break in criticisms against Sander, and at a rupture in rhythm, these meditations slip out of being in binary machines: question-answer, masculine-feminine, German-Russian, right-left (cf. Deleuze 2). The critics in a tug of war *rebegin*, through an interruption, to identify, or I should say misidentify, with Sander. The zigzagging motion (emotion, commotion) of accusations and counter-accusations, the disjunctivitis, eventually replaces them all in the zone of *betweens*. The two sides of resistance—the critics (formerly wasps) and Sander (formerly orchid), or Santner (formerly wasp) and Sander (formerly orchid)—both in the Round Table, provide the exemplar of being *in between.* The critics form a Sander image, but there is a critic-becoming of Sander, a Sander-becoming of the critics, a Santner becoming a Sander, a double capture since *what* each becomes changes no less than *that which* becomes.[34]

After about sixteen pages of the Round Table discussion, there is this opportune moment (*kairotic* break) when Adreas Huyssen interrupts the flow, and says: "I'm going out on a limb, but I would say that consciousness of the complexity of the victim and perpetrator roles and of how the two categories can mesh and slide is underdeveloped in German discourse. It's always either/or. Whether it's about German soldiers on the eastern front, about women, or anything else, the discussion gets stuck in the muck of victim versus perpetrators. There are historical reasons for that almost traumatic inability to differentiate further" ("Round" 106). And so then, we might anticipate that *the task of thinking* is to discover how to get unstuck, not so much, however, by learning how to differentiate between two, but by resituating the discussion somewhere in the heretofore excluded middle voice or in between. Not in the excluded element of the binary (not a negative deconstruction). But in a third position (to an affirmative deconstruction outside at the threshold of the binary, in a meshwork). Let us keep in mind the metaphors of Huyssen's statement of "limb," "mesh," and "slide." Let us anticipate the task of thinking within a *meshwork*.[35]

As the discussion moves out on a limb, Eric Santner ventures out on a very different limb. We have two limbs—

---

34 I am following and performing a slot-and-substitution formula with Deleuze's prose in *Dialogues* (2).

35 I take the term "meshwork" from De Landa ("Meshworks"), which, as he says, is another term for what Deleuze and Guttari refer to as "smooth space," the opposite of "striated space" (see *Thousand* 353, 369–73, 474–500).

Huyssen and Santner's—in search of a middle third that has nothing to do with arborescence at all. Santner says: Disjunctive thinking "is very stark in Sander's short story ["A Telephone Conversation with a Friend" In *The Three Women K*] which Annette [Michelson] mentioned. At some level, the opposition is reduced to a competition for funding. Whose memory-work is going to be funded—memory-work about the Holocaust, or memory-work about women's past and suffering?" (106). So the issue becomes one of an obsessive struggle over canonization and, so to speak, immortality. But there is a difference between what Huyssen and Santner are saying. Santner continues: "Moreover, the competition is accentuated because the narrator [of the short story] makes the larger claim that women's suffering is ultimately the product of Jewish monotheism. Sander's story suggests that behind the gesture of universalization may lie a sinister historicization, one which dates the advent of sexual violence with Jewish monotheism! For five thousand years the suffering has been going on. That is connected, I think, to the way the melodrama of breaking taboos gets overplayed in this film through [Sander's] self-dramatization as the one who is breaking the silence, discovering the statistics, and so on. The question arises, who constrained the discourse?" (106).

Again, there is an interesting, though not so unique, turn in Santner's exposition (of an argument). There is in Santner's thinking a representing of the Jews as prior perpetrators to their own victimage—they are caught in the Holocaust in their own origination of "sexual violence with Jewish monotheism." In other words, Santner is saying that the Judaic tradition set the trap and its own people got caught in it! But as Santner sees Sander's view in the short story and the film, so are women—German women—caught in this same universalization and historicization of "sexual violence." The German female in the story, Ms. K, points to "The destructive will in the Five Books of Moses" ("Telephone Conversation" 119). We should not forget, however, that Sander in the film *universalizes* the suffering of both German and Jewish women, especially the Jewish mother and daughter who come out of hiding during the so-called Liberation of Berlin, only to have to return in hiding. But again Santner would probably say—has said that Sander says—in response that this *universalization* itself has a "sinister historicization" behind it. Once again, Santner says that Sander is pointing at the Jews. All of Santner's interpretation is coming from his reading of the story and he is careful to point out that he is not interpreting the film by way of the story. But in Santner's interpretation Sander is less concerned with men against women and more concerned with Jews against women and vice versa. My sense, however, is that Sander situates herself critically and then thoughtfully in *between* each of these two groups in the story and perhaps in the film. (We will have to see.)[36]

---

36 It is not only a matter of scope-reduction, but of avoiding oppositions. In Sander's story, the female refuses to support her male friend's suggestion to help seek funding for a project of an "orthodox Jew" ("Telephone" 118); for such support would only take money away from German women. Santer insists that the theme and motive behind the story is competition for resources. But there is more. When the female character says that she could not place special interest in the project of the "orthodox Jew," her male friend immediately terminates the discussion by angrily saying, "'women's' [there is a long pause] 'pet issues' didn't interest him any more." Sanders then writes: "She got the impression that he had only just managed to stop himself from saying 'women's shit' or 'women's crap'" (120–21). She says, "Twenty years of women's liberation had now made it possible for a colleague to ask her, as a colleague, to do them a favour. But she still had no right to expect anyone to contend with her right to hold differing views. Indeed, [she] was not even sure that what she felt really did boil down to a differing view at all. That was precisely what she would have liked to work out with him" (121–22). The story is about *reception*, about a remembering and understanding that are restricted to one view.

In attempting to answer the question of "who constrained the discourse?" Santner continues:

> And I think—less in the film and more in the story—there is a sense that what has imposed these taboos [constraining discourse] has been the competition with the Jews and the task of bearing witness to Jewish suffering. This connects Sander's project to [Hans Jürgen] Syberberg, who has been very explicit about this competition. He believes that an obsession with Jewish suffering has been at the expense of attention paid to German suffering, and that now the time has come for this to end. He appeals to Germans to let go of the PC-ness that has always forced them to think about Jewish victims and never their own. I like to say that in German, 'PC' stands for 'proper coping' with the past. [Syberberg] wants Germany to bracket out these ideological pressures, go through the ruins, and remember their own suffering. It seems Syberberg ultimately wants to blame the Jews for making this impossible for the Germans. Such ideas really came to the fore in the mid-eighties with Bitburg and the Historians' Debate. I would agree with Andreas that the left won that debate, but after a latency period, the fall of the Wall restarted it. It sounds to me like Sander is taking a very Syberbergian position in claiming that it's time now to focus just on us. ("Round" 106)

Interesting enough, however, Huyssen jumps back into the conversation away from Santner's limb, to his own, and says: "I would want to defend [Sander] against the charge of complicity with Syberberg" (107).

Quickly, after returning to the question of numbers of victims, the conversation turns to Silvia Kolbowski, who says with others that Sander does not appear to identify with either the right or the left. Kolbowski says: "There's a way in which you might say she has tried to situate herself *in between these two discourses* [emphasis mine]. Or rather, she tries to occupy *another* ground" (107; Kolbowski's emphasis). A few pages later, Santner is saying, "there are times in the film when it seems as if [Sander] imagines that she is offering a kind of *neutral space for remembering.*" (111; emphasis mine). Similarly he says that Sander is "offer[ing] *a new kind of space* for the memory work" (111; emphasis mine). But in the closing section, there is agreement that Sander's film is "militant and yet occupies a middle ground" (112). The militancy is determined in this *evolving* and *revolving* interpretation by the closing presentation of the lines from *Penthesilea*. But the neutral space, the middle ground, the *in-between* is indeterminate in this *involving* experimentation by reopening the question concerning *Liberators Take Liberties*. At the end of the binary-machine there are compossible rebeginnings. In what Virginia Woolf calls "an unsubstantial territory" (*Waves* 185). At least in respect for thinking. Reading. Writing. Filming Rape. I am not saying that Sander is becoming Woolf. Rather, I am saying that "we" can also experimentally read Sander as becoming middle, as working in the same post-critical a-positionality as Deleuze is. (Which is what I am alluding to in the film still of the Russian soldier and the German woman in their tug of war for the bicycle that is becoming a unicycle.) Some of those meditating on her film, in relation to her having opened a neutral space or a new kind of space, have begun rethinking what has been already thought about *Liberators Take Liberties* in dis/order to find something vital and new.

Pagan Meditations (Eros)

> There is no event, no phenomenon, word or thought which does not have a multiple sense. A thing is sometimes this, sometimes that, sometimes something more complicated—depending on the forces (the gods) which take possession of it.
>
> Gilles Deleuze, *Nietzsche* (4)

I want to return to *the question of Eros*. In the film *BeFreier und Befreite*, as determined by various critics' resistance to it, there are in particular two themes that receive the most critical attention: That of genocide and procreation (Thanatos-Eros) and that of the "genocide of love" (a metaphor meant to be taken as *rape for revenge*). I cannot not take up the question of Eros again and for reasons that will become additionally more purposive as we proceed. As Michelangelo Antonioni says, and we will focus on eventually, *we are sick with Eros*, for *Eros is sick*.

There is something perpetually problematic in Freud's Eros-Thanatos pairing or forces of life/death instincts (*SE*, XVIII: 7–64; XXI: 118–24; 132–33, 137–41), just as there is something equally problematic in Sander's film in the love-genocide pairing. (The two pairs are rather analogous in their relation to war, rape, and children. And the drive to be [the living] dead.) Jean-Pierre Vernant tells us: "Thanatos and Eros, Death and Desire are neighbors" ("Feminine Figures" 97). But there is something perpetually problematic not only about the pairing but also about Eros himself. In taking up the question of Eros, I am going to leave aside Freud and Vernant and turn to another force within psychology-anthropology, Ginette Paris, who examines the question of Eros in terms of an ecology of polytheism, which is an ecology of human personalities that may be in or out of balance. Like others, she views gods figuratively, yet culturally, as driving forces. Paris writes that we socially make ourselves known by the forces that pull and shape us. She says, "Greek polytheism was not, as Judeo-Christianism [sic] is, a religion of afterdeath; it is not a 'religion' at all, but stands closer to an ecology of the living" (3).

For Freud, the myths (Oedipus, Eros) name his reasoned-rationalized meditations on instinctual drives. For Paris, "A myth is a support for meditation upon one's relationship with oneself, others, nature, and the sacred. In contrast to a meditation [that] seeks to find a void, a 'pagan' meditation allows all images, all possibilities to arise, all the fabulous personages who inhabit us, until... we perceive the web of their relations" (4). The meditations of the Round Table—Huyssen, Santner, Kolbowski—are the works of these "pagani" waging experiments in the *pagus*, that is, in the border or in between zone, where genres of discourse are in conflict over the meshwork of their linkages (cf. Lyotard, *Differend* 151). Paris engages in similar meshworks. On our way to Eros and his replacement in the pairing Eros-Death, I will summarize Paris's several possible meshworks. The first is Aphrodite-Ares.

Eros, when linked with Thanatos, leads to irrepressible death. But when Aphrodite, instead of Eros, is linked with Ares, according to Paris, there is a lessening of aggression. Paris explains that this relationship can best be understood in terms of *Pax Romana* (80). This may illustrate the relationship, but then it is not ideal by any means. Paris argues, however, as "Christians, it is difficult for us to conceive of this essential bond between Aphrodite and Ares: Greek wisdom, unlike Christian, implied that the one [peace, water, hyper-femininity] did not come without the other [war, fire, hyper-masculinity]. The Christian utopia is so attractive that we cannot admit without anxiety that one cannot have Aphrodite without Ares, peace without combat, pleasure without suffering" (80).

In terms of cause-effect, Paris argues, "the suppression of the aggressive pole in the Christian myth, represented by the myth of Ares, occurred at the same time as the suppression of the Aphrodisiacal-sexual pole.... [T]he repression of rage and anger (Ares) drives out also the pleasure, tenderness, and laughter of Aphrodite" (81). Paris argues that rape and aggression "appears to be a symptom, not of the return of Ares, but of his negation. Repression of the physical expression of aggressive energies leads to a disordered explosion of violence. Ares is not Aphrodite's rapist but her lover. Neither with women nor with the elderly does Ares want to fight, but with real adversaries. Delinquent violence ... strikes for the sake of striking; [the delinquent] rapes a woman because he does not know what love is. This violence is a revolt against a world in which the physical, aggressive energy has no outlet, a world which has been deserted as much by Ares as by Aphrodite" (81). Negation (repression) is the source of violence.[37] But according to Paris, it is not a repression of either Ares or of Aphrodite, but both. Their life-enhancing powers exist *between* them. Paris goes to the next ratio of gods, this one between Aphrodite and Adonis. She writes: "Passing from Ares to Adonis is a bit like passing from the virility of the cowboy to that of a gracious and emotional Valentino" who lacks the psychological maturity necessary and, therefore, is "ephemeral" (87–88). "The Adonis-type of man survives as long as he is 'protected' by stronger women, but in a male competitive world he is too vulnerable" (89). Finally we get to Eros. Paris asks: "[W]hy speak of Eros when Aphrodite [the mother] is concerned? Why have we

---

37 I argue this point in *Negation*. What Paris says of psychology, Bataille says of economics. Energy must be wasted. If it is repressed in a *restricted* economy, it will be explosive, leading to wars. If it is expressed as waste without return, grossly or artfully, in a *general* economy, it possibly can be *lived with*. (See Bataille, *Accursed*.)

masculinized the divine figure of Love?... Shall we relate [Freud's] preference... to his declaration that the 'libido is male'? And if the libido is male in a psychology dominated by the myth of Eros, would the inverse reasoning be correct? That is,... would sexual energy become feminine again" (90–91). Paris says that while Aphrodite "represented the universal principle of sexual attraction, the young Eros seemed to 'specialize' in... love relationships between males" (92–93). Paris continues: "[T]he [canonized] darling of the philosophers, represented... the love which unites the pederast and the pre-adolescent boy.... The platonic philosophers seemed to equate... bodily love, heterosexual love, the preference of Aphrodite to Eros, and being of low birth, and... homosexual love, lived within the head and heart rather than through the body, and being of a higher level of consciousness.... This tendency prepared the way for the anti-Aphrodisiacal monotheism of the Christian theologians as much as for a Freudian psychology" (93). The ecology of mind-body is upset. In subordinating Aphrodite and women, Paris argues, the philosophical tradition favored a homosocial space.[38] Paris says, "a similar disequilibrium may be found in an exclusively feminine world" (95). We are left with the question Is there any way out of these binary machines?

---

38 Paris's argument—though difficult to determine—is not necessarily against the practice of homosexuality (gay or lesbian), but contingently so, if it subordinates a woman or women. The same would be the case in the practice of heterosexuality, turning women into the subordinate sex.

Aphrodite, The Shadow Narrative I

> "Youth preoccupied with women and resolved to fight": politics as juvenile delinquency. Ortega [y Gasset] is thinking, as Freud did also, of a connection between fraternal organization and exogamy, conceived as form of "marriage by capture." The band of brothers feel the incest taboo and the lure of strange women; and adopt military organization (gang organization) for purposes of rape. Politics as gang bang. The game is juvenile, or, as Freud would say, infantile; and deadly serious; it is the game of Eros and Thanatos; of sex and war.
>
> Norman O. Brown, *Love's Body* (15)

Ginette Paris allows us heuristically to see the value of Aphrodite in ratios with male gods. But Paris's own advocacy for Aphrodite makes her blind to the implications in an account that she gives of Aphrodite's role in the Trojan War. We are left with ever-returning questions and images: Is *to negate* the negative that Eros represents and thereby to affirm Aphrodite *to create* a shadow narrative? Is *to favor* Aphrodite over Eros or any other god *to establish* the conditions for a shadow narrative? Son and Mother? Imminently reversible with the outcome the same? Perhaps every mythical, master narrative has a shadow narrative. And a shadow of a shadow. Presenting, yet absenting, sexual violence. A shadow narrative can be a double articulation of a dark side and a *mise en abyme*. Christopher Frayling, speaking of rape in cinema, relates: "The camera tended to tilt at the last moment toward a symbolic icon (such as a shining white reproduction of Canova's *Eros and Psyche* in the 1932 *Dr Jekyll and Mr. Hyde*), or the celluloid image tended discreetly to dissolve seconds before the ghastly act was committed—in the case of James Whale's *Frankenstein*, this *created* the impression that the little girl had been raped—and the audience had to be satisfied with distorted shadows on the opposite wall and the retribution of people like us" (174–75; Frayling's emphasis). Shadows and Caves? And yet, lamenting the loss of light that would cast a shadow, lamenting the loss of a shadow itself, Jean Baudrillard writes: "Our only shadow is the one projected onto the wall opposite by atomic radiation. These stencilled silhouettes produced by the Hiroshima bomb. The atomic shadow, the only one left to us: not the sun's shadow, nor even the shadows of Plato's cave, but the shadow of the absent, irradiated body, the delineation of the subject's annihilation, of the disappearance of the original" [*Illusion* 105; cf. Deleuze, *Difference* 268].

On one page Ginette Paris can be discussing the loss of balance in Aphrodite's relation to Ares and how this can contribute to rape in societies (81), and four pages later, Paris can be talking about Aphrodite and Paris (of Troy) and implicitly the rape of Helen,[39] and have no sense of the implications of what she is saying. Her whole discussion of this rape is caught up gloriously in terms of *fight* in love and *courage* among lovers.

In a section titled "Men, War, and Women"—which for me recalls Sander's subtitle of "War, Rape, and Children"— Ginette Paris discusses the Aphrodite-Ares ratio and its relation to how Aphrodite comes to be "at the origin of the Trojan War" (85): The god Eris (who signifies discord and strife) was not invited to the wedding of god Thetis to the mortal Peleus. Eris responds to the insult by casting the "apple of discord" before those present at the wedding. On the apple is written "For the Fairest." The apple with its message has its effect on three gods: Hera, Athena, and Aphrodite. Zeus intervenes and, as usual, he asks a mortal,

---

39 (Ginette) Paris and Paris (of Troy)! Here is another possible confusion in names between author and character.

in this case, Paris, to resolve the discord. Hera offers power; Athena, glory in battle; and Aphrodite, Helen of Sparta. Paris favors the latter.

Having related the narrative, Ginette Paris says: "The bond between Aphrodite and Ares, among its many significations, expresses the belief, deeply rooted amongst the Greeks that, [sic] men fight for women and that the origin of war is fundamentally a rivalry for them. The most illustrious example is obviously the *Iliad*. This belief was so strong among Greeks that even Herodotus...felt obliged to explain that 'perhaps' there was a rivalry for women in the origins of the Trojan War" (85–86. See Herodotus, *Histories* 1.1–4).[40] What is missing in Ginette Paris's discussion, however, is some realization that Aphrodite contributes to a rape narrative as the originating event. If we are to substitute, as she is suggesting, Aphrodite for Eros, for the reasons she gives, then, *what* would we gain that would be life-furthering? Either god, male or female, son or mother, takes us to death.

Paris made it clear earlier that rape is caused by the negation of Ares (81). Moreover, she argued that there needed to be a balance between Ares and Aphrodite. Hence, there would be the non-suppressed aggressive energies of Ares but there would have to be a necessary equilibrium (homeostasis) between binaries of Ares and Aphrodite to keep these energies in check. But for some reason or other, Paris begins to discuss love as "fight," as combat, and that love requires courage in the fight (84). So then, it is both Ares and Aphrodite that must contain

---

40 I discuss the rape of Helen and her defense by Gorgias in *Negation* 235–306. Helen, abducted, or captured for marriage (stolen for the property that is hers) fits into the kinds of "rape" listed by Brownmiller (see the list in the index, *Against* 465; about Helen, see 33). I discuss Sylvia Likens and the number of ways that she was "raped" according to Brownmiller's list in *Sexual Violence*.

each other in an equilibrium. But Aphrodite expresses her love of fighting also through mortals. Paris writes: "Even if [Aphrodite] does not fight her own battles, she quickly involves the men around her in combat" (85). (Perhaps she is caught in repression-compulsion, and needs this extra-mythological outlet.) Ginette Paris warned us: When speaking of Ares, or male immortals, she says, "a similar disequilibrium may be found in an exclusively feminine [hyper-feminine] world" (95). But the encounter with Paris (of Troy) is toward the other; it is a fostering of sexual violence in mortals. Paris makes it clear that Aphrodite "never fights directly" but through mortals such as Paris and that she is "at the origin of the Trojan War" (85; cf. Meagher 26–31), in that she intervenes by having Paris abduct (rape) Helen and thereby contributing to the mass bloodshed and undoing of so many. These interventions have nothing to do with containment or equilibrium (homeostasis) but everything to do with *killing* or *dying* and not *living*. There is something so dark in Ginette Paris's rendering of Aphrodite as *a fighter for love*. This god (recall Heidegger's "Only a god can help us now") is not the one who can help human beings! There is much less hope being offered by way of Aphrodite and much more through Norman O. Brown in *Life Against Death*.[41] But that is another story that I leave to my readers, as I now turn to what happens when in the feminine world equilibrium (in the binary) is lost to a hyper-feminine (sexual) violence that becomes as cold as an Apollonian war can and is the norm in today's battles.[42]

---

[41] Brown gives a compelling account of the problems with Eros in both *Life Against Death* and in *Love's Body*. See Brown's *Apocalypse*, especially the last chapter.

[42] Ginette Paris speaks of Apollonian war (81). She mentions events in WWI as well as alludes to WWII, specifically the French and the German soldiers (86–87).

Baise-Moi, The Shadow Narrative II

> Few people know that there were about a million...women-soldiers in the Red Army. I now drive to Minsk and ask them if they ever approached a man and told him: Man, come!?
> Helke Sander, *BeFreier* (114)

In Sander's film *BeFreier und Befreite*, the Russian soldiers would call to women by saying, "Come Women, Come!" This was the infamous call to be raped. In Virginie Despentes's novel *Baise-Moi* and in the film version with Coralie Trinh Thi, there is a similar, though reversed, command. The phrase *Baise-Moi*, to the uninitiated, might literally mean *Kiss-Me*; to others the expression would mean *Fuck-Me*. In the United States version of the novel and film, the title is rendered as *Rape-Me*. What keeps the work from being successful as a simple, yet complex, reversal—everything is imminently reversible—of sexual violence perpetrated by men, now perpetrated against them by two women, is that it is totally indiscriminate violence against anyone and for no apparent reasons. If the aesthetic of the film, however, is offered as being outside the realm of judgment (Kant), but offered in the realm of an experiment (Deleuze), the film remains unclear as to *what it is* or *what it is searching for* in its hot and cold mixture of Arian and Apollonian acts of violence. Even the two characters, Nadine and Manu, are not clear as to who they are in their works and why they are performing them.[43])

---

43 The film is itself searching for What women might do in a rape culture, but the film even undercuts such a process of thinking. Le Cain has speculated on the metafictional characters in the film, thinking about their own motives and directing their own actions. Despentes, in writing the novel, is more explicit in the omniscient point of view, suggesting the women are fated. For the metaphor of the spider and web, fate, see 155, 238. The novel ends: "Those things that had to happen. You think you can escape them" (244). Cf. Noe's *Irréversible*.

As the violence builds, there are two possibilities: Either the two women are more male than male, hyper-male. Or they are hyper-feminine. In their hyper-subjectivities, they are perhaps neo-Amazons. They are perhaps, the voice that says, "I'm Andrea, which means manhood.... My *nom de guerre* is Andrea One; I am reliably told there are many more; girls named courage who are ready to kill" (Dworkin, *Mercy* 333). They are perhaps women known as *Les Guérillères* (Wittig).

If the film's purpose is to portray an attempt at rethinking, reinventing, experimenting, through *autopoesis*, what the new female must be to survive masculine violence or what women must do to teach men that they must stop being violent, then, as this mono*man*ical point of view unfolds, this purpose un/just destroys itself along with the two women and a long line of apparent innocents. The two characters choose only to will nothingness. In as much as the film is about *the call to come* (a call to a community of avenging angels), it never realizes the possibilities of becoming. It stays in the register of mimesis, imitating male violence against women. (In this sense, Despentes's and Coralie Trinh Thi's film realizes, beyond Margie Strosser's wildest dreams, a revenge narrative against men as well as women and children.) *Baise-Moi*—both as film and novel—is un/just all shadow narrative (this time, all undifferentiated sexual violence). One built on an Aphrodite-Thanatos principle. In the context of this discussion, *Baise-Moi* can be seen as a shadow narrative of Sander's ending to *BeFreier und Befreite*, which attempts to negate male sexual violence and to affirm a *call to arms*. First, the *call*; then a shadowy-mirrored crime spree.

The first twenty or so minutes of the film attempts to lay the groundwork for *why* there is violence toward men. The character Manu is raped by a gang of men, and Nadine, who is a prostitute, is perpetually put upon by her Johns.

Some how or other by chance Manu and Nadine meet each other and begin to talk and speak of going on the road together. (The film obviously invites a comparison with *Thelma and Louise*.) But as the narrative unfolds on the road, there is nothing but gratuitous violence against any and everyone, women as well as men. In the novel, a child as well as adults. There is a scene that originates at an ATM machine, with a woman withdrawing money, and then a cut to her down the street up against a wall being robbed and shot by Nadine in the neck and head. (The gun is touching her head. We do not see Nadine. The blood splatters up on the brick wall.) It is all very coldly done, without any hesitancy. Later when Nadine with Manu reflects on the killing, she recalls feeling bad for a short while, but feels nothing now. There is a scene with an architect in his house, where the two women go to seduce him into opening his safe, to rob him of diamonds. It only proves to be another strange scene—less developed in the film, more fully developed in the novel—in which the architect builds while the women, "Avenging Angels" (*Baise-Moi* 221), see themselves as being called "to teach you [the architect] what losing means" (220). It is a resentful scene with those who have lost in life, taking on those who have succeeded in life. In the novel, the man is colored in less radiant-saintly terms, since he has DeSade on his bookshelves and a porn film (225, 228). They shoot him in the head and then urinate on his face. There is scene after scene of such killings. Most memorable and commented on by critics of the film is a scene toward the end in a sex club in which both women kill everyone methodically and save a special "killing" for a man who Manu penetrates with her hand gun and shoots in the anus.[44] This scene is not in the novel.

---

44 See Reynaud, who writes about the killing of the child in the shop scene and the killing of the man in the sex club.

Perhaps it is traded for another scene that is not in the film, in which Nadine shoots a little boy and his grandmother and then two shop girls (153–60)! The film, while starting as a revenge film, turns into something else. From kiss me, no; to fuck me, no; to rape me, no; to kill me. It is a film issuing a kiss of death against life. Killing sex, killing life, the life-force itself.

(A Closing, yet reopening parenthesis: Penthesilea's acts of violence in Kleist's play are against Achilles—not every man—but against her double—and so, then finally against herself as well. When critics find fault with Penthesilea's actions, they often say that she took on the job of killing Achilles herself, instead of allowing for justice through her group, her state-community of Amazons.[45] Nothing could stop Penthesilea from killing herself. I cannot repeat this enough: When the slave girl in Christa Wolf's *Cassandra* calls to Penthesilea, "Come join us" [118], leave the killing and dying to others who would will nothing for themselves, Penthesilea refuses—she has lost all equilibrium—and is killed by Achilles and mutilated. She ignores the third alternative of *Come Live with us*. She ignores the call toward community. But not to stand in contradiction to becoming, as in becoming with Achilles in Kleist, Penthesilea in Wolf's rendering refuses to become an assemblage in community.

And yet again, of course there is the community of the raped and dead, whom we memorialize. At the end of *Baise-Moi*, Manu is shot apparently by a man who is protecting himself from her attempt to hold him up. Nadine

---

45 See Deleuze, *Essays Critical* 79; *Thousand* 244. However, cf. Agee xxvii. I am not losing sight of the possibility that in Kleist's play Achilles becomes woman while Penthesilea becomes dog (see *Thousand* 268). However, in Christa Wolf's *Cassandra* the death of Penthesilea is not a becoming with Achilles, but a refusal to become community, when the slave girl calls her to form an assemblage, a new community of minor(atarian) people.

hears the exchange of gunfire, leaves the car and runs into the building and kills the man and takes Manu to the edge of the lake, covers and pours gasoline over her, and memorializes by cremating her. Nadine attempts to end her own life, but is caught and arrested. To face death by the state. This time Thelma is dead, but Louise is captured. There are other endings: I cannot stop thinking of the memorialization in the conclusion of Andrea Dworkin's *Mercy*: "[T]hen you will remember rape; these are the elements of memory, *constant, true, and perpetual pain*; and otherwise you will forget—we are a legion of zombies—because it burns out a piece of your brain" (321–23; Dworkin's emphasis). I cannot stop thinking of the memorialization in the conclusion of Monique Wittig's *Les Guérillères*:

> Moved by a common impulse, we all stood to seek gropingly the even flow, the exultant unity of the Internationale. And aged grizzled woman soldier sobbed like a child.... The great song filled the hall, burst through the doors and windows and rose to the calm sky. The war is over, the war is over, said a young working woman next to me. Her face shone. And when it was finished and we remained there in a kind of embarrassed silence, a woman at the end of the hall cried, Comrades, let us remember the women who died for liberty. And then we intoned the Funeral march, a slow, melancholy and yet triumphant air. (144)

So now the women can work through their grief and melancholy by initiating a mourning narrative. Being called—either in a pragmatic or ontological vocation—becomes an important issue in these works. Violence, trauma, melancholy, then, apparently mourning.

Hiroshima Mon Amour, The Mourning Narrative

> Antiquity never ceased to lament the horrors of the Trojan war, as we never cease to lament the day of Hiroshima; if we want to make history, let us forget that once and for all, though everything comes from there. The ancient history comes from the end of Troy, as our new history comes from the end of Hiroshima; let us not forget it.
>
> Michel Serres, *Rome: The Book of Foundations* (40)

> The postwar generations have... inherited not guilt so much as the denial of guilt, not losses so much as lost opportunities to mourn losses. But perhaps more important... postwar generations have inherited the psychic structures that impeded mourning in the generations of their parents and grandparents. Foremost among such structures is a thinking in rigid binary oppositions, which form the sociopsychological basis of all searches for scapegoats.
>
> Eric Santner, *Stranded Objects* (34; qtd. by Levin, "Taking Liberties" 77)

There can be a problem with thinking with the heuristic metaphor of the gods. There is no better relation in replacing Eros with a female god (goddess). What remains is a turning from one God and from multiple gods-in-ratios to a radical multiplicity. What remains is a radical indifferentiation, a *becoming woman*, which is not grounded in a metaphysic of mimesis, nor in a provisional essentialism or a master narrative with a shadow narrative; rather it is *a becoming in between*. Deleuze and Guattari write: "A becoming is neither one nor two, nor the relation [ratio] of the two; it is the in-between" (*Thousand* 293; cf. Levi, *Cinema* 138–60). They say: "When Virginia Woolf was questioned about a specifically women's writing, she was appalled at the idea of writing 'as a woman.' Rather, writing should produce a becoming-woman as atoms of womanhood capable of crossing and impregnating an entire social field, and of contaminating men, of sweeping them up in that becoming" (*Thousand* 276).⁴⁶

But there can also be a problem with the Freudian mourning narrative.⁴⁷ This section is about the mourning narrative in *Hiroshima Mon Amour*, but it also concerns an experimental narrative without a narrative. Virtually, it concerns the implication of a bloc of two narratives— both mourning (without rigid binaries) and experimenting (forming a becoming). I will get to this film with its experiments eventually. What is important now is that I return to the Question of *Eros* in relation to *Thanatos* as reworked and un/worked by way of Deleuze in his discussions of cinema (in *Cinema 1* and *2*) and finally in "A Life" (*Pure Immanence*). Afterwards, we will see two bodies in bed embracing libidinally two lives (2 X "a life"), *a*semiotically (*a*cinematically) across two narratives that are not narratives, while having been super-imposed over two more bodies in the holocaust of Hiroshima embracing two deaths. One can see these, *a*semiotically, as linked in an assemblage of in betweens (cf. Oates, *Rape: A Love Story*).

Eros (redux): There is the theme of vitalism in Deleuze (*What is Philosophy?* 213–18). Deleuze attempts to rethink the whole problematic of subjects of desire under negation, who suffer from "weary thought, incapable of maintaining [themselves] on the plane of immanence" (214).

---

46 As Spivak says, the word "woman" misfires ("Feminism" 217). The word "woman" is both an essentialist category and a concept-metaphor. (Cf. Deleuze and Guattari, *Thousand* 275–76.)

47 See Freud, "Mourning and Melancholy" in *SE*, XIV: 237–58. For the Germans not being able to mourn the war, see Alexander and Margarete Mitscherlich, especially Ch. 1, section 9, "Is There Another Way to Mourn?" and also Eric L. Santner, *Stranded Objects*. Cf. Rickels; Forter. Perhaps the most ingenious ways of mourning, though still founded on an economy of sacrifice, are found in Ulmer's "Abject Monumentality" and Mauer's "Proposal."

For Deleuze, what drives the world is a vital force (power [*dynamis*], immanence [imminence], potentiality [impotentiality][48]), specifically, libido, or Eros.[49] But "there are interferences" that inform the whole of the plane of cerebral thinking. Deleuze explains: "This is because each distinct discipline is... in relation with a negative." But "if [all negatives, or categorical imperatives] are still distinct in relation to the cerebral plane, they are no longer distinct in relation to the chaos into which the brain plunges. In this submersion it seems that there is extracted from chaos *the shadow of the 'people to come'* [emphasis mine]: mass-people, world-people, brain-people, chaos-people" (*What is Philosophy?* 218). But the shadow *can be* a renegating shadow not unlike the shadow that follows closely, but grows weary eventually, behind Zarathustra. The shadow says to Zarathustra that it is tired and it wants to go home to rest. It is tired, for it has chased after Zarathustra, who has an unquenchable desire to light out for the de/territorializations. Instead, the shadow has a negative, restless desire to be secure. Zarathustra tells his shadow: "To those who are as restless as you, even a jail will at last seem bliss.... Beware lest a narrow faith imprison you in the end... For whatever is narrow and solid seduces and tempts you now" (Nietzsche 387). Zarathustra tells his shadow to return to the cave—the Platonic site of shadows—for Zarathustra says, "even now a shadow seems to lie over me.

---

48 See, e.g., Rajchman's *Constructions* and *Deleuze Connection*; Daniel Smith, "Introduction" to Deleuze's *Essays Critical* xi–liii. For cinema's influence on philosophy, according to Deleuze, see Flaxman, ed. *Brain is the Screen*.

49 For Deleuze and Guattari, vitalism can mean many different things, which would require a book of its own. See Butler, *Subjects of Desire*, who starts with Aristotle's statement that all men desire (have an appetite) to know. This vocabulary of drives and libido, though used by Deleuze and Guattari, can be rather problematic, for they do have alternate vocabularies, as Guattari makes obvious (see *Chaosmosis* 126).

I want to run alone so that it may become bright around me again" (387). Zarathustra *would like to learn to live finally*!

Deleuze would agree with Ginette Paris that Eros has lost its way in this world. In *Cinema 2*, he writes: "If we are sick with Eros, Antonioni said, it is because Eros is himself sick; and he is sick not just because he is old and worn out [weary] in his content, but because he is caught in the pure form of a time which is torn between an already determined past and a dead-end future. For Antonioni, there is no other sickness than the chronic. Chronos is sickness itself" (24).[50] What is wanted, as suggested, is a "people to come." In his discussions of post-WW II films, Deleuze sees Directors after the Holocaust attempting to rethink Eros as well as Chronos, not in terms of following a substitute god such as Aphrodite, but in terms of an immanent (imminent) Libido in its relation to *a life* and images in cinema moving from Chronos to Aion (cinema time in irrational cuts), moving from definite space to any-space-whatever, from black and white—shadows—to pure colors (a chaos) absorbing faces and characters (see *Cinema 1* 117–22; *II* 166–68). Deleuze is thinking at the thresholds, or in the interstices of the binary of Eros/Thanatos or Aphrodite/Thanatos and of the unary of (master) narration; he is thinking the outside as a third term.[51]

---

50 Antonioni, speaking of his characters' preoccupation with sex, says: "But this preoccupation with the erotic would not become obsessive if Eros were healthy, that is, if it were kept within human proportions. But *Eros is sick*; man is uneasy, something is bothering him. And whenever something bothers him, man reacts, but he reacts badly, only on erotic impulse, and he is unhappy. The tragedy in *L'Avventura* stems directly from an erotic impulse of this type—unhappy, miserable, futile" (qtd. in Chatman, *Antonioni* 56; emphasis mine; qtd. from Antonioni, "A Talk With" 51). Other films with this theme are *Night*, *Eclipse*, and *Red Desert*.

51 Cf. Canning 342–43. While Deleuze acknowledges the traditional vocabulary of binary terms, he constructs an outside vocabulary of third

Eros is a bond(age). A link, holding all things together. Deleuze sees these Directors, experimenting by forming, inventing, creating new filmic concepts such as "indiscernibility" between subject and object in bondage (*Cinema 2* 23). Peter Canning describes the old Eros of "bond(age)" as that of "the name of the Father" (343). Canning's description of the event: "A new order of time [aion, or aeon, a child playing with dice] begins when the signifier of the father, theoretically foreclosed by science but remaining as transcendental category, structure of understanding, is removed by an act of Deleuzian-Spinozist philosophy, and the real 'absence of link' emerges in and for itself without representation, an opening in time, becoming outside, future, launching a process of another nature, and calling for creation of a new kind of love, an immanent libido without ego or object or subject. For it was finally the transcendental-erotic subject-form that chained the ego to its object in love and hate, that chained the social images and movements to one another in delusional consensus, and that thirsted for salvation and transcendence to another world beyond the world" (343). The world to come. What we can see in *BeFreier und Befreite* is a reportage of the old, sick Eros and a thinking about how to reach the new; what we do see in *Baise-Moi* is the old Eros of sexual bondage and violence run amuck. What the new Directors create is a new Eros of *indiscernible passages between images* and the *transition from one sensation to another*. The new Directors are makers of new concepts, new sensations with their affects and percepts, which are new experiments in

---

terms [*immanence* that is imminence, *sensation* that is not a subjective state, *affect* that is not feelings, *percept* that is not perception, and *between* that is a preposition cum proposition that produces yet takes no object. For sensation and its two types, affect and percept, see Deleuze and Guattari, *What is Philosophy?* 163–99; Rajchman, *Deleuze Connections* 134–35; Massumi, *Parables*.

linkages. I have been abstract enough. Let us cut to a few exemplars.

Exemplars of "A Life": Earlier we spoke of Deleuze's exemplar of *the wasp becoming of the orchid and the orchid becoming of the wasp* (*Dialogues* 2–3). Deleuze in "A Life" speaks of another experimental linkage, or of immanence (imminence) or becoming, this one in literature. I am going to quote his description at length:

> What is immanence? A life... No one has described what *a* life is better than Charles Dickens [in *Our Mutual Friend*].... A disreputable man, a rogue, held in contempt by everyone, is found as he lies dying. Suddenly, those taking care of him manifest an eagerness, respect, even love, for his slightest sign of life. Everybody bustles about to save him, to the point where, in his deepest coma, this wicked man himself senses something soft and sweet penetrating him. But to the degree that he comes back to life, his saviors turn colder, and he becomes once again mean and crude. Between his life and his death [Eros and Thanatos], there is a moment that is only that of *a* life playing with death. The life of the individual gives way to an impersonal and yet singular life that releases a pure event freed from the accidents of internal and external life.... *It is a haecceity no longer of individuation but of singularization: a life of pure immanence, neutral, beyond good and evil....*
> But we shouldn't enclose life in the *single moment* when individual life confronts universal death. A life is everywhere, in *all the moments* that a given living subject goes through and that are measured by given lived objects: an immanent life carrying with it the events or singularities that are merely actualized in

subjects and objects. This indefinite life does not itself have moments, close as they may be one to another, but only *between-times, between-moments*; it doesn't just come about or come after but offers the immensity of an empty time where one sees the event yet to come and already happened, in the absolute of an immediate consciousness. (28–29; emphasis mine)

Somewhere in *between* the man and those helping him lies a pure affect of indiscernibility, that is, of desubjectivation, a singularization. A becoming of each other. As Flaubert becomes *"Madame Bovary, c'est moi"*; et cetera.[52] All assemblages. All blocks of becoming. As Deleuze says: "We are not *in* the world, we become with the world" (*What is Philosophy?* 169). Everything participates with everything else. We live in a participatory radical of multiverses. It is a passion (an intensity) according to G.H.[53] A realization and actualization of this virtuality will be experienced by the coming community of people on the new earth (see *What is Philosophy?* 201–218; cf. Agamben, *Coming*).

The mourning narrative that best rethinks becoming experimentally is this time in cinema, *Hiroshima Mon Amour*. Marguerite Duras's "synopsis" is very precise about how movement-image is replaced by time-image (from *chronos* to *aion*).[54] (Movement-image requires an emphasis on cause and effect, whereas time-image emphasizes sense-effect, *sens*ation, a third *sens*. Directions. Redirections.) She rehearses the situation of the lovers with

---

52 See Daniel Smith's "Introduction" to *Essays Critical* for additional exemplars; and Deleuze's *Dialogues* 36–76.

53 See Lispector's *Passion*, in which the character *becomes roach* and becomes, thereby, indifferentiated into "a vastness" (96–97). For a full discussion, see my *Negation* (228–29).

54 See Caruth's discussion of *Hiroshima Mon Amour* in *Unclaimed Experience*.

two coextensive places, two incompossible worlds, two monads, Hiroshima and Nevers (France). The French woman with no name has finished all but one last scene of a film of peace in Hiroshima. The Japanese man with no name is an "engineer or architect" (8).[55] They are married to others. Their meeting is by "chance" (8). Duras prepares a time-image of aion through which to introduce the almost-anonymous characters. Duras writes: "In the beginning of the film...we see mutilated bodies—the heads, the hips—moving—in the throes of love or death [Eros or Thanatos]—and covered successively with the ashes, the dew, of atomic death—and the sweat of love fulfilled" (8). Then the bodies of the French woman and Japanese man *emerge* from and become superimposed over the bodies in death. We have a double capture of death and love, love and death. (Eros is sick.) And yet, incipient life emerges. The woman says, "she has seen everything in Hiroshima." She is referring to the photographs and displays at the Hiroshima Memorial. But the man rejects "the deceitful pictures" (8), saying, "You saw nothing in Hiroshima. Nothing" (15). The woman, insists: "I saw *everything. Everything*" (15; Duras's emphasis). In the synopsis, Duras explains: "[T]heir initial exchange is allegorical. In short, an operatic exchange.... All one can do is talk about the impossibility of talking about Hiroshima" (9). This affair, this one night, Duras says, "takes place in the one city of the world where it is hardest to imagine it: Hiroshima.... Between two people as dissimilar geographically, philosophically, historically, economically, racially, etc. as it is possible to be. Hiroshima will be *the common ground* (perhaps the only one in the world?) where the universal factors of eroticism, love, and unhappiness will appear in

---

55 The man-as-architect is in Antonioni's *L'Avventura*. Sandro, who is preoccupied with sex (suffers from eros sickness), cannot design for life. He is at odds with his calling in life, and consequently with living.

an implacable light" (10; emphasis mine). What we know is only the impossibility of knowing Hiroshima. The French woman remains a tourist, making a film about peace for virtual tourists. She tells the Japanese man: "Like you, I too have tried with all my might not to forget. Like you, I forgot. Like you, I wanted to have an inconsolable memory, a memory of shadows and stone. *(The shot of a shadow, 'photographed' on stone, of someone killed at Hiroshima.)*" (23; Duras's emphasis). What we eventually realize about Hiroshima, as a memorial, is that it is a new *sens* of grounding (*abgrund*). The Japanese man is right in saying that she knows *nothing*. When nothing becomes everything, "sense," as Deleuze claims, becomes "extra-being" (*Logic* 31). A "*third estate*" (32; Deleuze's emphasis).[56]

The whole first section of film is inundated with tourists visiting the memorial. But there is more to the film, for out of this impossibility of mourning the loss of the object, the woman and the man invent *a life*. Verging on incompossibilities. In doing so, the woman and the man leave behind public mourning and enter an exchange of a story that allows for a becoming. Duras makes clear that they are in love and that this is not yet another exemplar of a sickness of Eros. Moreover, because they are in love, the woman can tell her story of Nevers (11). Of loss. But theirs is not a private mourning. Again, there is neither public nor private mourning. This film is a double capture of the failure of mourning and the alternative of *sens*ation, unmourning, and antimemory.

The woman tells her story of Nevers (10). She has never told this story to anyone. Duras's sketch: In 1944, the

---

56 This is the impossible moment. At this point in this chapter. With perhaps a most important assignment about an assignation. Therefore, I am passing it on to you, the readers: Your assignment, if you choose to accept it, can be found in the Excursus, under chapter 2. Beginning with Bataille's "Concerning the Accounts."

townspeople shaved her head and her parents placed her in their cellar, where she was to stay for however long it would take.[57] Waiting. Until a *singular moment* of Liberation when there is the conjunction of the killing of her lover and the bombing of Hiroshima (12). A Life. In the woman's telling of this story, Nevers becomes, in Deleuze's vocabulary, a *percept*. Daniel Smith explains: "What the percept makes visible are the invisible forces [in shadows] that populate the universe, that affect us and make us become: characters pass into the [shadows of the virtual] landscape and themselves become part of the compound of sensations" ("Introduction," *Deleuze* xxxiv). Characters become part of the circuitry of what Deleuze calls "the crystal-image, or crystalline description," a joining of the actual and virtual images (*Cinema 2* 68–69). "These percepts," Smith reminds us, "are what Woolf called 'moments of the world,' and what Deleuze terms 'haecceities'" (xxxiv) or what Deleuze himself refers to as "sheets of past" (*Cinema 2* 98–125). The two geographical locations and events in time (aion) form, again as Smith suggests, "assemblages of nonsubjectified affects and percepts that enter into virtual conjunction" (xxxiv). Creating a Life. It is worth repeating: As Deleuze says, "We are not in the world," for when the neuronic circuitry shifts, "we become with the world" (*What is Philosophy?* 169).

Deleuze, in *Cinema 2*, sees Duras and Resnais thinking in terms of "sheets of past" which are incommensurable and which are by allusion incompossible worlds. As Deleuze says about Resnais, "Everything depends on which sheet you are in" (120; cf. 129–31). Deleuze explains:

---

57 Recall earlier other doubly articulated "sheets of past": The *loves* that also occurred during Liberation in March through May of 1945 in Berlin. Sander in *BeFreier* reminds us that there were German women who fell in love with the enemy (Russians or U.S., British, French allies)—which was read as collaboration—only to lose their love.

> There are two characters [in *Hiroshima Mon Amour*] but each has his or her own memory which is foreign to the other. There is no longer anything at all in common. It is like two incommensurable regions of past, Hiroshima and Nevers. And while the Japanese refuses the woman entry into his own region... the woman draws the Japanese into hers.... Is this not a way for each of them to forget his or her own memory, and make a memory for two, *as if memory was now becoming world*, detaching itself from their persons? [...] Throughout Resnais' work we plunge into a memory which overflows the conditions of psychology, memory for two, memory for several, memory-world, memory-ages of the world. But the question as a whole remains: what are the sheets of past regions of several memories, creation of a memory-world, or demonstration of the ages of the world? (117–19; emphasis mine)

It is at this point that Deleuze takes up the parathethod of topological stretchings, which is not unlike casuistic stretchings, as a means of answering his question. In many ways, or *wayves*, the topological stretchings are comparable to Woolf's expression in *Mrs. Dalloway* of passing through London, "slic[ing] like a knife through everything" (11). It is remarkable what a single slice through a sheet of potential cartographical spatial and temporal paper can do, along with a half-twist of stretching, re(mis)configuring a map of the city or of the world from two sides (Hiroshima-Nevers) into one side (see Deleuze, *Cinema 2* 119). Finally, Deleuze writes: "Resnais has always said that what interested him was the brain, the brain as world, as memory, as 'memory of the world.' It is in the most concrete way that Resnais... creates a cinema which has only one single character, Thought" (122).

*Sens*ation (or "Bicycle-less neo-realism"): Deleuze begins *Cinema 2* discussing the creators of concepts in cinema "rediscover[ing] the power of the fixed shot" (22). Antonioni begins to think of doing "without a bicycle—De Sica's bicycle, naturally" (23). The reference is to the film *The Bicycle Thief*. Deleuze writes: "Bicycle-less neo-realism replaces the last quest involving movement (the trip) with a specific weight of time operating inside characters and excavating them from within (the chronicle)" (23; cf. 17). Antonioni says, "Now that we have today eliminated the problem of the bicycle ... it is important to see what there is in the spirit and heart of this man whose bicycle has been stolen, how he has adapted, what has stayed with him out of all his past experiences of the war, the post-war and everything that has happened in our country" (qtd. by Deleuze 284–85, n. 40). The bicycle will no longer move in space as a movement-image (*Cinema 1*) but in aion as a time-image (*Cinema 2*), by way of various intensities. *Sens*ations. Redirections. This rider of the bicycle, now without a bicycle that may remain but a memory as in a photograph, a still frame, will be made into a multiplicity—less a subject and more a multiplicity. (Recall the German woman in a tug of war over her bicycle with the Russian soldier.) John Rajchman explains that a multiplicity, made from a pragmatics of *sens*, is outside the binary of public and private. Multiplicity is a third *sens*ation.[58] "The problem of 'making multiplicities' or 'constructing multiplicities' is ... a problem of life—of 'a life,' ... an indefinite life" (83). Singularities. "Singular occurrences." "Something ineffable" (85). A third *sens*. Of moments that compose *a life* (cf. Duras 68). A redirected one.

In part 2 of the *Hiroshima Mon Amour* film script,

---

58 I respectively refer to Rajchman's *Deleuze Connections* 80, and to Barthes's "Third meaning [Sens]."

Duras describes the scene as such: "(*A swarm of bicycles passes in the street, the noise growing louder, then fading*)" (29; Duras's emphasis; cf. 34–35).[59] Later in the midst of the woman's relating the story of Nevers, she tells the Japanese man: "[M]y hair is now a decent length. I'm in the street with the people" (67). In these images of the bicycle, there is mobility, flight, as there is in the dialogue of leaving the man and returning home. She is leaving, as she left her German lover in Nevers, the Japanese man. We can actually see her on the bicycle or in the plane physically leaving. But we can hear her also affirmatively forgetting. Leaving in itself. It is not just a physical leaving of Nevers (on a bicycle) and then Hiroshima (in a plane), but a series of moments with peculiar affirmations that make for multiplicities. Or blocs ("swarms") of bicycles in first a movement-image and then a time-image. She is taking leave, taking, forgetting, yet re-momenting, place. It is not memento, but momenting. She and the Japanese man are forgetting each other (68, 73, 83). Forgiving. Re-forging, Everything and nothing. Becoming world-people. They are dis/engaging by way of antimemory. As Deleuze and Guattari chime: "Memory, I hate you" (*What is Philosophy?* 168; cf. *Thousand* 294–95). She leaves rigid binaries (subject-object) for the extra-being of outside multiplicities. A vastness. Coextensive lives. There is this repeated refrain of affirmative forgetting and then the making of multiplicities, becomings, a bloc of percepts and affects. Both have dis/engaged by way of not just mourning but of unmourning. Both have returned from the dead (cf. Flaxman 42). Both now share a life in a

---

59 The bicycles are motor propelled. The woman's bicycle in Nevers, to Paris, is human propelled.

becoming world. Filled with moments. They are done with mourning and any incipient melancholy.

Unmourning: John Rajchman, commenting on memory, memorials, and mourning-melancholy, writes: "Affect in Spinoza becomes the sensation of what favors or prevents, augments or diminishes, the powers of life of which we are capable each with one another; and it is in something of this same 'ethical' sense that Deleuze proposes to extract clinical categories (like 'hysteria' or 'perversion' or 'schizophrenia') from their legal and psychiatric contexts and make them a matter of experimentation in moves of life in art and philosophy, or as categories of a philosophico-aesthetic 'clinic.'... Freud tried to understand 'melancholy' (and its relation with the arts) in terms of the work of mourning concerning loss or absence. But Deleuze thinks there is a 'unmourning' that requires more work, but promises more joy. Considered in philosophico-aesthetic terms, melancholy might then be said to be the sensation of an unhappy idealization, and the real antidote to it is to be found not in rememorization and identification, but in active forgetting and affirmative experimentation with what is yet to come" (*The Deleuze Connections* 132–33).

Antimemory: Deleuze and Guattari, in *A Thousand Plateaus*, write: "*Becoming is an antimemory*. Doubtless, there exists a molecular memory, but as a factor of integration into a majoritarian or molar system. Memories always have a reterritorialization function. On the other hand, a vector of deterritorialization is in no way indeterminate; it is directly plugged into the molecular levels, and the more deterritorialized it is, the stronger is the contact: it is deterritorialization that makes the aggregate of the molecular components 'hold together.' From this point of view, one may contrast a *childhood block*, or a becoming-child, with the *childhood memory*: 'a' molecular child is produced... 'a' child coexists with us, in a zone of proximity or a block of becoming, on a line of deterritorialization that carries us both off—as opposed to the child we once were, whom we remember or phantasize, the molar child whose future is the adult. 'This will be childhood, but it must not be my childhood,' writes Virginia Woolf. (*Orlando* already does not operate by memories, but by blocks, blocks of ages, block of epochs, blocks of the kingdoms of nature, blocks of sexes, forming so many becomings between things, or so many lines of deterritorialization.) Wherever we used the word 'memories,' we were saying becoming" (294; Deleuze and Guattari's emphasis; cf. Bergson, *Creative Evolution* 312–13; de Certeau, *Practice* 108).

CHASTE CINEMA III+?

Reading and Writing Revenge Fantasies

> "Nothing is ever to be *posited* that is not also reversed and caught up again in the *supplementarity of this reversal* [*reversement*]."
> Luce Irigaray, *This Sex* (79, Irigaray's emphasis)

Yes, rape (in cinema) has a history (e.g., Haskell). And so does revenge (e.g., Read; Horeck; Heller-Nicholas; Projansky). Perhaps rape and revenge began at the same time and have exhibited parallel complementary traces that contribute to the development of subjectivity. Rape and then revenge; or, Revenge and then rape; or still, Rape as revenge. But Revenge for What? Perhaps rape and revenge inform the very narrative structure of violence called history. As Laura Mulvey says: "sadism demands a story" ("Visual" 14). We could equally say that a story demands sadism. A sadist. Indeed, either may be in the other. Perhaps a sadist, such as de Sade, as many commentators have argued, can teach us in his dialogues something by way of his interlocutors.[1]

---

1 See these various commentators who generally read de Sade's various works as performing the dark side of reason (Enlightenment): Le Brun, *Sade: A Sudden Abyss;* Klossowski, *Sade: My Neighbor*; Frappier-Mazur, *Writing the Orgy*; Weiss, *The Aesthetics of Excess*. Also see this

I want to *turn* now to a woman's revenge story that has as its script *You rape me, I kill you*. In *my turn*, I will deal with *imminent reversibility*.

Wendy Hesford (Strosser's *Rape Stories*): As a case in point, Hesford addresses the reversibility based on revenge in Margie Strosser's video *Rape Stories* (1989) and takes a stand against it, just as I do. But Hesford's take is by far more complicated than this simple reversal (based on the principle of an eye for an eye) suggests.

Hesford starts from Teresa de Lauretis' discussion (*Technologies* 31–50) on the reversal of *violence of rhetoric* in relation to the *rhetoric of violence*. De Lauretis contends, "the representation of violence is inseparable from the notion of gender, even when the latter is explicitly 'deconstructed' or, more exactly, indicated as 'ideology.' I contend, in short, that violence is engendered in representation" (33). There is no doubt that "violence is engendered in representation," along with rhetoric becoming rhetorics! The problem is that a powerful way of attempting to escape the metaphysics of representation is both negative and nonpositive-affirmative deconstructions. *The violence of rhetoric* drifts, as Paul de Man would say, into "a reading, not a decodage," with readings unto readings unto a *pure rhetoric, which means rhetorics* (*Allegories* 9), displacing in *the rhetoric of violence* the fact that violence is engendered, that sex is forced on women and some men, making them sexually normed as "women," as objects used in certain life-denying ways (De Lauretis 37).[2] No matter how much

---

edition with introductions by Jean Paulhan and Maurice Blanchot to Marquis de Sade's *Complete Justine, Philosophy in the Bedroom, and other Writings*.

2 De Man's infinite rhetoricity (transversibility) is informed by his reading of C. S. Peirce. While de Man engages in a poststructuralist reading, Lauretis's is a "realist" reading (*Technologies* 38–42). Predispositions

anyone tries to control logos (language), however, through identification, non-contradiction, and excluded middle, logos does what logos desires—makes impossibility possible. Whether we like it or not. At best, we can take note of it when we notice it. (Here comes a tsunami.) In as much as human beings speak, we are also spoken.[3] There is, consequently, the idea of mis-trusting logos (a language, any language). Hence, the presumption that misology leads to misanthropy (See Plato, *Phaedo* 89d-90).

To combat this drift of reversibility and beyond, Hesford has one over-riding goal and primary application in respect to the fantasy of revenge in Strosser's video. The "goal," as Hesford says,

> is not to look at survivors' representations as mirrors of historical or psychic realities but to consider how realist strategies authenticate survivors' representa-

---

toward reading Peirce determine, as Hesford might say, the differences between "the materialist 'real' (historical reality) and the psychoanalytic 'Real' (resistance to symbolization)" (196). See Butler, *Bodies*, 1–55; Ronell, *Stupidity* 95–163. De Lauretis-Hesford's take on materialist reading can be read with Hengehold's reading Foucault, hysterization, and the second rape.

3 From Aristotle through Cicero to the present, rhetoric has been developed to teach speakers (writers and readers) to control the flow of logos (language). Historians of rhetoric have continually tried to separate the tropes from the topoi, the latter being supposedly the very essence of rhetoric. But there is no way to rid tropes from topoi, conceptual starting places. Later, with Ricoeur's hermeneuts of suspicion, especially, Nietzsche and Freud, as well as my addition of Heidegger, logos speaks human beings. Marx is usually included, but I can accept such an inclusion only if Marx is not a "Marxist." My sense is that Lyotard, in *Libidinal Economy*, has embarrassed Marxists. And so have Žižek (*Sublime Object of Ideology*) and Sloterdijk (*Critique of Cynical Reason*). What I am saying here is heretical on several levels, which I have already explained in detail in *Negation* and *Sexual Violence*. But really, a challenge was offered in favor of my position, way before I knew I had a position, by Ijsseling (*Philosophy and Rhetoric in Conflict*). See my summary in *Negation* (170–73), in fact, see the whole book.

tions. I use the terms *realist* in this context to refer to conventions and strategies of representation that signify that which is deemed 'true' and presume a measure of objectivity. Thus, the 'textual anxiety' that sustains this project is the desire to rescue the concept of agency from the anti-humanist assaults of poststructuralism in ways that do not configure agency outside of culture and its discourses but reconfigure personal and political agency as embodied negotiations and material enactments of cultural scripts and ideologies. For example, in order to account for the pain that women endure to claim agency in the context of sexual violence, we need to understand rape as both a material and a discursive site of struggle of cultural power. (197; Hesford's emphasis)

Hesford is "consider[ing] how ["realist"] strategies of appropriation can subvert dominant rape scripts even as they establish complicity with them" (197; cf. Leonardo).

Hesford responds to what she sees as the political weaknesses of poststructuralist reading practices for feminism and women.[4] Therefore, Hesford recognizes what I stated above, but would not accept what appears to be the inevitable flow of logos. Hence, our differences. So much depends on what is taken for our *relations* with *logos*!

Hesford's application centers on a series of readings of *Rape Stories* done with great care, asking, what is gained by Strosser's calling on a particular strategy of reversal? Hesford says, "The victim rewrites the rape narrative of male power by constructing herself [through a reversal] as [the] one who inflicts pain and violation; the survivor

---

4 See my thoughts on deconstruction in *Negation* (207–33).

maims and disarms the phallus and then distributes the fragments among other female rape survivors" (207).

To add to Hesford's critique—because I agree with Hesford's take on the trope of revenge—what I find ethico-politically counter-productive in Strosser's video is that it is not only reactionary, vengeful, and suffering from *ressentiment*, but it is also a call for a counter-narrative of sacrifice and resurrection. While there are countless narratives of rapes of women (it is an ur-script as I have pointed out), should the man who raped Strosser be murdered, mutilated, and cut into slivers and distributed to other women who have been raped? No doubt, the prevailing answer by readers would be understandably YES! For those who have not viewed the video: Toward the end, Strosser fantasizes killing the rapist and cutting his corpse into wafer-like slivers and distributing them to women to eat.[5] Hence, a sacrifice for communion. A call put out: *Do this in remembrance of me!* The ramifications of this fantasy-act are numerous, from a Christian story of incorporation and resurrection to a parodic reversal of Freud's story in *Totem and Taboo* of the slaying of the father and the consuming of his flesh by the brothers (*SE*, XIII: 1–161; cf. Hamacher 1–81). Here instead of a band of brothers, a band of sisters. Either way, someone is sacrificed. Either way, a community is established at the expense of the other. Either way, Strosser is saying: Do this in remembrance of all our sisters who have been raped.

But perhaps Hesford and I, though differently, are making too much of what we see as a script of revenge. After all, the script is just a thought, a fantasy, in a film/video, just like all those ancient mythic narratives of rape founding new communities. We might reason: What is

---

5 Strosser's work is not near—actually, it is not even comparable—to Meir Zarchi's *I Spit on Your Grave* (1978). But I have only read about Zarchi's film. I refuse to view it.

good for the goose is good for the gander. And for the gosling?[6] Everything is reversible! And improperly proper for a sacrificial economy. And yet, have we uncovered a limit?

I want to examine—diatactically—my own mixed responses to Strosser's video, for they open up for me some things about the video and Strosser's purpose for making it that complicate issues greatly. My ethic in thinking, reading, and writing is not dialectical resolutions (from standing above), but diatactical self-criticisms (from mis-understandings within and around the rhetoric of violence and the violence of rhetoric) (cf. White, *Tropics* 4). I must, as I hope others will, be suspicious of every thought spoken and written, for I am not the master of what I say or write. Nor, I would insist, is anyone. I will try to rehearse my responses and then comment on them and how I see the video as an *experiment against* canonized ways of reading rape and as an *experiment*, intended or not, for a pedagogy of reading (viewing) rape stories (cf. Projansky; Cuklanz). And yes, equivocations will mis/inform the flow.

Much of what I see and re-see, however, will be, in my contrary attempt to explain my viewing experiences, informed by the thinking of tactical poststructuralist theories. Some rather radical and even disconcerting for me at times. What I find peculiar in my experience with the video was that *while I was reading the video, the video was reading me*. It is not unusual that in some genres

---

6   My allusion here is to Ovid's story, in *Metamorphoses*, of Philomela. As the story goes: Tereus is married to Procne. They have Itys as their son. The narrative begins with Tereus raping Procne's sister, Philomela. Let us recall, if only with a casuistic stretching by analogy, that Procne for revenge kills her and Tereus' son *Itys* (*It was*) and then serves *Itys* up for the unwitting incorporation by the father. The generosity of Being (*Itys, it is, it gifts*) in this counter-scenario is subverted with violence begetting violence. With the eternal return of the same. (See, *Sexual Violence* 28–31.)

CHASTE CINEMA III+?

objects can read their subjects, whether male or female or third possibilities (Deleuze, *Cinema 1* 81; cf. Perniola 39–58; Elkins, *Object*; Baudrillard, *Revenge*).[7] What I am saying about viewer-video (subject-object) relations can be interpreted as a form of reciprocity, or reversibility itself, if not reconciliation, which I see as potentially, though dormant, in all thoughts and things, but it is not any mere reversibility that leads unquestionably to revenge as we see in Strosser's theme of revenge. I would think, as Christa Wolf does, that there is a "third alternative" (106–07, 118): Namely, "living" the various textual lives within the text, for example, in Wolf's work, the fall of Troy.

To this end, I am going to follow this *topos* as well as *chora* of *reversibility*. I am aware that Jean Baudrillard insists that today, given the "systems" we live in, reversibility in mythology is not possible. We are stuck, he insists, in "irreversibility" (*Revenge* 25), just as he refuses to go with "transversality" (33). More important for me, however, is to counter-insist on reversibility in "mythologies" (25), that is, in mythomorphic discourses that are the foundations of thinking, reading, writing. I will make much of this insistence as we proceed. Why? Because reversibility can lead to, and I believe *it is* leading toward, a *transversibility*, or rather a transvaluation of values that will enhance living (cf. Irigaray, *This Sex* 79–80). But I am getting ahead of myself.

At First Viewing: I received the video as being composed of, edited with, more than Strosser's telling her story. I received the video as having several different narrators, each telling her separate story ("Rape Stor*ies*"). I viewed it as an anthology of stories. Upon additional viewings,

---

7 And of course this reversal is made even clearer by paratheorists of Object-Oriented Ontologies, or OOO).

however, I reversed my original position and began to see that it was Strosser's telling alone, with the implication that her telling was one of many "Rape Stories." Therefore, I moved from the idea of many narrators to one (with the potentiality of many stories). Either way, what I began additionally to think was that the video was interrogating me, or more broadly that the video interrogates the viewer—that this was a video titled "Rape Stories" that also attempts to create the illusion, for the viewer, of going through the ordeal of having to make a statement concerning what is *taking place* (in the video) and then having to defend it. Most peculiar, as I began to critique the video, I simultaneously found myself being critiqued. This was no simple matter that critique of others is also self-critique. I discovered that I was becoming others and that the video is pedagogical in a distributed, non-privileged, non-canonized way.

To extrapolate further, what I find remarkable about Strosser's video is that it places me and perhaps other viewers into many different subject or mute (tongue cut out) interlocutor positions such as a police detective listening to a report made by a woman who has been raped, but which in a later scene has the same woman becoming that very detective watching and interrogating the viewer. Subject/object(abject) reverses to object(abject)/subject. In one story or subject position, it is many stories and subject-object positions. As Virginia Woolf might say, the apparent entities "are edged with mist. [They] make an unsubstantial territory" (*Waves* 185). Entities (subjects/objects) become singularities who take on, or taken by, some *apparatus* (*dispositif*) greater than the radical-collective eye of the fly.[8] There are all kinds of such productive-turn-para-

---

8   For apparatus, see Agamben, *What is an Apparatus?*, as well as Deleuze "*What is a* Dispositif?"

doxical reversals, as well as metamorphoses, in the video that test us as viewers, male or female (cf. Pribram; Projansky). That test the exuberance of our very being. (I am aware that I am mixing, conflating, my viewing experiences of *Rape Stories* with other potential viewers' experiences. In as much as Hesford's viewings are an invitation to see it her ways, my viewings are an invitation as well to see it my wa*yves* [*ways, waves, yes* as affirmations]. I do not see these various wa*yves* as antithetical. Rather, I see these wa*yves*, as Gayatri Spivak might say, as establishing the conditions for "saying 'yes'" to the text-video a second and third time [see "Feminism" 212].)

This video *Rape Stories* is many things, but it is, to borrow a critical phrase, a "test drive" as well (Ronell). When I view the video, I am tested. So while I agree with De Lauretis and Hesford that the reversibility displaces the literate "fact" that violence is en-gendered and that rape scripts go unchallenged, I still see that, because of reversibility, in another sense, rape scripts go perpetually challenged, and I can be taught, as other female and male viewers can be taught, what it may be *like* to be interrogated by the law, or as often claimed, raped again. (To be sure, this teaching, or pedagogical move by Strosser, can be viewed as a simulation [reality] of what it must be like to be *raped again*. See Smart 34–35; Estrich 60–62; Hengehold 98–100.) Strosser's video can teach the viewer both *how* to listen and more importantly *how* to hear rape stories when told—and "we" are told—in quite different and subtle ways. (I am referring to Strosser's telling the viewers that, when she tells men that she has been raped, she tries to situate the stories to make them tell-able. She tells a man, "I hate parking garages because I was raped. And invariably, the man would say, I never knew anyone who was raped before. And I would say, that's what you think; they just never tell you.")

Reversibility can be pharmakonic.[9] Part of which can be life-enhancing. And yet, any such part, or counterpart, can put out a call for a script of transgression. Revenge. Which after all is said and undone is what *Rape Stories* attempts to do, to transgress, and to accomplish transgression by way of mirror images, which are plentiful in the video. And as Hesford argues and reminds us these strategies based on mirroring (a woman is raped; therefore, a woman should fantasize revenge against the rapist) are productive of only the same (206–12). As long as we dwell in the Symbolic (exchange and death), however, we are left with the question of where do women go for a life-enhancing scripted response that does not send them looping back to fantasizing about "empowerment" by way of revenge? Or contra-power? The Symbolic (along with simulation) has its various pedagogical mirroring stages. But it is not near enough to avoid the *psychoanalytic Symbolic and Real* and take up with the so-called *materialist real* to find the scripts. After all, the two, as Slavoj Žižek argues, homologically uphold *each other*: The Freudian-Lacanian and the Marxian views are both concerned with "the secret" of the dream and of the commodity (*Sublime* 11–16; cf. Horeck 1–13; Rose, *States* 3–4). Scripts as texts for life or filmic action are potentially Ovidean texts.[10]

I consider myself, at this *moment*, a Bergsonian materialist that would not attempt to separate his thinking from the Symbolic—Lacan, Kristeva, Žižek's S/symbolic and Real—except when passing over into the zone of indeter-

---

9 For a discussion of *pharmakon*, see Derrida, *Dissemination*. It is not a matter of choosing to think pharmakonically. Thinking is pharmakonic.

10 We can read Žižek as a poststructuralist himself. Žižek reads Lacan, however, as espousing a view that "is perhaps the most radical contemporary version of the Enlightenment" (7). But Žižek argues, "the moment we see it 'as it really is,' this being [i.e., this thing that is "the paradox of being"] dissolves itself into nothingness or, more precisely, it changes into another kind of reality" (28).

mination where *third* (non-transcendental, non-simulated) *figures* will have flourished (Bergson, *Creative* 126; cf. Kittler, *Discourse*; *Gramophone*).

Subsequent Viewings: I viewed the video all the way through the first time and thereafter numerous times the first day that I received it.[11] The second day, I viewed the video through stops and restarts. Forwards/backwards. Backwards/forwards. Browsings. Repeatedly. Studying the scenes. Taking notes. Making more notes, while recalling how I was hailed to view the video by way of Hesford's readings.

Let us stop and take notice of the fact that I have been calling Strosser's work a "video" and not a film. Hesford calls it a "film" (200). The organization—*Women Make Movies*—that distributed *Rape Stories* called it a videotape, which distinguishes it from other offerings that the organization calls films. (The works, at the time of my ordering/viewing, came in two basic formats of either 16mm, with a few in 35mm, film or in generic analog video. These expressions of difference by the WMM organization are more in terms of format and do not allude to a theory/genre specifying particular conventions of film vs. video making. The video is now distributed by scribe.org.)

So, Why am I calling the work a video? And is there a difference between a film and a video? The latter question is generally answered with a Yes.[12] The former question is

---

11 The video was originally available from Women Make Movies <http://www.wmm.com/>. Presently, available from Scribe Video Center <http://scribe.org/catalogue/rapestories>. Cf. Lennon and Ono's film *Rape* (December 1969).

12 Yvonne Spielmann focuses on the technical differences between various media, including film and video. But in the opening chapter, she spends much time reviewing exceptions to technological differences. She points to and thereby reminds me of Bolter and Grusin's take on *remediation*. They write: "If the logic of immediacy leads one either to

best answered by my saying that I am insisting on *thinking* the work *a video* for the reason that it allows me to use the term, genre or paragenre, heuristically in rethinking *Rape Stories*. If the work can take me on a test drive, I in turn can take the work on a test drive. In fact, I would say that the work invites me to take this reversal seriously. If for no other than heuristic, herethic, heuretic reasons. And for, as I announce in the *Preamble*, the task here is *meditation* through *remediation*.

My calling *Rape Stories* a video changes the *conditions* for the possibilities of reading any rape stories as De Lauretis would and Hesford does. I am less disagreeing with Hesford's reading, which is informed by the cultural and academic scripts of reading films; I am more so attempting, rather, to account for Hesford's reading of rape scripts, real/ism, and how "realist strategies can authenticate survivors' representations" (197) in *Rape Stories*. This approach that would avoid, or work around, the violence of rhetoric is important to both De Lauretis and Hesford, and yet, it is equally important to all previous, parallel discussions concerning the inoperative, unavowable, coming community (cf. Alexandra Juhasz's work). But the importance of the approach rests on the notion that a liberating subject of modernity is necessary to do

---

erase or to render automatic the act of representation, the logic of hypermediacy acknowledges multiple acts of representation and makes them visible. Where immediacy suggests a unified visual space, contemporary hypermediacy offers a heterogeneous space, in which representation is conceived of not as a window on the world, but rather as 'windowed' itself—with windows that open on to other representations or other media.... In every manifestation, hypermediacy makes us aware of the medium or media and (in sometimes subtle and sometimes obvious ways) reminds us of our desire for immediacy" (33–34; qtd, 302–03). Additionally see Bellour, *L'entre-images*; Jameson, "Reading"; Ulmer, "One"; Ronell, *Finitude's Score*.

political work. This subject is, however, as Greg Ulmer argues,

> formed in the apparatus of literacy, dependent on a specific historical configuration of technology, institutional practices (a written model of knowledge and law) and the behaviors of selfhood (the humanistic ideology of individualism). Is this apparatus still in place? The debate about the constructed nature of the human subject among humanists, Marxists, and deconstructors is one *symptom* that things are changing. The institutions organized by the apparatus of literacy express a nearly universal condemnation of a new institution whose organization reflects a new apparatus—television, representing the electronic apparatus (different technology, institutional practices, and personal behaviors). ("One" 259; emphasis added. Cf. Heath, "Turn"; Nancy, *Being* 1–99.)

But besides the distinction between film and video, I have in mind also Deleuze's distinction between *classical* and *modern cinema*, which are comparable in their differences with the previous pair. Specifically, I am thinking of Deleuze's *Cinema 1* and *Cinema 2*, in which he develops the differences between classical and modern, with the later radically decoding (deterritorializing) subjectivity, or any center of feigned authority and control. As is well known—and therefore I will give only a brief description here—Deleuze is working out of a Bergsonian ontology of monism with memory (mind) and matter as indistinguishable, or "*movement-image* and *flowing-matter* [as] strictly the same thing" (*Cinema 1* 59; Deleuze's emphasis). Subjective and objective perceptions, going through a *distributed perception*, slide into a third of "liquid perception"; or additionally put, solids become liquids that, in turn, become "gaseous perceptions" (dispersive and nonhuman) (71–86). What Deleuze has in mind as an exemplar for the latter-third is "Vertov's non-human eye, the cine-eye [which] is not the eye of a fly or an eagle.... Neither is it... the eye of the spirit endowed with a temporal perspective.... [I]t is the eye of *matter*, the eye *in* matter, not subject to time" (81; emphasis added. Cf. Deleuze, *Negotiations* 54). This eye is radically molecular and distributed. Which is brought about in cinema through "flickering montage... photogramme-shot [frame still shot]... hyper-rapid montage... re-recording" (85). According to Deleuze, what Vertov aims for and achieves is "the genetic element of all possible perception, that is, the point which changes, and which makes perception change, the *differential* of perception itself" (83; emphasis added). Besides movement-image, there is time-image, which introduces the "irrational cut," no longer based on metonymic (cause/effect) or synedochic (part/whole) relations but paralogical-conductive relations, with the interstices bringing forth "the new image of thought" (*Cinema 2* 214–15; cf. 179–82; cf. Doane). The irrational cut is outside of the realm of the so-called rational cut (castration itself). For Bergson and Deleuze, "the universe... is metacinema" (*Cinema 1* 59), is brain (*Cinema 2* 189–224), in its relation with human beings *after* human beings' brain, that is, after the posthumanist turn. As Deleuze says, "cinema produces reality" (*Negotiations* 58; cf. *Cinema 2* 262) by circulating and decirculating its characters and hence its viewers through "cerebral circuits, brain waves" (60; cf. Kittler, *Gramophone* xl-xli). Metacinema forms a potential pedagogy and a canon that is perpetually de-canonized.

As we move from film (modernism) to video (postmodernism or late capitalism), or from classical through modern cinema, the more we lose the conditions of subjectivity (agency), narrative representation and memory, as well as rational cuts, and the more we rediscover the conditions for cracking-up subjectivity (Deleuze and Guattari, *Thousand* 198–200; Deleuze, *Cinema 2*, 167) into haecceities and singularities (Agamben, *Coming* 17–20; cf. Perniola 22–38). Which are by far more resistant to domination than subject-object relations. We have not yet arrived at this crack-up of subjectivity into singularities, to the degree it will occur, but all signs (symptoms) indicate we are drifting—for good, bad, or in-difference—to a greater degree in this direction. Just as we drifted from orality to literacy, we are now drifting from literacy (print culture) to electracy (electronic culture).[13] And finally to the conditions of imminence (coming politics and community). But this is not to say that any one of these modes of being is left behind or disappears, for they all remain and begin to crowd and mob memory itself (see Burgos). We move hence from *imminent reversibility* to *imminence* (always already on the verge of happening). But this sketch needs to be a full argument, or a more forceful post-annunciation, than I can possibly give here.[14] But we will have to re-live through it, perhaps for a while in the desert—a fate

---

13 We should keep in mind Freud's "Screen Memories" (*SE*, III: 301–22); Deleuze's notion that the "brain is a screen" (see, e.g., the interview "Brain" in Flaxman 366; also, *Cinema 1* 56–63; *Cinema 2* 189–224) which echoes back to Bergson's thinking (*Matter and Memory* and *Creative Evolution*) and recalls recent "intellectual" cinema. Moreover, we should keep in mind Havelock (*Muse*), Ulmer (*Teletheory*; *Heuretics*; *Internet*), and Ronell (*Telephone*) on distinctions among oral, literate, and electronic-digital cultures. Also, see Burgos, "Memento"; Murray, "Digital Incompossibility"; Hansen, "Seeing With the Body"; Johnston, "Machinic Vision." And especially see Kittler, *Gramophone* 129–33, who argues, "Total use of media instead of total literacy: sound film and video cameras as mass entertainment liquidate the real even" (133). Most devastating is Kittler's *Discourse Networks*.

14 Baudrillard best describes the implosion of time and space, the loss of ethos (or subjectivity, agency), logos (reason), pathos (community). See *Transparency*; cf. Virilio *Open Sky*.

accomplished—first to think it as a back-formation, or metaleptic production (Levinas, *Totality* 22–30; cf. Blanchot, "Prophetic," *Book* 79–85). The writing-reading-thinking as backwards! Or as a *chiasm* (Irigaray, "Invisible" 151–84). At least, this sketch can suggest, however, *where* I am coming from in dis/respect to this test drive. If there is an exemplar for this *condition of imminence* it is to be found performed (virtually, deformed) in Jonathan Nolan's story "Memento Mori"[15] (which his brother, Christopher, made into the film *Memento*). But it is the story—not only the film—though the story and the film, the two different apparatuses, keep collapsing in on each other—that I refer to as exemplars of what is coming to our post-medium communities. It is the story, curiously enough, that carries the germs of an electronic apparatus. The story is, in my thinking, a story of transitions-interruptions and not one of restricted, but general arrival.

Interruptions as Other Viewings (*Memento*): In the story, Earl (in the film, Leonard Shelby), the man who suffers from a blow to the head as he attempted to save his wife from getting raped and murdered, tries to remember but cannot. (Or so we are led for the most part to believe in the film.) His "condition" for being has changed. Though he would think sustained difference, he thinks repetition. In the film, Leonard asks, *Have I told you about my condition? Of possibilities?* He perpetually attempts, nonetheless, to remember, to return himself back to that event of real violence (the originary moment), but he perpetually and circularly fails, even with the prosthesis of writing notes

---

15 Nolan's story was published in *Esquire* (March 2001), and can be found on the Web at <http://www.esquire.com/entertainment/books/a1564/memento-mori-0301/>. For the film *Memento*, see the script (Nolan, *Memento*), a selection of articles (Kania), and the making of the film (Mottram).

all around him (on the walls, mirrors, on front and back of photographs, on the ceiling and even more so on his body). As he reads these notes, he can remember them for about ten minutes and then he slips into a total state of confusion, which is not a beginning but an interruption, an experience of finitude, starting over again reading. Leonard's signature is the ten-minute script replayed in loops throughout the story as well as the film on its way to becoming a video near us. Leonard and the viewers along with him loop the loop in reversible order to some apparent origin of crime. An *image* of rape. Every ten minutes, Leonard experiences the depletion of self. Of subjectivity itself. Of individuation. The cognitive conventions of the subject-Leonard as a prosecutor declaring a particular subject a criminal—means, method, motive, and opportunity—disappear.

Leonard uses his "writings" as a means of establishing a point of stasis. He *reads* what he has *written* on the back of a Polaroid *photo* of Teddy: "Don't believe his lie He is the one Kill him [sic]." He does this knowing that he does not know. And yet, he thinks knowing, thinks he has a grounding freed from subjective distortion by the facts written down on paper or tattooed across his body. As Deleuze might say about Earl/Leonard, "defenseless against a rising of the ground which holds up to [them] a distorted or distorting mirror... all determinations become bad and cruel" (see *Difference* 152–53). Earl/Leonard's thinking is finally accomplished in a total state of cynicism. Someone's gotta pay. Or be sacrificed. To close this debt. This rape. As he says in the last scene of the film, which is the first of the chronological scenario, "I have to believe in *a world outside my own mind* [or brain]. I have to believe that my actions still have meaning, even if I cannot remember them. I have to believe when my eyes are closed, the world is still here. Do I believe the world is still here? Is it still out there? Yeah! We all need mirrors to remind ourselves where we are. I'm no different" (emphasis added). Then after a pause, he says: "Now, where was I?" Thus ends, yet ever re-begins for us, the film. The image, in the mirror, of thought.

In any court of law, this *story* → turn *Polaroid-photos* → turn-*film* → turn *video* would most likely be thrown out. This metamorphosis of story-turn-video could not even be shown as evidence to convict Earl or Leonard, for video, as *l'entre-image*, is subject to what the court would see as *cynical cuts*. In this story that is morphed into a film, *there is the incipient, yet residual beginnings of video itself*. Not only does this story without a story, attack the conventions of literacy itself, and not only does it pass through the conventions of film, as a transitional form, but it also replaces us nearby, if not well inside, the material conditions of video. It is a huge leap to say so, but as Ulmer might say, this film without a film is approaching "video thinking as a kind of hymn [elegy] to writing ("One" 262; Deleuze, *Cinema 2* 166–67).

Earl/Leonard writes to the point of having messages to himself tattooed-written in reverse on his body so that he can read them in a mirror: On his arm, he reads, "I RAPED AND KILLED YOUR WIFE." And on his chest he sees a tattooed sketch of a man, like a "police sketch." Earl/Leonard perpetually yet only momentarily asks, Who is the "I" of "I RAPED AND KILLED YOUR WIFE." Earl/Leonard wants to track down this sketch of a man and get revenge for his wife's death and pain. But the voice in Earl/Leonard, the remaining thread of what was, forever re-looped, says, "So the question is not 'to be or not to be,' because you aren't. The question is whether... revenge matters to you. It does to most people.... But the passage of time is all it takes to erode that initial impulse. Time is theft.... And as for the passage of time, well, that doesn't really apply to you anymore, does it? Just the same ten minutes, over and over again. So how can you forgive if you can't remember to forget?" (story, online). This voice (over) in the story as well as the film that speaks and taunts Earl/Leonard (about revenge) will also disappear. As the film nullifies itself, so do the taunts. At best, for us it is an oral or literate residue of a convention of narration and point of view, a nostalgia that will eventually withdraw from us altogether. As guilt or conscience will have withdrawn. With the conditions of the possibilities of revenge gone, which means the subject (agent) gone, so then goes *ethos*. Which is haunt, place, *topos*. Home. Without any takers or buyers. The crying of our lot. Disappearance.

The problem is not just the violence of rhetoric as portrayed and explained by De Lauretis and supported and reinformed in terms of rape scripts by Hesford. The problem is not just owing to the use of poststructuralist reading (bad) habits. The problem, rather, is the on-going result of cultural drift, the growing loss of *habitus*, of symbolic exchange, which poststructuralism and literacy-turn-electracy studies are *disclosing* to us. We are moving toward the posthuman period becoming an ellipsis (e.g., see Steigler, *Technics*, I and II; cf. Pearson, *Viroid Life*). In as much as Strosser's video resituates us as subjects, or objects, or even abjects in the rape stories, the apparatus of video itself resituates us. The change in the media—*intermedia*—changes us. As I have tried to suggest electrate conventions even in literacy, a short story, or in a film, can function as videography, drifting (reversing, transversing) where they so desire, changing both the story/ies and us.

There is every good reason to believe that Strosser was, in fact, raped. Because she said she was. But when Strosser's rape "story"-turn-"stories" are re-rendered in video, or film/video, uncontrollable proliferation begins to occur. There should be every good reason to believe that Leonard's wife was, in fact, raped and killed by an unknown man, but the telling in film-video, given the rapid cuts and layering of scenes, toward the end, which is the rebeginning, casts doubt, suggesting that Leonard himself might be the perpetrator. Which leaves us with the additional impossible problem of his inability to form new memories. Even the *brain-mind*, as cinema, and *memory*, as screen memories, are given to irrational (or non-rational) cuts, or as some might claim, cynical cuts. The medium does become both the mass/age and the mess/age.

The media of "Memento Mori" (print) and *Memento* (film-video) are devastating. Catastrophic. Quite allegorically (literally), Earl/Leonard is dead ("the question is not 'to be or not to be,' because you aren't"). The question is whether or not Earl/Leonard wants to kill or not kill the (a) man who raped and killed his wife and killed him. Or put similarly, wants revenge. And yet, existentially, there is the question of *living on* in his death. Posthumanly. Let the dead bury the living (cf. Kittler, *Gramophone* 124–33).

CHASTE CINEMA III+? 173

> The abyssal inclusion of video as call of conscience offers no easy transparency but requires a reading; it calls for a discourse. As we have been shown with singular clarity in the Rodney King case and, in particular, with the trial, what is called for when video acts as the call of conscience is not so much a viewing of a spectacle, but a reading, and, instead of voyeurism, an exegesis.
>
> Avital Ronell, "Trauma TV," *Finitude's Score* (312)

A Peculiar (Now Impertinent) Reading: Before this interruption explaining why I called *Rape Stories* a video, why I wanted to disclose the conditions for different-differential readings, and then why the eventual loss of reading as an ethico-political problem, I began with what I referred to as a "peculiar" reading, which I will continue. I initially viewed the video as being composed of a number of women sequentially telling their rape stories, though of course I made the assumption that the primary story—the first one told—was Strosser's. Hence, while the story was one in its repetitiveness, it was also many stories of women raped and forced (obsessively, like the ancient mariner) to tell their stories. (I have analyzed the video and accounted for nine sections.[16] I can only invite my readers to view this video to follow my discussion.)

---

16 There are, as I count them, nine sections to *Rape Stories*. Each section is titled by Strosser herself in a designation of time, which I place in italics. I open each with only the starting monologue.

- The video opens in black with audio in the background: "In 1979 I was raped. These are my stories."
- Section 1, in color, is of a lone woman viewed at a distance walking in an Urban, quasi-industrial setting. There are two separate shots. The voice over begins, "*The earliest memory* I have of rape fear was when I was about six or seven years old and we lived in the country."
- Title shot: *Rape Stories*
- Section 2, in color, is of a woman (in a talking-head view) beginning, "*Now ten years later [1989]*, I still think of the rapist. Actually,

In part, what led me to *many* instead of *one* storyteller

  I don't think about the rapist but think about rapists in general or about being rape.... But I do think about the rapist, too. What happened to him?"
- Section 3, in b/w and the longest section, begins, "*Two Saturdays ago*" [1979] with another talking-head camera view supposedly of Strosser (or a different woman altogether playing Strosser [?]), speaking into a microphone, saying, "Okay, well, two Saturdays ago, I was up late with Susan...." The speaker gives a full account of her going outside to buy cigarettes and returning and letting a man who was a stranger into the building and then the elevator with her and of being raped by him while he held a knife to her throat.
- Section 4, in color, is of two women in jogging shorts, with the shot limited to a frontal view of their tee-shirts and shorts with arms moving as they are apparently jogging. This section begins, "*The day after the rape* I wore sunglasses all the time. I was afraid to meet other peoples' eyes, because my look was frightened, accusing. I felt transparent through the eyes."
- Section 5, in b/w, takes place in a room, perhaps a laundry basement, with a woman walking around holding a clamped light, while she momentarily picks up a cat, and then returns to walking around. The voice over says, "*For a long time* I never entered a room without looking for another way out. If I couldn't see it, I wouldn't go in."
- Section 6, in color with a steady camera shot at night, takes place inside a car in the flow of traffic with street lights passing. The voice over says, "*Right after the rape* I was working as an assistant editor on a documentary film about high-fashion models called *Beautiful Baby, Beautiful*. All the editors were women. And we worked in a nice apartment on Central Park West. So it was an extremely secure kind of environment."
- Section 7, in color, same woman with camera shot as in section 2, saying, "*I still have this nightmare* about the rape. Sometimes. The nightmare is that I'm in my lobby."
- Section 8, in color, women in a pool floating with face up. The voice over says, "*On the night of the rape*, after I was released from the emergency room, I went home and sat in a hot bath tub. And tired to soak off the rapist."
- Section 9, in color, same woman with camera shots as in sections 2 and 7, saying, "*One day* it occurred to me that I would feel a lot better if I got rid of the rapist. So I started fantasizing about killing the rapist."
- The credits are shown with the background audio of an elevator opening and people walking in and out.

was the sequential shift from the woman telling her story in what I have labeled section 2 ("Now ten years later") to section 3 ("Two Saturdays ago"). I took the person in section 2, which is right after the title shot, to be Strosser herself. The contrast between the women in sections 2 and 3 is so distinctive in the way the two women look that I simply did not see them as the same woman. (After rape, is there metamorphosis as Ovid suggests? Or perhaps, in a rather negative term, a "hysterization," as Freud suggested? [see Hengehold 98–100].) It was more than the fact that one section is in black and white and the other is in color; it is a whole host of differences in terms of movement-images (loops) and time-images (cuts).

Later, however, when rereading Hesford, I discovered that she says, "Two Saturdays ago" (or my section 3) is "spliced into" the whole 1989 narrative of the video (200). This was puzzling for me. In looking for some support for Hesford's interpretation, I returned to the *Women Make Movies* Online Catalog and read the following statement: "In October 1979, Margie Strosser was raped in the elevator of her apartment building. *Two weeks later, she asked a friend to interview her about the incident* [emphasis added]. Ten years later, she remembers and recounts the rape, revealing the emotional texture of the experience and the reshaping of the event *through memory*. Between these two distant and disparate versions of the same story, slips a third, that of *the video narration*, which integrates the experience over time, revealing the process of recovery. Candid and intimate, *Rape Stories* speaks to women's common fears and the importance of telling our stories, however painful" (emphasis added)[17]

With this explanation for the relation of time between

---

[17] <www.wmm.com/Catalog/pages/c167.htm>. No long available at wmm.com.

section 2 and 3, I still found it difficult to see Section 3 *as real*, for the movement-image, the sensory-motor scheme appears to break down in its over-playing of scripts (e.g., the microphone and the self-conscious comment about it [Oh, "I'm on microphone," so I should speak directly into it]; the reaching for the cigarette and the holding it in hand [the planned filming of the cigarette episode, zooming away in such a way and with perfect timing and then, when the cigarette script is accomplished, zooming back to the original subject-camera distance]; the fixing of hair; the phrasing of some comments and asides such as telling why she is amending her earlier versions of the story for the sake of truthfulness—in other words, all appear to be as scripted and rehearsed and, therefore, as cues to be sent to the viewer-readers to see-read the "actor's" and filmographer's tone [i.e., their practiced attitude toward what they are saying and doing]). And yet, I ask myself What is a "real" (representation of a *realist*) response to a camera and a report to spectators after having been raped? I felt a deep stupidity (Ronell, *Stupidity*; Shaviro, *Cinematic* 201–39), when confronted with the question of *actuality* or *reality*. I heard an ethical scream coming from within me. I wanted to believe that this scene *is* real, but I felt stupidly pressured into having to accept this scene *as* real, when the scene itself was telling me, perhaps by way of film-literary conventions, that it *is* apparently not real. Not a documentary. But staged. And yet, are not documentaries staged! (Did we not discuss this matter earlier when thinking about Elke Sander's *Liberators Take Liberties*!) My confusion was placing me into the position of interrogating and assessing my "reading" of *Rape Stories*. I was undergoing a metamorphosis and hysterization. Approaching, perhaps, the conditions of a Lacanian *real*.

As I recall viewing the Strosser's film or video, I am

now additionally aware that, as a video, it is comparable to George Holliday's video tape of Rodney King's being beaten and shown on TV and then in court. I can see now that the Holliday's video is undercut by the TV presentation (the cutting short and the framing of the video on TV next to the talking heads) and can also see now that the full video is similarly undercut, so to speak, by the defense attorney's reading of it in court frame by frame by frame (cf. Ronell, *Finitude* 312–24; Gooding-Williams 42–43, 51–53, 58–62, 65–69).

Everyone, including Strosser, is employing the logic of the cut, yet reframing the cuts, or in terms of collage re-motivating by detaching and reattaching the cuts elsewhere. And whether for experimental, juridical, political purposes (see Ulmer, "Object" 92–93). In other words, the Holliday-King video has two showings (on TV and in court) and two primary outcomes among others (one at first apparently determined, the other undetermined, or overdetermined, and dismissed as evidence). Which is more truthful? The edited version on TV with the talking heads or the so-called raw (uncooked footage of the entire video)? Or yet again the so-called raw (uncooked) footage that the attorney stirred and cooked—let simmer—through his reading of it in court frame by frame? (cf. Burke, *Counter-Statement* 66).

We have come to learn—or have been reminded—that video, like photographs, is portable and more malleable than film once it is released and placed in public places. Video is just cut and recut and shown on TV, now on YouTube or wherever, while studios have their film cut in copyrighted trailers or full versions. (The exception to video trailers' being fixed, however, is the growing interest that video-enthusiasts and hobbyists have for downloading from the WWW re-editing trailers. Through bricolage, montage, collage.) TV entertainment news would not likely show a scene from a new film just anyway it wished, while it does show a scene from a video as it so wishes. When film is recut, it is later a Director's cut. Or a censor's cut. In general, a residue of authority follows film. Eventually, a residue of authority disperses—i.e., disappears—in video. Again, the Holliday video, in its final cut, was thrown out of court. Just as eye-witness accounts are thrown out.

I am presuming not just a difference between film and video or TV and video, with video watching TV and vice versa—Ronell has discussed this relationship—or a difference between classical and modern cinema—Deleuze has already accomplished this end. I am pointing, rather, to a difference between two videos hesitantly becoming one. I am pointing to a difference introduced by the logic—any-logic-whatever—of the cut. Specifically, in respect to *Rape Stories*, I am pointing to differences and repetitions owing to a *spliced* video (section 3, "Two Saturdays Ago" [1979]) being introduced within a full, narrated 1989 video called *Rape Stories*, with the former, in a sense, re-cutting the latter perpetually not just in reversals but potentially in imminent transversals. The introduction of this foreign body into the larger body revs up the immune system to reject it. But it is not that simple. For this organ without a body, as Slovaj Žižek might say, remains an "incoherent, excessive supplement" (*Organs* 87). In retrospect now, I can only ask, How is the splicing of a 1979 video into the 1989 video changing the corpus? How is it functioning as an intruder. While the WMM online statement points to the voice over ("*the video narration*, which *integrates* the experience over time*") as narrative suturing the two scenes together ("two weeks later" and "ten years later"), I did not take note of this "video narration" when viewing the film. Why? Because it was, rather, the *cut* and then the *movements* that in another sense for me *narrated* the experience. Deleuze explains:

> Cinema always narrates what the image's movement and time make it narrate. If the motion's governed by a sensory-motor scheme, if it shows a character reaching to a situation, then you get a story. If, on the other hand, *the sensory-motor scheme breaks down to leave disoriented and discordant movements* [which it does for me in the section 3, in B/W, as I described the movements being disorienting, with the woman at the microphone], then you get other patterns, *becomings* [a plane of immanence, assemblages, blocs] rather than *stories*. (*Negotiations* 59; emphasis added)

I should have realized that I should not have been confused about the number of *stories* (as well as tellers), but redirected by the *blocs*. Of various—not experiences—but movements, affects, sensations.

Strosser, or so I believe, directs the splicing and inserting. (Christopher Nolan, similarly, inserts a chronological, quasi-documentary, in black and white, in *Memento*, so that the rest of the film, told in reverse, might be more easily followed. And yet, the counter-documentary also makes for immense thematic complications and productive confusions.) It is that way in the age of mechanical reproduction. But someone might object that all "movies" (cinema, film, video analog and digital) are subject to being cut and spliced and, in fact, that is how they are made. Or might object that while the Holliday video was cut by others, the Strosser video-film has not subsequently been cut by others. Of course. But it is not just any cut I am referring to in respect to *Rape Stories*. I am attempting to talk about a quite different logic of the cut from one that Occam's razor might intend, to supposedly simplify the story or to add to a tighter economy of communication.[18] It is not just a matter of who makes the cut or when or how many times the cut has been made. I am talking about *a logic of the cut*—virtually, any paralogic of the fold—that turns any celluloid or analog/digital film/video into a *direct* statement or a telling of *theory* itself (see Small, *Direct Theory*; Ulmer, *Teletheory*). By design or by chance. To make my point even more heretical: I am not so certain now that Strosser's video is, as Hesford claims, a pro-fantasy-revenge story or stories. There is too much in the video that complicates that ever-so-easy reading and invitation to critique it as such. The video is highly reflexive and deflective. The video is more exuberant in terms of creating a view of video making itself as such. Video is, *as* intermedia can be, an aesthetic of confusion, any-space-whatever and wherever. The logic of the cuts in *Rape Stories* adds to a certain uncertain

---

18 In discussing editing, I use Ackham's razor to exemplify the distinction between rational cuts (castration, the principle of negative dialectic being applied) and irrational, or nonrational cuts (vagination, or folding). Though I call on this difference, I generally agree with Shaviro's Deleuzean take that the sign of lack (negation) is not helpful or accurate in discussing editing or suturing, that instead editing augments (i.e., shows the "ontological instability of the image," but thereby adds exuberance, opens up excess) (see *Cinematic* 34–43; cf. Heath, "On Suture" in *Questions* 76–112; Silverman, *Subjects* 194–236, and *Acoustic* 10–13; Copjec, "Cutting Up" in *Read* 39–64; Žižek, *Organs* 87–90). Similar to Shaviro (Deleuze), I am interested in movement, affect, sensation. I continue this discussion through chapter 2 and thereafter. Interestingly, Valerie Solanas in *Scum Manifesto* and Avital Ronell in her introduction to the second edition point to an *editing* (SCUM suggesting "society for cutting up men") that looks forward to Strosser's fantasy of cutting up her rapist into slivers and distributing (ironically, through contra-power, disseminating) them. But most interesting is Ronell's discussion of Solanas's ideas-concepts in terms of editing men: "'Cutting up' no doubt conjures castrative glee, insinuating carving up, morcellating men. Yet [it] also pens other semantic possibilities of which Valerie was fond: laughter, montage, editing" (11).

extra confusion or amplification between literacy and electracy, but a productive confusion. While the video is about rape stories (supposedly through a proposed constative-performative act of *mimetic* revenge), the video is also about unmaking a video about rape stories and revenge (through a proposed deformative act of grafting, montage and collage). The video post-critically mimes itself as an object of study. While, therefore, there is the suggestion of revenge through castration, there is the counter-suggestion of forbearance through invagination. Or through a series of folds. Not only does Strosser propose to cut up her perpetrator into slivers and to distribute them as communion, but also she is cutting up her film-video into slivers and distributing it anyplace wheresoever. It is, as if Strosser is filming-writing—video*graph*ing—and becoming Mrs. Dalloway, "slic[ing] like a knife through everything" (Woolf 11). Over all, this film-video is about moving from consubstantiality to unsubstantiality. While it has an epistemic-ethico-political purpose (knowing and doing), it also has an aesthetic dimension (making). And yet, it has a post-Aristotelian-Kantian-aesthetic dimension of the "informe," or "formless" as well as of the "deform"ative (unmaking) (see Bois and Krauss, *Formless*; Sallis, *Double*).

In an electronic age, film-video is sent pirated in cuts across the world. We expect this outcome from photography and film-video to *file.mov*. It is impossible to control these passages. They chronically misfire. Going beyond any single aim. Film-video *becomes*, in as much as Strosser's "Rape Stories" does, "thin slices of space as well as time" distributed, becomes assemblages of accidental details (see Sontag 4–5, 22–23, 105–10; Ray 13, 24–39). Many videos—as direct theory or tell a theory—are made as such, needing no, but remain open to, additional cuts and invaginations. Many of us, aware of the cutting and distributions of these virtual-incompossible worlds, bring those presuppositions and conditions to bear on viewing film-video. *Rape Stories* invites me—invites *us*—to expect such self-reflexive, self-reversal-transversal remarkings of it.

All of which is to say, then, that, the body-corpus of Strosser's film-video, with an ironic twist—call it the *revenge* of object over subject—is becoming sliced into thin singularities and distributed to a (coming) community of sorts. (One way or another we are asked to consume a corpse, corpus.) It is as if the film by way of video is becoming "filmic." The entire film. Which, according to Barthes, would mean the film is becoming beyond description, obtuse, slipping into the third *senses* (*Image* 64–65). Or as Deleuze might say, it is as if the film is becoming "nothing other than slivers of crystal-images" (*Cinema 2* 69). It is not that I feel less stupid when viewing *Rape Stories* as a video. I am aware that I am responding to the video by way of a misnaming (a mistaken/ness) and a parabasis (an interruption), both of which are stupidities of other kinds. It is that I, too, become forgetful.

But something else wants to be said. In terms of *materiality*, we are moving from *techne* (potentiality) to *atechne* (impotentiality). In terms of *reading* film, we are moving from film through video (as intermedia) to TV. But video again calls us. As Ronell says: "[W]hat is called for when video acts *as the call of conscience* is not so much a viewing of a spectacle, but a reading, and, instead of voyeurism, an exegesis" (*Finitude* 312; emphasis added. Cf. Heidegger, *Being* 317–35). Ronell speaks of "TRAUMATV" (TraumaIn-Visability). Obviously, Strosser's *Rape Stories* is an account of the traumatic event. Ronell says, as Cathy Caruth does, however, that reading trauma is *reading the impossible*. (While this notion of reading trauma comes out of psychoanalysis, which De Lauretis and Hesford want to avoid, this notion is equally about psychoanalysis *and* technology.) For Ronell, the trauma is "a phantom text," "hidden from televised view" and "the Rodney King beating is a metonymy of a hidden atrocity." She continues, "Under nocturnal cover, nomadic, guerrilla video captures no more than the debilitating discrepancy, always screened by television, *between* experience and meaning.... This is why it could prove nothing but this discrepancy in a court of law [in Napa Valley].... The repeat performance of a frame-by-frame blow shows how this text became nothing more than the compulsive unfolding of a *blank citation* [emphasis added]." And finally, Ronell says: "*this is the truth of video*, the site of the neural gleam that knows something which cannot be shown" (324–25; emphasis added). As we know—but I insist on repeating—the court eventually threw out the video as evidence and fell back on *eye*witness accounts. As Ronell argues through Shoshana Felman and Dori Laub, "'the trial both derives from and proceeds by a crisis of evidence, which the verdict must resolve.' As a sentence, the verdict is a force of law performatively enacted as a defensive gesture for not knowing" (325; qtd. from Felman and Laub, *Testimony* 18). To date, no judge, as far as I know, has thrown out secreted-hidden videos made by the rapist, showing himself raping the victim. But that day may come sooner than we think.[19]

---

19 Coincidentally, as I originally wrote this section, a judge had to call a mistrial of the Gregory Haidl and Jane Doe case (Santa Ana, trial in Orange County) that involved a video of a group rape. Several teenage males drugged a teenage female and raped her. It was not necessary for the judge to throw out the video, for the defense-jury did. The defense was able to redescribe the video as the making of an amateur porn film and called on an expert witness to say that Jane Doe, who was "allegedly" in a stupor, unconscious, during the making of the video, was not in a *full* stupor but conscious enough to resist! Recent report: <http://www.ocregister.com/articles/doe-241830-videotape-jane.html>. Perhaps one of the most infamous cases that involved a video is that in Canada of Paul Bernardo and his wife, Karla Homolka, who raped and killed on video Karla's sister, Kristen French. There was a conviction. "Key events in the Bernardo/Homolka case": <http://www.cbc.ca/news/canada/

I have tried to illustrate that both film and video give new, yet diminish older, conditions of possibilities: Both, but more so potentially video, break up literary (print culture) conventions, *becoming* "filmic," and both break up the subject as well as memory, *becoming* the "third meaning [*sense*]."[20] Additionally, as Deleuze says: "Any creative activity has *a political aspect and significance* [just as Strosser has]. The problem is that such activity isn't very compatible with *circuits of information and communication*, ready-made circuits that are compromised from the outset. All forms of creativity including any creativity that might be possible in television, here face a common enemy. Once again it's a cerebral matter: *the brain's the hidden side of all circuits*, and these can allow the most creative tracings, less 'probable' links" (*Negotiations* 61; emphasis added). In other words, cinema-film-video (the metacinema, the brain's hidden side) is our best alocus for creative discoveries that will work around the, heretofore, intractable circuits of the informatics of domination.

Both film/video and TV, as we have seen, have the capacity to make Rape (sexual violence) Chaste. And yet, there is a double capacity at work. There is a pharmakonic effect: While one side incapacitates potentiality, the other opens up something new (impotentialities), something

---

story/2010/06/16/f-bernardo-homolka-timeline.html> and "Tapes made by Bernardo destroyed" by Canadian government: <http://www.cbc.ca/news/canada/story/2001/12/21/bernardo011220.html>.

20 Barthes writes, "The filmic is not the same as the film, is as far removed from the film as the novelistic is from the novel (I can write in the novelistic without ever writing novels)" (65). The filmic and the novelistic are the remainders. In terms of economy, then, Strosser's film signals for us a becoming by way of "useless expenditure" (Barthes *Image* 55; Bataille, *Accursed*), becoming "lovable" (see Barthes 59; Agamben *Coming* 2), becoming radical singularities and "whatever beings" (Agamben 1–2). In this third sense, the film is not just for the present community of wanting revenge, but for the coming political community of the obtuse or whatever beings.

vital in terms of capacities. Out of the impossible can come possibilities. As a case in point, I have in mind what Barthes calls the "filmic" and characterizes as a certain uncertain obtuse element in film (as in Eisensteinian, Vertovian, but in any, experimental film). He says that the filmic "outplays meaning—subverts not the content but the whole practice of meaning [into the third meaning, *sens*e]" (62). That is, it subverts the whole practice of informatics. In this subversion, there is—I would venture to say again and again—an uncanny movement from *constative* through *performative* to *deformative* (cf. Sallis *Double* 85–106). To post-cinematics. What this drifting out of a binary, which is imminently-reversible-turn-transversal anyway, leads to is a third figure of *sens*e, a third figure that challenges, if not erases, what has gone for content, meaning, altogether (cf. Deleuze, *Logic* 28–35). *Sens* is our alocus of impotentiality for resistance.[21]

Barthes explains further: "A new—rare—practice affirmed against a majority [i.e., dominant] practice (that of signification), obtuse meaning appears necessarily as a luxury, an expenditure with no exchange [as in Bataille's accursed share]. This luxury does not *yet* belong to today's politics but nevertheless *already* to tomorrow's" (62–63; Barthes's emphasis). Barthes's allusion to *tomorrow's politics*, I take, to be in an obtuse, future anterior, yet metaleptic allusion to *a politics* put forth in Nancy, Blanchot, Agamben, Ronell, *and Waters'* discussions of a community without a community. From disappearance does come compearance (see Nancy, *Inoperative* 28, 30). Not a politics of revolution-evolution, but involution.

But I am getting way ahead of myself. Again. And yet, it is ever important that this forthcoming community, which

---

21 If there is a challenge on the horizon, a challenge that would take us back to an informatic domination, it may very well be neurocinematics (see Hasson et al.). But not to worry!

Strosser's video awaits a viewing in, is one without revenge, one that, as Agamben writes, "can have hope only in what is without remedy" (*Coming* 102; cf. Nietzsche, *Zarathustra* 249–54). But without remedy is to be taken as the "irreparable," which has another, third *sense*. We will approach it later. I leave much unsaid and unacknowledged that wants to be ethically screamed. Therefore, let me rebegin and try again by thinking, reading, writing my continuing notes.

(To be continued.)

EXCURSUS
THE ASSESSMENT-TEST EVENT

WHAT DOES VITANZA *gain for readers* by re-informing the traditional "Table of Contents" (TOC) with an *imagined* DVD list of extras (supplements)? After all, this is a book about cinema. Virtually, it is a book, as Vitanza suggests in the *Preamble*, that takes a post-critical approach, suggesting that the book-that-is-not-a-book is an object of post-criticism (Ulmer).

WHY DOES VITANZA open *Chaste Cinematics* with what he refers to as a *Preamble*? Which is not an introduction or preface, contrary to traditional definitions? Why does he ask his readers if they are still with him? And then why does he basically at the end tell the reader *to forget it all*? What purpose and whose interest might it serve? To forget? And why this assessment-test event! To re-begin with?

RATHER THAN THE *Preamble*—which makes clear that a reader can enter the book at any point—do you think that you might want, first, to read the footnotes (or in retrospect, you should have read the footnotes), from beginning to end?

But if you are so habituated to read from the front through to the so-called end and you have done so, then, you have already missed the opportunity to read differently. And yet! Simply start over and over. Again and again. Do not worry about being a promiscuous reader. You are redeemed from any imagined sin when approaching and re-approaching this book.

The index—but there is no index—perhaps could have given you some sense of what Vitanza values in the book. Who or what gets cited and what is said about them? What concepts and puncepts get listed and how are they sutured together across pages? In other words, the index could have suggested to you what to look for while reading. Why not make your own index? And send it to Vitanza.

IN CHAPTER 1, Vitanza refers to fluxes and fugues as well as modernity. Also, he uses such images as the *desert* and eventually *waves*. What purpose do they give to the reading, your readings?

IN CHAPTER 1, Vitanza primarily plays off of DVD "extras" when he turns to the three polylogues that address each of the three films. Is he not pretentious in speaking for others, even if he knows them and they, him? You might want to examine the etymology of the word "pretentious." If you have read Plato's Socratic dialogues, you have read imaginary works. There is no sympathy here for the difference between real and fictive.

IN CHAPTER 1, Vitanza refers to the etymology of the word "Chastity" as central to his discussion of rape (sexual violence). He asks the readers to study the various etymologies. What do you find in the etymologies, as well as histories of (appropriations of) this word? Consider, *to begin with*, such contexts as "cult of chastity" or "politics of chastity." Or the ever so proper name "Chastity."

IN CHAPTER 1, Vitanza discusses the conflict between Mozart and Salieri. So as to rethink the play and film, view

THE ASSESSMENT-TEST EVENT

the film *Mozart's Sister*. And then ask yourself how you would, or how we ourselves might, insert Nannerl Mozart into that masculine, homosocial conflict over recognition and fame? And yet, What does this question presume? Another option: Write a brief summary for a film yet to be realized with the inclusion of Nannerl Mozart. What and how would Mozart's sister change the story of this *chaste* film?

IN CHAPTER 1, Milan Kundera and his character discuss childish, prank occurrences and how they change the world. Kundera's novel *Immortality* is filled with *test drives*. Read the novel and locate each test (Agnes's, Rueben's, etc.) and compare them to the tests that you confront during reading *Chaste Cinematics*. (A clue: Agnes goes on a test drive, by leaving a main highway and taking a "quieter route." What happens to Agnes when she takes this detour? Why is it significant to the narrative? What does all of this have to do not only with test drives but also with the discussions in *Chaste Cinematics*? You might start in *Immortality* on page 257.)

IN CHAPTER 1, without any delay whatsoever, Vitanza begins to direct you, the reader of this book, to his other two books on the topic: *Negation* and *Sexual Violence* (both abbreviated titles)? Why does he do so, for what purpose? The big question, however, is that he is intermittently assigning you to read other books by others elsewhere. Why? The interruptions? Why this test-drive theme (Ronell)?

IN CHAPTER 1, Vitanza makes much of Lobstora raping Divine in *Multiple Maniacs* (1970). (See Figure 1.)

Evidently, Vitanza does not know that perhaps John Waters was influenced by the film *When Dinosaurs Ruled*

Figure 1. Divine is raped by Lobstora in *Multiple Maniacs*.
(Photograph by Lawrence Irvine, © New Line Cinema).

the Earth (1970), which has a prehistoric crab attempting to consume (rape?) the character played by Victoria (Cecilia) Vetry (pseudonym, Angela Dorian). See Figure 2 for a pic of the cut scene.

This similar pic had been supposedly cut yet saved by Baxter Philips in the book *Cut: The Unseen Cinema* (74). What more can you find out about this relation between *Multiple Maniacs* and *When Dinosaurs*? Had Waters viewed this scene and copied the parallel in *Multiple*, or did someone at Hammer Film Productions see Waters's scene? Or is there a third+ film with the same imagery? Or is this merely, but wildly so, an analog at best? And if so, then, how to explain? ... And yet, you just might search online for *Lobster Films*, which is a company that collects and preserves old films as well as produces new films, especially documentaries! <http://www.lobsterfilms.com/>. There's more. But what can you make of or un-make with them? Good hunting.

Figure 2. Victoria Vetri and the crab. Unused promotional still for *When Dinosaurs Ruled the Earth*.

FOLLOW-UP: How DID we get from the Swan and Leda to a crustacean and Divine? How did we get from birds (the Spirit) swooping down and raping a woman to a lobster or a crab scuttling over to a woman to rape? Let us not forget that Deleuze and Guattari identify a lobster, a crustacean, as God (see *Thousand Plateaus*)! So the question, among others that precede it, is how did we get from the gods as rapists to crustacean as rapist? Of course, we are left with a question that makes no sense! Unless we recall that lobsters and crabs have the two pincers. The double bind. And so then, What?...You might want to read/study René Girard's *To Double Business Bound*.

IN CHAPTER 1, in various discussions of *the divine*, Vitanza refers to the word "intervention" three times. In terms of a divine + intervention, informed by and with tragic-comedic takes in the discussion of the antics of Avenarius in Kundera's *Immortality*, you should view Eli Suleiman's film *Divine Intervention*. Of special interest is the "army post scene." Make of it, what you will. (How would you interject Suleiman into the polylogue?) Thereafter, view Claire Denis's *Friday Night*. Make of it, what you will, in terms of *Divine Intervention*. (And what might Denis add to the polylogue?)

VITANZA OPENS CHAPTER 2 by reporting and discussing a series of scenes from Helke Sander's film, under the rubric: *Research: (Facts, Statistics, Testimony)*. He states, however, that he has changed the order of the series as found *in the film itself*, making for a completely different series in his discussion. He explains that he has rearranged-re-mixed-repurposed the sequence for a different rhetorical affect. The shooting and editing script, so to speak, takes up now with the following series of scenes in *Chaste Cinematics*:

a. Sander claims to be the first to make the mass rapes public;

b. Sander explains that the "catalyst" for researching the event was Frau G's story of being raped and wanting revenge;

c. Sander claims she thereafter turned to seeking "real information for the film" (i.e., statistics);

d. Sander discusses the anecdote of only one woman, raped, who claimed to be a "war casualty";

e. then, finally in Vitanza's sequence, Sander turns to the anecdote of a woman who had been raped by a Russian soldier. The woman tells a former German officer who says, if it had been his wife, he would have killed her. The woman says: "I wanted to live, not be killed."

Presuming that you have or will actually view the film or read the book of the film, or both, how might you respond to Vitanza's change in the sequence? What has been variously achieved by Vitanza's cut?

IN CHAPTER 2 and earlier, Vitanza discusses the *filmic* as opposed to *film* (Barthes). His extensive discussion comes when he refers to the tug-of-war over the *bicycle* between the Russian soldier and the German woman. Do you think that Vitanza is merely engaging in a private, esoteric viewing of the *filmic*? Again, What does the *bicycle* have to do with anything? Vitanza connects it with events in De Sica's *The Bicycle Thief*. Is this connection far-fetched? In fact, through out most of the book, Vitanza makes what he calls conductive linkages (Ulmer).

IN CHAPTER 2, Vitanza begins to work with *shadow* and *mourning narratives*, initially with *Baise-Moi* and then *Hiroshima, Mon Amour* as such narratives. There is an assignment for you in chapter 2, note 56, about the latter film on mourning. But before working on the assignment, you need *first to read/study* John Hersey's *Hiroshima* (1946). Then, read/study Bataille's "Concerning the Accounts Given by the Residents of Hiroshima" (1947) and Reynolds's "Toward a Sovereign Cinema" (2010). Thereafter, consider Bataille's discussion of the "impossibility" of recalling and representing the event of Hiroshima and especially in the *flashing light* of the film. Additionally, read Claude Lanzman's similar, though quiet different take, on the Holocaust, "The Obscenity of Understanding." Thereafter, read LaCapra's *Writing History, Writing*

Trauma. When accomplished, return to a viewing of film *Hiroshima, Mon Amour.* After doing so, reconsider the assignment in terms of not only the assignation in the film but also in terms of remembering and mourning, the *event.* (Be sure to take the next three assignments, below, into consideration as well.)

As an afterword-afterimage, in relation to the film *Hiroshima, Mon Amour,* you might want to view Aazaki's *White Light/Black Rain* (2007) as well as Wells's *24 Hours after Hiroshima* (2010). And let us not forget Claude Lanzmann's 9+ hour film, *Shoah.* The complete text is available. Recently, Lanzmann has written a memoir. How would you compare Lanzmann's interviews with Sander's?

Vitanza, in chapter 2, refers to the use of the expression "the genocide of love" as an explanation put forth by an interlocutor for why there is rape in war. Twice, in the chapter, Vitanza adds a citation in reference to discussion of "the genocide of love." Vitanza suggests: "(cf. Oates, *Rape: A Love Story*)." What do you make of Vitanza's suggestion to read and compare Oates's novel rape and love with genocide and love? In other words, how can such a connection be!

At the close of chapter 2, Vitanza calls on the peculiar paratopoi of *unmourning* and *antimemory.* Assuming that you find Vitanza's reading of *Hiroshima Mon Amour,* across these two paratopoi, compelling, or let us say suggestive, you might attempt to rethink Andrea Dworkin's proposal for Rape Museums as Vitanza discusses the proposal in *Sexual Violence* 181–82. Do you think that such museums, as with most museums, if not all, would also end up being sites for tourists? (Have the camps and Holocaust museums in great part become sites for tourism?)

Would not Dworkin, like the Japanese man in *Hiroshima*, finally have to say to tourists, "you have seen nothing. Nothing. Of rape." The assumption here is that Dworkin is serious about Rape Museums. If so, how would you solve the problems of obscenity? In other words, how would you not traffic in the very scenes of rape that you would memorialize? But then, as the Japanese man says, what does it mean to have seen "Nothing"!

AT THE CLOSE of chapter 2, Vitanza discusses, in passing, Deleuze and Guattari's paraconcept of *antimemory*. They write: "Memory, I hate you" (*What is Philosophy?* 168). Do you think that Deleuze and Guattari are turning their backs on the ethical necessity, the very obligation for *the call of care*, to remember the atrocities of Auschwitz as well as any other atrocities? Whatever you think, be careful, doubly careful. You might want to spend some time researching and reading Cathy Caruth's *Unclaimed Experience* as well as Caruth's collection of articles in *Trauma*. So as to avoid, if possible, a double bind.

IN AN FOOTNOTE to chapter 2 and in the body of chapter 3, Vitanza includes John Waters in the bloc of those working toward an inoperative, unavowable, coming, calvacade of perverts in community: Nancy, Blanchot, Agamben, Ronell, *and Waters*. What is Vitanza thinking? Is this not *sacrilegious*? How to explain? Perhaps there is a possible answer in the polylogues in chapter 1.

AN INTERRUPTING QUESTION: How have you experienced Vitanza's use of quotations leading into each chapter and each section? Normally, such quotations *lead* or *orient* the reader. Do you find that some of the quotations are otherwise in as much as they can interrupt the flow and, thereby, disorient the reader? Why would Vitanza want to mislead and to disorient the reader?

IN CHAPTER 3, Vitanza responds to Wendy Hesford's reading of Margie Strosser's *Rape Stories*. Given that he obviously agrees with Hesford—being against revenge as well as the will to avenge—what precisely is Vitanza finding fault with, nonetheless, in Hesford's presumptions? Perhaps, the word "fault" suggests here *a fault in the ground of reason*, an architectonic shift that makes the ground move and tumble. Therefore, given the *fault* in the grounding (diminishing *Grund*, increasing *Abgrund*), the presumption of reason appears to be that *the rhetoric of violence* becomes, as Hesford finds fault with, *the violence of rhetoric*, and vice versa. As Vitanza argues, however, logos (the principles of reason, language itself, including film language) is potentially (and more so impotentially) violent! Bringing forth a plethora of dissoi- polylogoi. He argues that "realist strategies" are also subject to reversals as well as transversals? Feminist commentaries strongly suggest that such is the case. For a start, see and study Alexandra Juhasz's work. Therefore, what array of contingencies and anxieties—with the *abnorm* always already becoming the norm—would a realist-strategic attempt be confronted with?

Might it be that Vitanza's inferred fault in the ground of thinking, therefore, additionally shakes up the differences (becoming *différance*) between "video" vs. "film"? Or for that matter between "classic" and "modern" cinema? If so, why does Vitanza insist on calling Strosser's *Rape Stories* a video? Rather than a film? What do you find in his discussions to be an explanation?

IN CHAPTER 3, Vitanza interrupts the flow of the prose and begins to discuss Christopher Nolan's film *Memento*. What is gained? What impact might this interruption (or this moment of *finitude*) have on the idea—Leonard Shelby's idea—of revenge? Does the interruption in some way put you in a loop also. That way, you as a reader find yourself, doubly so, in an ex-status of reversibility? Waiting for a third figure? Never completing the test event?

IN CHAPTER 3, Vitanza says he has never viewed *I Spit on your Grave* and refuses to do so, on the grounds that it is far too violent. And yet, in chapter 1, he has viewed *Baise-Moi*, which is certainly as violent if not more so. What's up?

THE *ALTERNATE ENDINGS* and the *Easter Eggs*? As for the alternate endings, based on the *principle of reversibility*—recall that Vitanza's discussion of the reversible arts in the *Preamble*—just how is, however, his suggestion for reversibility to be implemented? Is he serious?

As for both Easter eggs—a double yoke—Vitanza turns to the *principle of the irreparable*. For the first example, you might want to read, as Vitanza himself suggests, the whole of Dominique Laporte's *History of Shit*, which addresses the issue of *"one cannot fix a price on the loss of* [human] *shit"* (126).

IN THE SECOND example, is Vitanza demonstrating a loss of nerve? Simply capitulating to what might be impossible? And yet, as Vitanza well knows and has argued, out of the impossible comes the possible, or compossibility. In any case, you might want to read Agamben's *The Coming Community*, since Vitanza quotes the closing passage on the *irreparable* from that work. You might also want to read Derrida's *On Cosmopolitanism and Forgiveness*, which addresses the *irreparable* in terms of who can forgive. Also, read Giovanna Borradori's "Living with the Irreparable," in *Parallax* 17.1 (2011). 78–88. The *irreparable* is an ancient principle that informs and reforms the law. You might research the many ways that it has been applied and challenged in the world's courts.

ALTERNATE ENDINGS
WITH REBEGINNINGS
IRREVERSIBILITY?

> It was a movie about American bombers in the Second World War.... Seen backwards by Billy, the story went like this:... The formation flew backwards over a German city that was in flames. The bombers opened their bomb bay doors exerted a miraculous magnetism which shrunk the fires, gathered them into cylindrical steel containers, and lifted the containers into the bellies of the planes.
>
> Kurt Vonnegut, Jr., *Slaughter-House Five* (74).

Irreversibility: Have I mentioned this earlier? It returned in a newspaper thrown on my lawn. On a Sunday morning. It was a news story in the Life and Arts section. It was in part about Gaspar Noé's film *Irréversible*, which is a narrative told in reverse, just as *Memento* is told in reverse. Both are about rape and murder, extreme sexual violence, and re-membering: In *Memento* it is the character Leonard Shelby trying to remember but always ten or so minutes later forgetting everything and having to restart again. In his quest for revenge. An eye for an eye. (There is a lot of looping of scenes in *Memento*.) In *Irréversible*, it is the film itself trying to re-member, but again in reverse, forgetting in a final (but initial) scene what had been. Or so the film appears to be saying.

Irréversible begins with the ending. Two men are arrested, one is being carried off on a stretcher. They are Re: Vengers. It ends with the beginning. Max, the female, is in an idyllic scene, but with a write-over: "Time [chronos] destroys Everything."[1] The initial shot is of Max on an orange towel, lying on the greenest of grass, reading a book, and with children running and playing around her. The shot is vertical with her upside down and then, in an arc shot, righted. Finally-beginningly, the shot returns to the whirling motion. Midway in the film, where the fulcrum or lever, maintaining the pans of blind justice, might be located, Max is at a party with Marcus, her lover, and with Pierre, her former lover. They are happy and playful but then there is a quarrel. She leaves and, while on the street, from which she departs to cross over, takes an underpass. Into hell. Shot in all reds. There she is raped

---

1 The film *Irréversible*, a summary of the important scenes. The DVD identifies 16 scenes; below, I list 9.
- Credits are in reverse and acamera shots in a whirling motion through much of the film.
- Scene from Noe's previous film, *I Stand Alone*, with the butcher saying: "There are no bad deeds. Just deeds." The butcher recounts his crime of having raped his daughter.
- The police arrest two men (one on a stretcher). There is much homophobic invective.
- Marcus with Pierre searches for Le *Ténia* (Tape Worm). They are told he can be found at a gay night club called "The Rectum." The search ends with the bashing of a man's face with a fire extinguisher.
- Marcus and Pierre have just been told that Alex has been raped and her face kicked in by Le Ténia.
- Alex, in the street, takes an underpass. She encounters a man beating on a prostitute. Alex is in the way. Le Ténia (?) pulls a knife on her, rapes and sodomizes her. The scene is nine minutes long. The camera is on the ground (*Grund*), fixed on the rape.
- Alex is with Marcus and Pierre at a party. Alex quarrels with Marcus and leaves.
- Pierre and Alex wake and are intimate. Alex suggests she is pregnant.
- Opens with a tranquil, idyllic scene with Alex lying in the grass. Children playing. There is a note over the scene: "Time destroys everything." The scene dissolves into one of the universe whirling.

and sodomized and her face is bashed in, in a nine-minute scene with the camera running and capturing it all in a single, uncut shot. The scene at the beginning of the film, which is the end, is of Marcus and Pierre taking revenge on the man who allegedly attacked Alex, but the man is most likely not the man who raped Alex. In seeking revenge, however, what does that matter! Any stand-in will do, as René Girard and Christopher Nolan argue. The beginning is the end of the characters. Time has destroyed everything. Rape-time has undone everything. As Aristotle says about Troy, he could say about *Paris*, France: None of the sacking and raping and bashing of faces can be revoked. All is subject to the principle of irrevocability. But it is even more complicated, and yet, even more precise. The official press book for *Irréversible* offers this text, summarizing the film:

> Irreversible → Because time destroys everything → because some acts are irreparable → because man is an animal → because the desire for vengeance is a natural impulse → because most crimes remain unpunished → because the loss of a loved one destroys like lightning → because love is the source of life → because all history is written in sperm and blood → because in a good world → because premonitions do not alter the course of events → because time reveals everything → the best and the worst.

Is this the *inscription* that determines the film? These predications, qualities? Or can it also function as a *prescription*, something written at the top on a blank, wax tablet? "Because time reveals everything → The best and the worst." God's best and worst of all possible worlds? No, this is an inscription (one value divided into two), not a prescription (all that can be thought to be compossible).

Therein, in that difference, lies the test. Or Does the test lie in the in-different? Or in-difference. At the surface of the wax tablet?

This press book, with its *statements*, reminds me of the presocratic fragments. Which are the very *paradeigma* of thinking *as* testing, testing *as* thinking—which, as Agamben writes, is the improper "proper place of the example...always beside itself, in the empty space in which its undefinable and unforgettable life unfolds" (*Coming* 10). In this case, testing *as* thinking, reading, writing rape (sexual violence). As it variously unfolds. This press book, with its *fragments*, reminds me of Anaxamander's fragment, his celebrated (celibate) principle of the indeterminate—*to apeiron*—but as rendered by the attempter and experimenter Nietzsche, in his anecdotal testaments (*Philosophy* 25, 45–50). In writing about presocratic figures, Nietzsche gives three anecdotes for each. (Once he gets to three, he has thousands.) Nietzsche's take is not inscriptions, but coming-prescriptions. He writes the conditions for compossibility (with its incompossibilities). While Anaxamander is a "true pessimist" (45–46), Heraclitus is in-different to species-genus relations (50–69). Heraclitus situates One and Many, a radical multiplicity, in paralogical writings. Which means the One is not, yet is (see Heraclitus, e.g., fragments 45–47; cf. Badiou, *Being* 52–59). Anaxamander *is to* best and worst or to one and many *as* Heraclitus *is to* in-difference, *in-differentiae*. Heaviness or lightness? The test: What do you, my Dear Reader, choose? Do not be mislaid, misdirected, by a sense of the political over the aesthetic. After all, for both there is the beautiful and the sublime.

Nietzsche writes about Heraclitus: "Man is necessity down to his last fibre, and totally 'unfree,' that is if one means by freedom the foolish demand to be able to change one *essentia* arbitrarily, like a garment—a demand which every serious philosophy has rejected with the proper scorn.... Heraclitus... had no reason why he *had* to prove (as Leibniz did) that this is the best of all possible worlds. It is enough for him that it is the beautiful innocent game of the aeon" (63–64). But while Nietzsche writes about such thirds as Anaxamander and Heraclitus, he goes to other thirds as well, making, turning, them into new *conceptual personae* (Deleuze and Guattari, *What Is Philosophy?* 64), all incipient thirds (Thales, Parmenides, Anaxagoras, Empedocles, Democritus, Socrates). All men on their way to becoming something other than men or the other of women. Something of a third figure. Multiple maniacs!

Reversible Destiny: I also mentioned this rubric earlier. In *Sexual Violence*. Toward the end, yet rebeginnings (185–   ). There, I pointed to Aristotle and the irrevocability of Troy through Leibniz and the Palace of Destinies. And the new Anarchive. But this reversible destiny, as I see it now, appeared out of the corner of my eyes on Google.com. And then again, quite forcefully, on Amazon.com. But I, for some reason of timing, ignored it. Until I could no more. It returned in the form of a prompt—"you desire this one"—at Amazon.com on my monitor. It is a book *Reversible Destiny: We Have Decided Not to Die* by Arakawa and Madeline Gins. I could but laugh! Once I purchased this book, there was then the additional prompts of yet other books by Arakawa and Gins, so I was told, that I desired: *Architectural Body, The Mechanism of Meaning, Architecture: Sites of Reversible Destiny (Architectural Experiments After Auschwitz-Hiroshima), Helen Keller or Arakawa.* What Arakawa and Gins are interested in is designing, not tombs for our return to *humus* (see Harrison, "Hic Jacet"; Leary, *Design for Dying*), but bridges that will sustain life, living, not dying, living humanely or post-humanely, and not through the instant of our rape and death, soul murder. They are architects of entire community spaces. Of the new *humus*. I have just to attach their thinking to a community without a community, extracting death as such a community's basis, and then moving us on to living (cf. Jake Kennedy). But then, that will require a whole new book that would be a finishing of a trilogy with *Negation* and *Sexual Violence* (along with *Chaste Cinematics*) and what will become, in a tentative title, *Design as Dasein*. But I can say here now, saving much for later, that Arakawa and Gins's vision of architecture, the (new) earth, and space is one that does not rely on the old epideictic architechtonic discourse that gave us the palace of memory at Hiroshima or of Auschwitz, perpetuating death-holocaust in memory, memory in death, but gives us what they call a reversible destiny. For many people, of course, such thinking is, to put it politely, too optimistic. Perhaps too eutopian. Too sentimental. Childish. Too Primary Narcissistic. (Such childish omnipotence!) For many people—given to death, in love with entropy until death—there can be no other way but death. Heidegger tells us: "As potentiality-for-Being, Dasein cannot outstrip the possibility of death. Death is the possibility of the absolute impossibility of Dasein. Thus death reveals itself as that *possibility which is one's ownmost, which is non-relational, and which is not to be outstripped*. As such, death is something *distinctively* impending" (*Being* 294; Heidegger's emphasis). Etceteras. May they (those who would die), then, RIP. But Arakawa and Gins rethink bodies living in peace and a space of a "bridge of reversible destiny/the process in question" (see the various writings and graphics in *Reversible Destiny*; cf. Taylor, "Saving Not" in *Nots* 96–121). This bridge (or Sebold's tunnel revisited) has many "rooms" that a visitor has to pass through:

Bodily Conjectural at Light → In the Recesses of the
Communal Stare → The New Missing Link → Diffuse
Receding Gauge → Companion to Indeterminacy →
Volume Bypass → Points of Departure Membranes →
The Where of Nowhere → Edges of Apprehending →
Inflected Geometry → Accrual Matrix → The Planet's
Cry → Than Which No Other → To Not To Die/The
Helen Keller Room → Reverse-Symmetry Trans-
verse-Envelope Hall → Gaze Brace → Assembly of
Latent Perceivers → Cradle of Reassembly → Forming
Inextinguishability

With the help of Arakawa and Gins perhaps we can rebuild Troy as a bridge (or tunnel) through the Palace of Destinies To Not-To-Be-Raped Again and Again, Not-to-Die. In the meantime, we will learn from the Palace of Destinies to subtract our present situation by *wayves* of *multiPLIcations*. Multiple Maniacs!

But it is not just with the vision of these two anarchitects (well, only one left now, since the other died) that we can search for reversibility over and against irreversibility, but it is also with Michel Serres himself who opens up the compossibility of simultaneous reversible irreversibility and irreversible reversibility. Serres rewrites himself, re-including what he had cast away as reactionary reversibles. Reaching for a third. Serres asks and answers: "What is an organism? A sheaf of times. What is a living system? A bouquet of times" (*Hermes* 75). Serres, in detail, explains:

> It has not been inelegant to conclude that the organism combines three varieties of time, and that its system constitutes a temporal sheaf.... Background noise, the major obstacle to messages, assumes an organizational function. But this noise is the equivalent of thermal disorder. Its time is that of increasing

entropy, of that irreversible element which pushes the system toward death at maximum speed. Aging, for example, is a process that we are beginning to understand as a loss of redundancies and the drifting of information into background noise. If the integration levels function correctly as partial rectifiers and transform the noise of disorder into potential organization, then they have *reversed the arrow of time*. They are rectifiers of time. Entropic irreversibility also changes direction and sign; *negentropy* [emphais mine] goes back upstream. We have discovered the place, the operation, and the theorem where and with which the knots of the bouquet are tied. It is here and in this manner that time flows back and can change direction. Due to the numerous reversals of the temporal vector, the fluctuating homeorhesis acquires a fleeting stability [homeorhesis, an open, dynamic system, in contrast to a homeostatic one]. For a moment the temporal sheaf makes a full circle. *It forms a turbulence where opposing times converge.* Organization per se, as system and homeorhesis, functions precisely as a converter of time. We now know how to describe this converter, as well as its levels and meanderings, from whence come anamnesis, memory, and everything imaginable. (81–82; emphasis and bracketed statement mine. Cf. *Parasite* 182–89)

Multiply Principles, Fly towards Transversals: When confronted with disjunctions, when affronted with two philosophers, *write a third one*. When confronted and affronted with whatever it is, write a third transversal one. As *Serres* himself does. When stuck, multiple y.our principles. Write of a sheaf of multiple times, in multiple, simultaneous *sens*es, directions. Multiply multiples. Incompossibilities.

Do not think of simply and only reversing the particular incompossibility; for it can, more often than not, lead to revenge. "Man would rather will *nothingness* than not will" (*Genealogy* 163; Nietzsche's emphasis). But it is, as Nietzsche continues elsewhere, more complicated and easily mis-acted—this willing. Nietzsche's Zarathustra teaches: "The will cannot will backwards;...that is the will's loneliest *melancholy*" (251). Rather, going to the past to redeem the present, go to the future anterior: Think, write, read nothing but y.our potentiality to not-think, not-write, not-read. *What was not.* In the future waiting for the past. For this purpose, we have sent Bartleby to the Palace of Destinies, to call the principle of irrevocability into question and thereby to claim *What was not.*

For a similar purpose, we can send Pip away from "Murray's Grammar" (*Moby Dick* 385) to Thomas Sebeok's impotential paragrammar of David Ingram's grammar and beyond to whatever paragrammars. Sebeok writes: In "Aymara (as spoken in Bolivia), the number of grammatical persons has been determined as 3 x 3, each compacting coactions between one pair of possible interlocutors. Simplifying somewhat, the following forms can occur: first person is addressor included but addressee excluded; second person is addressee included but addressor excluded; third person is neither addressor nor addressee included; and fourth person is both addressor and addressee included. These, then, yield nine categories of possible interreaction: $1 \to 2, 1 \to 3, 2 \to 1, 2 \to 3, 3 \to 1, 3 \to 2, 3 \to 3, 3 \to 4$, and $4 \to 3$. It is mind boggling to fantasy what the character of [C.S.] Peirce's metaphysic might have been had he been born a native speaker of Jaqui language" (Eco and Sebeok, *Sign* 7–8). It would equally be mind boggling to fantasize, say, in a Borgesean book of imaginary becomings, what the character Pip might become if born transversally across asystems of paragrammaticisms. Other modals and contingencies. ~~~~~ Pip, flying the mad fly's eye in an assemblage with the flying of a mad wasp. ~~~~~ Telling other stories, parastories. And yet, I must incite, through Alain Badiou's thinking *being* and *event*, even more so how mind boggling if we were to reconceive the character Pip in terms of a pure, rapturous break from even Jorge Luis Borges. From Deleuze. By subtracting the One and thereby increasing the conditions as compossible (*Manifesto* 33–39) and adding a complementary relation between set theory ("from Cantor to Groethendick") and literary discourse ("from Mallarmé to Becket") (*Being* xiv), we would find the child Pip in wildly and equally distributed heterogeneous domains of art, politics, science, and love.

EASTER EGG 1
THE IRREPARABLE,
AS THE OBJECT OF LOSS

Dominique Laporte (1949–1984) writes of *a lost object*—specifically, of human waste—that has several implications in his book: *Histoire de la merdre*, 1978 (*History of Shit*, 2000). (Search the Internet for the cover design for the 1978 edition, especially its illustration by Roland Topor.) First, Laporte's history begins with the Hygiene Act of 1539 in Paris. This act spins out other endless acts focuses exclusively on human waste. Additionally, this act determines that human waste, as a grounding, constitutes what a human subject or individual might be. In other words, as Rodolphe el-Khoury, one of the translators, explains, the history of shit constitutes the history of "bourgeois subjectivity" (x). The argument is that waste, especially human waste, could be used to grow food. Since food and human waste, as well as other animals' waste, however, are a serious problem for health, the hygienists ruled the day, arguing for precise collection and processing of human waste, which was perceived to be superior to other animal wastes. Hygienists saw their roles primarily as seeking the balance of the needs (*besoins*). Here is a sample of what Laporte sees as *the logic of the irreparable* at work:

> How are we to understand the hygienists' efforts to demonstrate that the loss of the object [human waste] would result in national disaster? How should we

consider their meticulousness in keeping records, in balancing figures, and in summing up accounts?... What is evident from this fantastic arithmetic is that *the object of loss is incalculable.* It is the priceless pretext that contorts arithmetic into marvelous and inconsistent figures and, in the end, demonstrates only that *one cannot fix a price on the loss of shit.* Dr. E. D. Bertherand, who considered cesspools and latrines from the triple perspective of 'hygiene, agriculture, and commerce,' introduced his communication to the agricultural Commission with the following epigraph: 'That which we lose through neglect, that which we fail to gain through ignorance, *is without price.*'

This sentence splendidly summarizes the driving impulse of the hygienist's project: an *irreparable loss* that must be replenished through an excess of attention and knowledge. It is thus no accident that—when it is a matter of fulfilling need—the manure of choice should be human. It is only fitting that shit should be the select object of bourgeois anthropocentrism.

(126; emphasis added)

EASTER EGG 2
THE IRREPARABLE, AS HOPE IN WHAT IS WITHOUT REMEDY

In a tunnel where I was raped, a tunnel that was once an underground entry to an amphitheater, a place where actors burst forth from underneath the seats of a crowd, a girl had been murdered and dismembered. I was told this story by the police. In comparison, they said, I was lucky.

> Alice Sebold, *Lucky: A Memoir*
> (cover, hardback edition)

I could not have what I wanted most: Mr. Harvey dead and me living. Heaven wasn't perfect. But I came to believe that if I watched closely, I might change the lives of those I loved on Earth.

> Alice Sebold, *The Lovely Bones* (20)

Like the freed convict in Kafka's *Penal Colony*, who has survived the destruction of the machine that was to have executed him, these beings [unbaptized children in Limbo] have left the world of guilt and justice behind them: The light that rains down on them is that irreparable light of the dawn following the *novissima dies* of judgment. But the life that begins on earth after the last day is simply human life.

> Giorgio Agamben, *Coming* (7)

Irreparable: But what if all of the above principles, along with Bartleby and Pip, should fail (might fail, even *ought* to fail)? What if we are stuck within Aristotle's logic of the irrevocable (*Nichomachean Ethics*, 1139b.1–13)? If so, then there is always the irreparable. Agamben says: "The

Irreparable is that things are just as they are, in this or that mode, consigned without remedy to their way of being. States of things are irreparable, whatever they may be: sad or happy, atrocious or blessed. How you are, how the world is—that is the Irreparable" (*Coming* 90). But this notion of the Irreparable does not mean there is no hope. There is a topological loop worked into the folding of the problem, or the problematizing of the fold. Agamben says: "We can have hope only in what is without remedy" (*Coming* 102).

I keep thinking of Foucault's scraps from the archive in *Archaeology*, but more so I keep thinking of Agamben's discussion of Auschwitz, enunciation, and the archive. There is such a hopeful passage toward the end (or rebeginnings) of *Remnants*: "*Between* the obsessive memory of tradition, which knows only *what has been said*, and the *exaggerated thoughtlessness of oblivion*, which cares only for *what was never said*, the *archive* is the unsaid or sayable inscribed in everything said by virtue of being enunciated; it is the fragment of memory that is always forgotten in the act of saying 'I.' It is in this 'historical a priori,' suspended between *langue* and *parole*, that Foucault establishes his construction site and founds archaeology as 'the general theme of a description that *questions the already-said* at the level of its existence' [*Archaeology* 131]—that is, as the system of relations between the *unsaid* and the said in every act of speech, between the enunciative function and the discourse in which it exerts itself, between the outside and the inside of language" (144; emphases mine).

This is a description of obsession and its hysterical other, or the hysterical third try (above), in which we placed and still place in, as a taking place of, hope. The *What remained unsaid*, the *What was not*, will have been said, will have become a being in the coming community, will have become through a series of lines of flight. There is the condition of the compossibility (of the archive, of the Palace of Destinies) of a rebirth of sub-jectivity in a superject, in an anarchi-ject or in some walking dead who knows and who speaks, who testifies to not only what has been, but what is to come. This rebirth is compossible, as Agamben says, in terms of human being, in terms of s/he turns *it*[1] who "is capable of not having language, because it is capable of its own in-fancy" (146). Human being, between two images of language, can appear out of Auschwitz, out of "the most radical negation of contingency," as the *Muselmann* (148) can appear—compear—as Primo Livi's paradox of the *Muselmann*. Agamben writes: "'The *Muselmann* is the complete witness.' It implies two contradictory propositions: 1) 'the Muselmann is the non-human, the one who could never bear witness,' and 2) 'the one who cannot bear witness is the true witness, the absolute witness'" (150; cf. 159–71). From everyone raped to the *Muselmann*, the ashes, the stones, the bones, the specters, the non-human—all speak. In radical emerging media. The raped open up new condition for the possibility of emergent media. Given what wants to be recalled. Spoken. I think of Susie Salmon.

And yet, *it* is, more so, the "silent murmur" in the archive (Foucault, *Archaeology* 27–28) or *it* is "the animal in flight that we seem to hear rustling away in our words" (Agamben, *Language* 107) that speaks. But as Agamben says, "the voice, the human voice, does not exist" in language (107). Again, the voice is not human. Made not human. Made into some other species. By way of the negative, we can but say "it is" not human, non-human. "It is"

---

1 *Ereignis*. Agamben, from Heidegger's *Being and Time*, writes-interpolates: "it is [it = *Ereignis*] only nameable as a pronoun, as It (*Es*) and as That (*Jenes*) 'which has sent the various forms of epochal Being,' but that, in itself, is 'ahistorical, or more precisely, without destiny'" (*Language* 102; Heidegger qtd. from *Being* 41).

intractable (108). "It" speaks *statements* that are not readable. How we respond to "it" in language "is ethics" (107).

> We walk through the woods: suddenly we hear the flapping of wings or the wind in the grass. A pheasant lifts off and then disappears instantly among the trees, a porcupine buries in the thick underbrush, the dry leaves crackles as a snake slithers away. Not the encounter, but this flight of invisible animals is thought. Not, it was not our voice. We came as close as possible to language, we almost brushed against it, held it in suspense: but we never reached our encounter and now we turn back, untroubled, toward home. So, language is our voice, our language. As you now speak, that is ethics. (108)

The nonhuman *taking place* toward the coming community, murmurs and rustles awaYvES: From the between of potentiality and impotentiality; from beyond good and evil; to and from Limbo. "[B]eyond perdition and salvation" (*Coming* 6). Hence, a (third figure of) the Irreparable.

DELETED SCENES

WORKS CITED

Abé, Kobo. *The Face of Another.* Trans. E. Dale Saudners. NY: Vintage, 2003.

———. *The Woman in the Dunes.* Trans. E. Dale Saunders. NY: Vintage, 1964.

Adair, Gilbert. *Flickers.* London: Faber and Faber, 1995.

Agamben, Giorgio. *What is an Apparatus?* Trans. David Kishik and Stefan Pedatella. Stanford: Stanford UP, 2009.

———. *The Coming Community.* Minneapolis: U of Minnesota P, 1993.

———. *Homo Sacer.* Trans. Daniel Heller-Roazen. Stanford: Stanford UP, 1998.

———. *Language and Death: The Place of Negativity.* Minneapolis: U of Minnesota P, 2006.

———. *Potentialities.* Ed. and Trans., Daniel Heller-Roazen. Stanford: Stanford UP, 1999.

———. *Profanations.* Trans. Jeff Fort. NY: Zone Books, 2007.

———. *Remnants of Auschwitz.* Trans. Daniel Heller-Roazen. NY: Zone Books, 1999.

Agee, Joel. "Introduction" to *Penthesilea.* NY: Harper-Collins, 1998. xi-xxix.

Akazaki, Steven, dir. *White Light/Black Rain: The Destruction of Hiroshima and Nagasaki.* HBO Home Video. 2007. Video.

Altman, Robert, dir. *Cross Cuts.* Criterion Collection. 1993. Film.

Antonioni, Michelangelo. "A Talk with Michelangelo Antonioni on His Work." *Film Culture* No. 24 (Spring 1962): 45–61.

Arakawa, [Shusaku], and Madeline Gins. *Architectural Body*. Tuscaloosa, AL: U of Alabama P, 2002.

———. *Architecture Sites of Reversible Destiny*. London: The Academy Group, 1994.

———. *The Mechanism of Meaning*. NY: Abbeville P, 1979.

———. *Reversible Destiny*. NY: Guggenheim Museum P, 1997.

Badiou, Alain. *Being and Event*. Trans. Oliver Feltham. NY: Continuum, 2005.

———. *Manifesto for Philosophy*. Trans. Norman Madarasz. Albany: SUNY P, 1999.

Barthes, Roland. *Camera Lucida*. NY: Hill and Wang, 1981.

———. "The Third Meaning." *Image Music Text*. Trans. Stephen Heath. NY: Hill and Wang, 1977. 52–68.

———. "Inaugural Lecture, *College de France*." *A Barthes Reader*. NY: Hill and Wang, 1983. 457–78.

———. *Roland Barthes by Roland Barthes*. NY: Hill and Wang, 1977.

———. *The Neutral*. Trans. Rosalind E. Krauss and Denis Hollier. NY: Columbia UP, 2005.

Bataille, Georges. *The Absence of Myth: Writings on Surrealism*. Ed. and Trans. Michael Richardson. NY: Verso, 2006.

———. *The Accursed Share*. Trans. Robert Hurley. Vol. 1. NY: Zone, 1988.

———. "Concerning the Accounts Given by the Residents of Hiroshima." Trans. Alan Keenan. *In Trauma: Explorations In Memory*. Ed. Cathy Caruth. Baltimore: The Johns Hopkins UP, 1995. 221–35.

———. *Divine Filth: Lost Scatology and Erotica*. Trans. Mark Spitzer. NY: Solar Books, 2009.

———. *Divine Filth: Lost Writings*. Trans. Mark Spitzer. NY: Creation Books, 2004.

———. *Guilty*. Trans. Bruce Boone. Venice, California: Lapis P, 1988.

———. *The Tears of Eros*. Trans. Peter Connor. San Francisco: City Lights Books, 1989.

———. *The Unfinished System of Nonknowledge*. Ed. Stuart Kendall. Trans. Michelle Kendall and Stuart Kendall. Minneapolis: U of Minnesota P, 2001.

———. *Visions of Excess: Selected Writings, 1927–1939*. Ed. Allan Stoekl. Trans. Allan Stoekl, Carl R. Lovitt, and Donald M. Leslie Jr. Minneapolis: U of Minnesota P, 1985.

Bataille, Georges, et al., Ed. *Encyclopaedia Acephalica*. Trans. Iain White, et al. London: Atlas P, 1995.

Baudrillard, Jean. *Baudrillard Live*. Ed. Mike Gane. NY: Routledge, 1993.

———. *Fatal Strategies*. Trans. Philip Beitchman and W. G. J. Niesluchowski. NY: Semiotext(e)/Pluto, 1990.

———. *The Illusion of the End*. Trans. Chris Turner. Stanford: Stanford UP, 1994.

———. *Revenge of the Crystal*. Ed. and trans. by Paul Foss and Julian Pefanis. London: Pluto P, 1990.

———. *Seduction*. Trans. Brian Singer. NY: St. Martin's P, 1990.

———. *Simulacra and Simulation*. Trans. Sheila Faria Glaser. Ann Arbor: U of Michigan P, 1994.

———. *Transparency of Evil*. Trans. James Benedict. NY: Verso, 1993.

Beauvoir, Simone de. *The Second Sex*. Trans. H. M. Parshley. NY: Vintage, 1974.

Bellour, Raymond. *L'entre-images*. Paris: La Différence, 1990.

Bergson, Henri. *Creative Evolution*. Trans. Arthur Mitchell. Mineola, NY: Dover, 1998.

Berleant, Arnold. Review of George W. Linden's *Reflections on the Screen* and Paul Weiss' *Cinematics*. *Philosophy and Phenomenological Research* 38.2 (December 1977). 266–68.

"Berlin 1945: War and Rape: 'Liberators Take Liberties [*BeFreier und Befreite*].'" Ed. Stuart Liebman. *October* 72 (Spring 1995). Special Issue.

Berman, Marshall. *All that is Solid Melts in Air: The Experience of Modernity*. NY: Penguin, 1988.

Blanchot, Maurice. *The Infinite Conversation*. Trans. Susan Hanson. Minneapolis: U of Minnesota P, 1999.

———. *The Book to Come*. Trans. Charlotte Mandell. Stanford: Stanford UP, 2002.

———. *The Unavowable Community*. Trans. Pierre Joris. Barrytown, NY: Staion Hill P, 1988.

———. *The Writing of the Disaster*. Trans. Ann Smock. Lincoln: U of Nebraska P, 1988.

Bois, Yve-Alain, and Rosalind Krauss. *Formless: A User's Guide*. NY: Zone, 1997.

Borges, Jorge Luis. *Ficciones*. Ed. Anthony Kerrigan. NY: Grove, 1962.

———. *Labyrinths*. Ed. Donald A. Yates and James E. Irby. NY: Penguin, 1964.

Brown, Norman O. *Apocalypse and/or Metamorphosis*. Berkeley: U of California P, 1991.

———. *Life Against Death*. Middleton, Connecticut: Wesleyan UP, 1959.

———. *Love's Body*. Berkeley: U of California P, 1966.

Brownmiller, Susan. *Against Our Will*. NY: Fawcett Columbine, 1993.

Burke, Kenneth. *Counter-Statement*. Second Edition. Berkeley: U of California P, 1968.

———. *Grammar of Motives*. Berkeley: U of California P, 1969.

Burgos, Nate. "Memento, Memory, and Montage." *C-Theory* (2001). Web. 21 May 2012 <http://www.ctheory.net/articles.aspx?id=321>.

Burroughs, William S. *Nova Express*. NY: Grove P, 1994.

Butler, Judith. *Bodies That Matter: On the Discursive Limits of Sex*. NY: Routledge, 1993.

———. *Subjects of Desire*. NY: Columbia UP, 1987.

Cahill, Ann J. *Rethinking Rape*. Ithaca, NY: Cornell UP, 2001.

Cahill, James Leo. "Anacinema: Peter Tscherkassky's Cinematic

Breakdowns: Towards the Unspeakable Film." *Spectator* 28.2 (Fall 2008). 90–101.

Campbell, Felicia. "Silver Screen, Shadow Play: The Tradition of the *Wayang Kulit* in *The Year of Living Dangerously*." *The Journal of Popular Culture* 28.1 (Summer 1994). 163–69.

Canning, Peter. "The Imagination of Immanence: An Ethics of Cinema." Ed. Gregory Flaxman *The Brain Is the Screen*. 303–25.

Caruth, Cathy, Ed. *Trauma: Explorations in Memory*. Baltimore, Maryland: The Johns Hopkins UP, 1995.

———. *Unclaimed Experience*. Baltimore: Johns Hopkins UP, 1996.

Casey, Damien. "Sacrifice, *Piss Christ*, and Liberal Excess" in *Law, Text, Culture* (June 2002). dlibrary.acu.edu.au/staffhome/dacasey/Serrano.html (viewed: October 19, 2003).

Chamberlain, Charles. "From 'Haunts' to 'Character': The Meaning of Ethos." *Helios* 11: 2 (1984). 97–108.

Chang, Iris. *The Rape of Nanking*. NY: Penguin, 1998.

Chesler, Phyllis. "What is Justice for a Rape Victim?" in *The Phyllis Chesler Organization* (Winter 1995). <http://76.12.0.56/index.php?option=com_content&task=view&id=229&Itemid=1> (viewed: December 18, 2008).

Clément, Catherine. *La Syncope: Philosophie du Ravissement*. Paris: Bernard Grasset, 1990.

Cohen-Pfister, Laurel, "Portraying Mass Wartime Rape in the Documentary: *BeFreier und Befreite* and *Calling the Ghosts*." *West Virginia University Philological Papers*. Special Issue on The Evolution of War and its Representation in Literature and Film. 50 (Fall 2004): 104–10.

Conley, Tom. "Conspiracy Crisis." *Polygraph* No. 14 (2002): 47–60.

———. "The Film Event: From Interval to Interstice." *The Brain Is the Screen*. Ed. Gregory Flaxman. 303–25.

Copjec, Joan. *Read My Desire*. Cambridge: MIT P, 1995.
Cuklanz, Lisa M. *Rape on Prime Time: Television, Masculinity, and Sexual Violence*. Philadelphia: U of Pennsylvania P, 2000.
Davis, D. Diane. "'Addicted to Love'; Or, Toward an Inessential Solidarity." *JAC* 19.4 (Fall 1999): 633–56.
———. *Breaking Up at Totality*. Carbondale: Southern Illinois UP, 2000.
———. "Finitude's Clamor: Or, Notes toward a Communitarian Literacy." *CCC* 53.1 (September 2001): 119–45.
De Certeau, Michel. *The Practice of Everyday Life*. Trans. Steven Rendall. Berkeley: U of California P, 1988.
De Landa, Manuel. "Meshworks, Hierarchies, and Interfaces." Web. 21 May 2012 <http://www.to.or.at/delanda/meshwork.htm>.
De Lauretis, Teresa. *Technologies of Gender*. Bloomington: Indiana UP, 1987.
Deleuze, Gilles. "The Brain is the Screen: An Interview." Flaxman, Ed, *The Brain is the Screen*. Minneapolis: Minnesota, 2000. 365–73.
———. *Cinema 1*. Trans. Hugh Tomlinson and Barbara Habberjam. Minneapolis: U of Minnesota P, 1986.
———. *Cinema 2*. Trans. Hugh Tomlinson and Robert Galeta. Minneapolis: U of Minnesota P, 1989.
———. *Dialogues*. NY: Columbia UP, 1987.
———. *Difference and Repetition*. Trans. Paul Patton. NY: Columbia UP, 1995.
———. "The Exhausted" ("*L'épuisé*"). Trans. Daniel W. Smith and Michael A. Greco. *Essays Critical and Clinical*. Minneapolis: U of Minnesota P, 1997. 152–74.
———. *The Fold*. Trans. Tom Conley. Minneapolis: U of Minnesota P, 1993.
———. *Foucault*. Trans. Seán Hand. Minneapolis: U of Minnesota P, 1988.

———. *Francis Bacon*. Trans. Daniel W. Smith. Minneapolis: U of Minnesota P, 2003.

———. *The Logic of Sense*. Trans. Mark Lester with Charles Stivale. NY: Columbia UP, 1990.

———. *Negotiations*. Trans. Martin Joughin. NY: Columbia UP, 1995.

———. *Nietzsche and Philosophy*. Trans. Hugh Tomlinson. NY: Columbia UP, 1983.

———. *Pure Immanence*. Trans. Anne Boyman. NY: Zone Books, 2001.

———. "*What is a* Dispositif?" In *Michel Foucault: Philosopher*. Ed. and Trans. Timothy J. Armstrong. NY: Routledge, 1991. 159–68.

Deleuze, Gilles, and Felix Guattari. *A Thousand Plateaus*. Minneapolis: U of Minnesota P, 1987.

———. *What is Philosophy?* Trans. Hugh Tomlinson and Graham Burchell. NY: Columbia UP, 1994.

De Man, Paul. *Allegories of Reading*. New Haven, Connecticut: Yale UP, 1982.

Denis, Claire, dir. *Friday Night*. Bac Films. 2002. Film.

Derrida, Jacques. *Archive Fever*. U of Chicago P. 1998.

———. *Dissemination*. Trans. Barbara Johnson. Chicago: The U of Chicago P, 1981.

———. *Of Spirit*. Trans. Geoffrey Bennington and Rachel Bowlby. Chicago: U of Chicago P, 1989.

———. *On Cosmopolitanism and Forgiveness*. Trans. Mark Dooley and Michael Hughes. NY: Routledge, 2002.

———. "Structure, Sign, and Play." In *Writing and Difference*. Trans. Allan Bass. Chicago: The U of Chicago P, 1978.

Despentes, Virginie. *Baise-Moi*. Paris: Florent Massot, 1993.

———. *Baise-Moi (Rape-Me)*. Trans. Bruce Benderson. NY: Grove P, 2003.

Despentes, Virginie, and Coralie Trinh Thi. *Baise-Moi*. DVD. Remstar, 2005.

Doane, Mary Ann. *The Emergence of Cinematic Time.* Cambridge: Harvard UP, 2002.

DuBois, Page. *Torture and Truth.* NY: Routledge, 1991.

Duras. Marguerite. *Hiroshima Mon Amour.* Trans. Richard Seaver. NY: Grove P, 1961.

Durkheim, Emile. *The Elementary Forms of the Religious Life.* Trans. Joseph Ward Swain. NY: Dover, 2008.

Dworkin, Andrea. *Intercourse.* NY: The Free P, 1987.

———. *Mercy.* NY: Four Walls Eight Windows, 1991.

———. *Scapegoat.* NY: The Free P, 2000.

Eagleton, Terry. *Walter Benjamin, Or Towards a Revolutionary Criticism.* NY: Verso, 1981.

Eco, Umberto, and Thomas A. Sebeok, Ed. *The Sign of Three.* Bloomington: Indiana UP, 1988.

Elkins, James. *The Object Stares Back: On the Nature of Seeing.* NY: Mariner Books. 1997.

Eliade, Mircea. *The Sacred and the Profane: The Nature of Religion.* Trans. Willard R. Trask. NY: Harcourt, 1987.

Epstein, Jean. "Bonjour Cinéma." Trans. Tom Milne. *Afterimage* 10 (Autumn 1981). 9–16.

Estrich, Susan. *Real Rape.* Cambridge: Harvard UP, 1987.

Fausto-Sterling, Anne. "The Five Sexes: Why Male and Female Are Not Enough." *The Sciences* (March/April 1993): 20–25.

———. *Myths of Gender.* 2nd Revision Edition. NY: Basic Books, 1992.

———. *Sexing the Body.* NY: Basic Books, 2000.

Felman, Shoshana, and Dori Laub. *Testimony.* NY: Routledge, 1991.

Féret, René, dir. *Mozart's Sister* (*Nannerl, La Soeur de Mozart*). Les Films Alyne. DVD. 2010. Film.

Flusser, Vilem. *Writings.* Ed. Andreas Ströhl. Trans. Erik Elsel. Minneapolis: U of Minnesota P, 2004.

Flaxman, Gregory, Ed. *The Brain is the Screen.* Minneapolis: U of Minnesota P, 2000.

Forman, Miloš, dir. *Amadeus*. Final Screenplay, 1982. Peter Shaffer. Warner Brothers. DVD. 1997. Film.

———, dir. *Amadeus Director's Cut*. Screenplay, Peter Shaffer. Warner Brothers. DVD. 2002. Film.

Foucault, Michel. *Language, Counter-Memory, Practice*. Ithaca: Cornell UP, 1986.

———. *Madness and Civilization*. NY: Vintage, 1988.

Frappier-Mazur, Lucienne. *Writing the Orgy: Power and Parody in Sade*. Trans. Gillian C. Gill. Philadelphia: U of Pennsylvania P, 1996.

Frayling, Christopher. "The House that Jack Built: Some Stereotypes of the Rapist in the History of Popular Culture." In *Rape*. Ed. Tomaselli and Porter. 174–215.

Freud, Sigmund. *The Standard Edition of the Complete Psychological Works of Sigmund Freud*. 24 volumes. Ed. James Strachey. London: Hogarth Press and the Institute of Psycho-Analysis, 1953–1974.

Fynsk, Christopher. *Infant Figures*. Stanford: Stanford UP, 2000.

Genet, Jean. *Our Lady of the Flowers*. Trans. Bernard Frechtman. NY: Grove P, 1963.

Ghiglieri, Michael P. *The Dark Side of Man*. Cambridge, Massachusetts: Perseus Books, 2000.

Gins, Madeline. *Helen Keller or Arakawa*. Santa Fe, NM: Burning Books with East-West Cultural Studies, 1994.

Gins, Madeline, and Arakawa. *Architectural Body*. Tuscaloosa: The U of Alabama P, 2002.

Girard, René. *To Double Business Bound: Essays on Literature, Mimesis and Anthropology*. Baltimore: The Johns Hopkins UP, 1988.

———. *Violence and the Sacred*. Trans. Patrick Gregory. Baltimore: The Johns Hopkins UP, 1979.

Godard, Jean-Luc. *Hail Mary*. (*Je Vous Salue, Marie*) Film. Gaumont and New Yorker Films, 1985.

Gooding-Williams, Robert, Ed. *Reading Rodney King, Reading Urban Uprising*. NY: Routledge, 1993.

Grindon, Gavin. "Alchemist of the Revolution: The Affective Materialism of Georges Bataille." *Third Text* 24.3 (2010). 305–17.

Gross, Zoe. "Excremental Ecstasy, Divine Defecation and Revolting Reception: Configuring a Scatological Gaze in Trash Filmmaking." *Colloquy* 10 (2009). <http://artsonline.monash.edu.au/colloquy/download/colloquy_issue_eighteen/gross.pdf>.

Grossmann, Atina. "A Question of Silence: The Rape of German Women by Occupation Soldiers." *October* 72 (Spring 1995): 43–63.

Guattari, Felix. *Chaosmosis*. Trans. Paul Bains and Julian Pefanis. Bloomington: Indiana UP, 1995.

Gysin, Brion. *The Process*. London: Paladin, Grafton Books, 1988.

Hamacher, Werner. *Pleroma—Reading in Hegel*. Trans. Nicholas Walker and Simon Jarvis. Stanford: Stanford UP, 1998.

Hammond, Paul, Ed and Trans. *The Shadow and its Shadow: Surrealist Writings on the Cinema*. Third Edition. San Francisco: City Lights, 2000.

Hansen, Mark B. N. "Seeing With the Body the Digital Image in Postphotography." *Diacritics* 31.4 (2001) 54–82.

Harrison, Robert Pogue. "*Hic Jacet*." *Critical Inquiry* 27 (Spring 2001): 393–407.

Hartley, Hal, dir. *Fay Grimm*. DVD. Magnolia, 2007. Film.

———, dir. *Henry Fool*. DVD. SONY Pictures, 2003. Film.

———. *Henry Fool*. Script. London: Faber and Faber, 1998.

———. "Responding to Nature: Hal Hartley in Conversation with Graham Fuller." In *Henry Fool*. vii-xxv.

Haskell, Molly. *From Reverence to Rape*. Chicago: The U of Chicago P, 1987.

Hasson, Uri, and Ohad Landesman, Barbara Knappmeyer, Ignacio Vallines, Nava Rubin, and David J. Heeger. "Neurocinematics: The Neuroscience of Film." *Projections* 2.1 (Summer 2008). 1–26.

Havelock, Eric. *The Muse Learns to Write: Reflections on Orality and Literacy from Antiquity to the Present.* New Haven, Connecticut: Yale UP, 1988.

Hayes, Julie Candler. "The Body of the Letter: Epistolary Acts of Simon Hantaï, Jean-Luc Nancy, and Jacques Derrida." *Postmodern Culture* 13.3 (May 2003). <http://pmc.iath.virginia.edu/issue.503/13.3NEWhayes.html>.

Heath, Stephen. *Questions of Cinema.* Bloomington: Indiana UP, 1981.

[Hegel, G. W. F.] *Phenomenology of Spirit.* Trans A. V. Miller. NY: Oxford UP, 1977.

Heidegger, Martin. *Being and Time.* Trans. John Macquarrie and Edward Robinson. NY: Harper and Row, 1962.

———. *"Der Spiegel* Interview" in *Martin Heidegger and National Socialism.* NY: Paragon, 1990.

———. *Parmenides.* Trans. Andre Schuwer and Richard Rojcewicz. Bloomington: Indiana UP, 1998.

———. *Poetry, Language, Thought.* Trans. Albert Hofstadter. NY: Harper and Row, 1971.

———. *What is Called Thinking?* Trans. J. Glenn Gray. NY: Harper and Row, 1968.

Heller-Nicholas, Alexandra. *Rape-Revenge Films: A Critical Study.* Jefferson, NC: Mcfarland, 2011.

Hengehold, Laura. "An Immodest Proposal: Foucault, Hysterization, and the 'Second Rape'." *Hypatia* 9.3 (1994). 88–107.

Herman, Judith Lewis. *Trauma and Recovery.* NY: Basic Books, 1992.

Herodotus, *The Histories.* NY: Oxford UP, 2008.

Hesford, Wendy S. "Reading Rape Stories: Material Rhetoric and the Trauma of Representation." *College English* 62.2 (November 1999): 192–221.

Hollier, Denis, and Hilari Allred. "The Dualist Materialism of Georges Bataille." *Yale French Studies* 78 (1990). 124–39.

Hollywood, Amy. "Bataille and Mysticism: A 'Dazzling Dissolution.'" *Diacritics* 26.2. (Summer 1996). 74–87.

———. *Sensible Ecstasy: Mysticism, Sexual Difference, and the Demands of History*. Chicago: U of Chicago P, 2002.

Horeck, Tanya. *Public Rape*. NY: Routledge, 2004.

Hussey, Andrew. *The Inner Scar: The Mysticism of Georges Bataille*. Amsterdam: Rodopi, 2000.

Hutcheon, Linda. *A Poetics of Postmodernism: History, Theory, Fiction*, NY: Routledge, 1988.

Ijselling, Samuel. *Rhetoric and Philosophy in Conflict*. The Hague: Martinus Nijhoff, 1976.

Irigaray, Luce. "The Invisible of the Flesh: A Reading of Merleau-Ponty's 'The Intertwining—The Chiasm,'" *An Ethics of Sexual Difference*. Trans. Carolyn Burke and Gillian C. Gill. Ithaca: Cornell UP, 1993. 151–84.

———. *This Sex Which Is Not One*. Trans. Catherine Porter. Ithaca, NY: Cornell UP, 1985.

Jameson, Fredric. "Postmodernism, or The Cultural Logic of Late Capitalism." *New Left Review* I/146 (July–August 1984). 53–92.

———. "Reading Without Interpretation: Post-Modernism and the Video-Text." In *The Linguistics of Writing*. Ed. Nigel Fabb, et al. NY: Methuen, 1987. 199–223.

Jay, Martin. *Downcast Eyes: The Denigration of Vision in Twentieth-Century French Thought*. Berkeley: U of California P, 1994.

Jed, Stephanie H. *Chaste Thinking*. Bloomington: Indiana UP, 1989.

Jelinek, Elfriede. *The Piano Teacher*. Trans. Joachim Neugroschel. NY: Weidenfelf and Nicholson, 1988.

Johnson, Sheila K. "Helke Sander's *BeFreier und Befreite: Krieg, Vergewaltigung, Kinder* and Postmodernism." *Pacific Coast Philology*. 28.1 (September 1993). 81–93.

Johnston, John. "Machinic Vision." *Critical Inquiry* 26 (Autumn 1999): 27–48.

Juhasz, Alexandra. "The Politics of the Realist, Feminist Documentary." *Screen* 35.2 (Summer 1994). 171–90.

(Republished as "They Said We Were Trying to Show Reality—All I Want to Show is My Video: The Politics of the Realist Feminist Documentary." In *Collecting Visible Evidence*. Vol. 6. Ed. Jane M. Gaines and Michael Renov. Minneapolis: U of Minnesota P, 1999. 190–215.)

Kania, Andrew, Ed. *Memento*. NY: Routledge, 2009.

Kennedy, Jake. "Gins, Arakawa and the Undying Community." *Culture Machine* 8 (2006). culturemachine.tees.ac.uk/frm_f1.htm (viewed: January 26, 2007).

Kipnis, Laura. *Marx: The Video*. Chicago: Video Data Bank, 1990. Video.

———. "Marx: The Video. A Politics of Revolting Bodies." In *Ecstasy Unlimited*. Minnesota: U of Minneapolis P, 1993.

Kittler, Friedrich A. *Discourse Networks 1800 / 1900*. Trans. Michael Metteer, with Chris Cullens. Stanford: Stanford UP, 1990.

———. *Gramophone, Film, Typewriter*. Trans. Geoffrey Winthrop-Young and Michael Wutz. Stanford: Stanford UP, 1999.

———. "Man as a Drunken Town-Musician." *MLN*, 118.3 German Issue (April, 2003). 637–52.

———. "Writing into the Wind, Bettina." *Glyph 7*. Baltimore: The Johns Hopkins UP, 1980. 32–70.

Kleist, Heinrich von. *The Marquise of O, and Other Stories*. Trans. and Introduction by David Luke and Nigel Reeves. London: Penguin, 1978.

———. *Penthesilea*. Trans. Joel Agee. NY: Harper-Collins, 1998.

———. *Penthesilea*. Trans. Martin Greenberg. New Haven: Yale UP, 1988.

Klossowski, Pierre. *Sade: My Neighbor*. Trans. Alphonso Lingis. Evanston, Illinois: Northwestern UP, 1991.

Koch, Christopher J. *The Year of Living Dangerously*. NY: Penguin, 1995.

Koch, Gertrud. "Blood, Sperm, and Tears." Trans. Stuart Liebman. *October* 72 (Spring 1995): 27–41.

Kristeva, Julia. *Desire in Language*. Trans. Thomas Gora, Alice Jardine, and Leon S. Roudiez. NY: Columbia UP, 1980.

———. *Powers of Horror: An Essay on Abjection*. Trans. Leon S. Roudiez. NY: Columbia UP, 1982.

———. *Tales of Love*. Trans. Leon Roudiez. NY: Columbia UP, 1987.

Kundera, Milan. *Immortality*. Trans. Peter Kussi. NY: Grove Weidenfeld, 1991.

Kramer, Lawrence. *After the Lovedeath*. Berkeley: U of California P, 1997.

LaCapra, Dominick. *Writing History, Writing Trauma*. Baltimore: The Johns Hopkins UP, 2001.

Lanzmann, Claude. "The Obscenity of Understanding: An Evening with Claude Lanzmann." In *Trauma: Explorations in Memory*. Ed. Cathy Caruth. Baltimore: The Johns Hopkins UP, 1995. 200–220.

———. *The Patagonian Hare: A Memoir*. Trans. Frank Wynne. NY: Farrar, Straus and Giroux, 2012.

———, Dir. *Shoah*. New Yorker Films, 1985. Film.

———. *Shoah: The Complete Text Of The Acclaimed Holocaust Film*. 10th Ed. NY: Da Capo P, 1995.

Laporte, Dominique. *History of Shit (Histoire de la merdre)*. Trans. Nadia Benabid and Rodolphe el-Khoury. Cambridge: MIT P, 2000.

Leary, Timothy. *Design for Dying*. San Francisco: Harper, 1997.

Le Brun, Annie. *Sade: A Sudden Abyss*. Trans. Camille Naish. San Francisco: City Light Books, 1990.

Le Cain, Maximilian. "Fresh Blood: *Baise-Moi*." (October 2, 2002) Web. 21 May 2012 <http://sensesofcinema.com/2002/feature-articles/baise-moi_max/>.

Leibniz, G. W. *Theodicy*. Trans. E. M. Huggard. La Salle, Illinois: Open Court, 1985.

Lennon, John, and Yoko Ono, dir. *Rape*. (1969). Film.

Leonard, Richard James. "The Cinematic Mystical Gaze: The Films of Peter Weir." Dissertation. University of Melbourne, August 2003.

———. *The Mystical Gaze of the Cinema: The Films of Peter Weir.* Austrilia: Melbourne UP, 2009.

Levi, Pavle. *Cinema By Other Means.* NY: Oxford UP, 2012.

Levin, David J. "Taking Liberties with Liberties Taken: On the Politics of Helke Sander's *BeFreier und Befreite*." *October* 72 (Spring 1995): 65–77.

Levinas, Emmanuel. *Otherwise Than Being or Beyond Essence.* Trans. Alphonso Lingis. Pittsburgh: Duquesne UP, 1998.

———. *Totality and Infinity.* Trans. Alphonso Linguis. Pittsburgh: Duquesne UP, 1969.

Liebman, Stuart, and Annette Michelson. "After the Fall: Women in the House of the Hangmen." *October* 72 (1995): 5–14.

Lispector, Clarice. *The Passion According to G. H.* Trans. Ronald W. Sousa. Minneapolis: U of Minnesota P, 1988.

Loraux, Nicole. *The Experiences of Tiresias.* Trans. Paula Wissing. Princeton, NJ: Princeton UP, 1997.

Lu, Chuan. Director. *City of Life and Death.* Media Asia, China Film Group. 2009.

Lyotard, Jean-François. "Acenima" in *The Lyotard Reader.* Ed. Andrew Benjamin. Cambridge, Massachusetts: Basil Blackwell, 1989. 169–80.

———. *The Differend: Phrase in Dispute.* Trans. Georges Van Den Abbeele. Minneapolis: U of Minnesota P, 1988.

———. *Libidinal Economy.* Trans. Iain Hamilton Grant. Bloomington: Indiana UP, 1993.

MacKinnon, Catharine A. *Only Words.* Cambridge: Harvard UP, 1993.

———. *Toward a Feminist Theory of the State.* Cambridge: Harvard UP, 1989.

———. "Turning Rape into Pornography: Postmodern Genocide." *Ms.* (July-August 1993): 24–30.

Marker, Chris, dir. *La Jetée/Sans Soleil*. (1962, 1983). Criterion Collection (2007). Film.

Marsh, James L., and John D. Caputo, Jerold Westphal, Ed. *Modernity and Its Discontents*. NY: Fordham UP, 1992.

Massumi, Brian. *Parables for the Virtual*. Durham: Duke UP, 2002.

Marx, Karl. *The Eighteenth Brumaire of Louis Bonaparte*. NY: International Publishers, 1963.

Marx, Karl, and Fredrick Engels. *Manifesto of the Communist Party*. Trans. Samuel Moore (ed. by Fredrick Engels) in 1888. Marx/Engels Internet Archive. Web. <http://www.marxists.org>. Offline version: Marx/Engels Internet Archive (marxists.org), 2000

Mauer, Barry. "Proposal for a Monument to Lost Data." Book chapter for Studies In Writing, volume 17, *Writing and Digital Media*, ed. Luuk van Waes, Mariëlle Leijten, Christine M. Neuwirth. West Yorkshire, England: Emerald Group Publishing, 2006. 287–310.

McCarthy, Sarah J. "Pornography, Rape, and the Cult of Macho," *Humanist* (September/October 1980). 11–20.

McCormick, Richard W. "Rape and War, Gender and Nation, Victims and Victimizers: Helke Sander's *Befreier und Befreite*." *Camera Obscura* 16.1 (2001): 99–141.

Meagher, Robert Emmet. *Helen*. NY: Continuum, 1995.

Mehlman, Jeffrey. *Revolution and Repetition*. Berkeley: U of California P, 1977.

Melville, Herman. *Moby Dick*. Ed. Alfred Kazin. Boston: Houghton Mifflin. 1956.

Miller, Henry. *Tropic of Cancer*. NY: Grove, 1994.

Miller, Paul (DJ Spooky). *Rhythm Science*. Cambridge: MIT P, 2004.

Millett, Kate. *The Basement*. NY: Simon and Schuster, 1979.
———. *The Basement*. NY: Simon and Schuster, 1991.

Mitscherlich, Alexander and Margarete. *The Inability to Mourn*. Trans. Beverley R. Placzek. NY: Grove P, 1975.

Mottram, James. *The Making of Memento*. NY: Faber and Faber, 2002.

Mueller, Cookie. *Ask Doctor Mueller*. Ed. Amy Scholder. NY: High Risk Books, 1997.

Mulvey, Laura. "Visual Pleasure and Narrative Cinema." *Screen* 16.3 (1985): 6–18.

Murray, Timothy. "Digital Incompossibility: Cruising the Aesthetic Haze of the New Media." *C-Theory* (2000). Web. 21 May 2012 < http://www.ctheory.net/articles.aspx?id=121>.

Nägele, Rainer. *Reading After Freud*. NY: Columbia UP, 1987.

Nancy, Jean-Luc. *Being Singular Plural*. Trans. Robert D. Richardson and Anne E. O'Byrne. Stanford: Stanford UP, 2000.

———. *Corpus*. Édition revue et complétée. Paris: Éditions Métailiée, 2006.

———. *The Discourse of the Syncope: Logodaedalus*. Stanford: Stanford UP, 2008.

———. *The Ground of the Image*. Trans. Jeff Fort. NY: Fordham, 2005.

———. *Dis-Enclosure: The Deconstruction of Christianity*. Trans. Bettina Bergo, Garriel Malenfant, and Michael B. Smith. NY: Fordham UP, 2008.

———. *The Experience of Freedom*. Trans. Bridget McDonald. Stanford: Stanford UP, 1993.

———. *The Inoperative Community*. Trans. Peter Connor et al. Minneapolis: The U of Minnesota P, 1991.

———. *The Sense of the World*. Trans. Jeffrey S. Librett. Minneapolis: The U of Minnesota P, 1997.

Nancy, Jean-Luc, and Abbas Kiarostami. *The Evidence of Film*. Trans. Christine Irizarry and Verena Andermatt Conley. Bruxelles: Yves Gevaert Publisher, 2001.

Nietzsche, Friedrich. *The Gay Science.* Trans. Walter Kaufmann. NY: Vintage, 1974.

———. *On the Genealogy of Morals and Ecce Homo.* Trans. Walter Kaufmann. NY: Vintage, 1969.

———. *Philosophy in the Tragic Age of the Greeks.* Trans. Marianne Cowan. NY: Gateway, 1996.

———. *Thus Spake Zarathustra* in *The Portable Nietzsche.* NY: Penguin, 1968. 103–439.

———. *Twilight of the Idols and The Anti-Christ.* Trans. R. J. Hollingdale. NY: Penguin Books, 1968.

Nikolopoudou, Kalliopi. "Elements of Experience: Bataille's Drama." In *The Obsessions of Georges Bataille.* Ed. Andrew J. Mitchell and Jason Kemp Winfree. Albany: SUNY, 2009. 99–118.

Noé, Gaspar, *Irréversible.* DVD. Nord-Ouest Production. 2003. Film.

Nolan, Chistopher, dir. *Memento.* Columbia. 2001. Film.

———. *Memento and Following.* NY: Faber and Faber, 2001.

Nolan, Jonathan. "Memento Mori." *Esquire* (March 2001) Web. 21 May 2012 <http://www.esquire.com/fiction/fiction/memento-mori-0301?click=main_sr>.

Noys, Benjamin. "George Bataille's Base Materialism." *Cultural Values* 2.4 (1998): 499–517.

Oates, Joyce Carol. *Rape: A Love Story.* NY: Carroll and Graf, 2003.

Ovid. *Metamorphoses.* Trans. Rolfe Humphries. Bloomington: U of Indiana UP, 1967.

Paris, Ginette. *Pagan Meditations.* Trans. Gwendolyn Moore. Dallas, Texas: Spring Publications, 1988.

Pavić, Milorad. "The Beginning and the End of Reading—The Beginning and the End of the Novel." *The Review of Contemporary Fiction* 18.2 (1998). 142–46.

———. *Dictionary of the Khazars: A Lexicon Novel in 100,000 Words.* Trans. Christina Pribićević-Zorić. NY: Vintage, 1989.

Pefanis, Julian. *Heterology and the Postmodern*. Durham: Duke UP, 1991.

Perniola, Mario. *Enigmas*. Trans. Christopher Woodall. NY: Verso, 1995.

Philips, Baxter. *Cut the Unseen Cinema*. NY: Lorrimer, Bounty Books, 1975.

Plaza, Monique. "Our Damages and Their Compensation." *Feminist Issues* 1.3 (1981). 1981.

Pontevia, Jean-Marie. *La peinture, masque et miroir*. Bordeaux: William Blake, 1984.

Pribram, E. Deidre Ed. *Female Spectators*. NY: Verso, 1988.

Projansky, Sarah. *Watching Rape: Film and Television in Postfeminist Culture*. NY: NYU P, 2001.

Rajchman, John. *Constructions*. Cambridge: MIT UP, 1998.

———. *The Deleuze Connections*. Cambridge: The MIT P, 2001.

Ramdas, Rodney. "The Acinema of Grandrieux: On *Un Lac*." I: Forests. *Lumen* (2011). <http://lumenjournal.org/>.

Rancière, Jacques. *Film Fables*. NY: Berg, 2006.

Rand, Harry. Review of Paul Weiss' *Cinematics*. *Leonardo* 10.4 (Autumn, 1977). 349.

Ray, Robert B. *The Avant-Garde Finds Andy Hardy*. Cambridge: Harvard UP, 1995.

Read, Jacinda. *The New Avengers: Feminism, Femininity, and the Rape-Revenge Cycle*. Manchester: Manchester UP, 2000.

Reising, Russell. *Loose Ends: Closure and Crisis in the American Social Text*. Durham, NC: Duke UP, 1996.

Resnais, Alain, dir. Marguerite Duras, Screenplay. *Hiroshima, Mon Amour*. Janus. 1959. Film.

Reynaud, Berenice. "*Baise-Moi*: A Personal Angry-Yet-Feminist Reaction." (September 2002). Web. 21 May 2012 < http://sensesofcinema.com/2002/feature-articles/baise-moi/>.

Reynolds, Anthony. "Toward a Sovereign Cinema: Georges Bataille's *Hiroshima Mon Amour*." *Literature / Film Quarterly* 38.4 (2010). 311–22.

Rickels, Laurence A. *Aberrations of Mourning*. Detroit, Michigan: Wayne State UP, 1988.

Ricoeur, Paul. *Freud and Philosophy*. Trans. Denis Savage. New Haven: Yale UP, 1978.

Rodowick, D. N. *Reading the Figural, or, Philosophy After the New Media*. Durham: Duke UP, 2001.

Ronell, Avital. *Crack Wars: Literature Addiction Mania*. Urbana: U of Illinois P, 2004.

———. *Dictation: On Haunted Writing*. Urbana: U of Illinois P, 2006.

———. *Finitude's Score*. Lincoln: U of Nebraska P, 1994.

———. *Stupidity*. Urbana: U of Illinois P, 2002.

———. *Test Drive*. Urbana: U of Illinois P, 2004.

Rose, Jacqueline. *States of Fantasy*. Oxford: Clarendon P, 1996.

Rosen, Philip, Ed. *Narrative, Apparatus, Ideology: A Film Theory Reader*. NY: Columbia UP, 1986.

Rosenbaum, Jonathan. "Intense Materialism: *Too Soon, Too Late*." *Sense of Cinema* (2000) Issue 6. <http://sensesofcinema.com/2000/6/soon/>.

Rosenzweig, Wiltrud. "Some Very Personal Thoughts about the Accusations of Revisionism Made Against Helke Sander's Film *Liberators Take Liberties*." *October* 72 (Spring 1995): 79–80.

Round Table. "Further Thoughts on Helke Sander's Project." *October* 72 (Spring 1995): 89–113.

Russell, Dominique. *Rape in Art Cinema*. NY: Continuum, 2012.

Sade, Donatien-Alphonse-François. *Complete Justine, Philosophy in the Bedroom, and other Writings*. Trans. Richard Seaver and Austryn Wainhouse. Intro. By Jean Paulhan and Maurice Blanchot. The American Edition. NY: Grove P, 1965.

Sallis, John. *Crossings: Nietzsche and the Space of Tragedy*. U of Chicago P, 1991.

———. *Double Truth*. Albany: SUNY P, 1995.

Salva, Victor. dir. *Powder*. Hollywood Pictures. 1995. Film.

Sander, Helke, dir. *BeFreier und Befreite* ("Liberators Take Liberties"). February, 1992. Film.
———. "Remembering/Forgetting." *October* 72 (1995): 15–25.
———. "A Response to My Critics." *October* 72 (1995): 87–88.
———. *The Three Women K*. London: Serpent's Tail, 1991.
Sander, Helke, and Barbara Johr, Ed. *BeFreier und Befreite*. Munich: Kunstmann, 1992.
Santner, Eric L. *Stranded Objects*. Ithaca, NY: Cornell UP, 1990.
Sartre, Jean-Paul. "Introduction" to *Our Lady of the Flowers*, by Jean Genet. NY: Grove P, 1963. 9–57.
———. Preface to Henri Alleg, *The Question*. Trans. John Calder. NY: G. Braziller 1958.
———. *Saint Genet*. NY: George Braziller, 1981.
Schirmacher, Wolfgang. "The City as *Geviert*: Questions Arising from a Philosophy of Architecture, Sentence Building." *Architecture-Theory-Criticism*. Ed. N. Hellmayr. Freyberg: Graz, 1993.
———. "Cloning Humans with Media: Impermanence and Imperceptible Perfection." *Poiesis*. 2 (2000): 38–41.
———. "Homo Generator: Media and Postmodern Technology." *Culture on the Brink*. Ed. Gretchen Bender and Timothy Druckrey. Seattle: Bay P, 1994. 65–79, 82.
Schreber, Daniel Paul. *Memoirs of My Nervous Illness*. Cambridge, Mass.: Harvard UP, 1988.
Scott, Charles E. *The Question of Ethics*. Bloomington: U of Indiana P, 1990.
Scott, Joan. "The Evidence of Experience." *Critical Inquiry* 17 (Summer 1991): 773–97.
Sebald, W. G. *On the Natural History of Destruction*. Trans. Anthea Bell. NY: Random, 2003.
Sebeok, Thomas A. "One, Two, Three Spells UBERTY." In *The Sign of Three*. Ed. Umerto Eco and Thomas A. Sebeok. Bloomington: Indiana UP, 1988. 1–10.
Sebold, Alice. *Lucky*. Boston: Back Bay Books, 2002.
———. *The Lovely Bones*. NY: Little Brown, 2002.

Sedgwick, Eve Kosofsky. *Between Men*. NY: Columbia UP, 1985.
Serres, Michel. *Hermes*. Ed. Josue V. Harari and David F. Bell. Baltimore: The Johns Hopkins UP, 1982.
———. *The Parasite*. Trans. Lawrence R. Schehr. Baltimore: The Johns Hopkins UP, 1982
———. *Rome: The Book of Foundations*. Stanford: Stanford UP, 1983.
Shaffer, Peter. *Peter Shaffer's Amadeus. With a New Introduction to the Film Edition by the Author*. NY: Signet, New American. 1984.
———. *Peter Shaffer's Amadeus: A Play. With an Introduction by the Director Sir Peter Hall and A Wholly New Preface by the Author*. NY: Perennial, 2001.
———. *Amadeus. A Play by Peter Shaffer. With a Postscript by the Author*. UK, 1984.
Shaviro, Steven. *The Cinematic Body*. Minneapolis: U of Minnesota P, 1993.
———. *Post Cinematic Affect*. NY: John Hunt Publishing, Xero Books, 2011.
Sherman, Cindy. *Untitled Film Stills*. NY: Rizzoli, 1990.
———. *The Complete Untitled Film Stills*. NY: Museum of Modern Art, 2003.
Siegert, Bernhard. *Relays: Literature as an Epoch of the Postal System*. Trans. Kevin Repp. Standford: Standford UP, 1999.
Silverman, Kaja. *The Acoustic Mirror*. Bloomington: Indiana UP, 1988.
———. *The Subject of Semiotics*. NY: Oxford UP, 1983.
Skoller, Jeffrey. *Shadows, Specters, Shards: Making History in Avant-Garde Film*. Minneapolis: U of Minnesota P, 2005.
Sloterdijk, Peter. *Critique of Cynical Reason*. Trans. Michael Eldred. Minneapolis: U of Minnesota P, 1987.
Small, Edward. S. *Direct Theory*. Carbondale: Southern Illinois UP, 1994.
Smart, Carol. *Feminism and the Power of Law*. NY: Routledge, 1989.

Smith, Daniel W. "Introduction" to *Deleuze, Essays Critical and Clinical*. xi-liii.

Solanas, Valerie. *SCUM Manifesto*. Second Edition. Intro. Avital Ronell. NY: Verso, 2004.

Spielmann, Yvonne. *Video: The Reflexive Medium*. Trans. Anja Welle and Stan Jones. Cambridege: MIT P, 2008.

Spivak, Gayatri. "Feminism and Deconstruction, Again: Negotiating with Unacknowledged Masculinism." *Between Feminism and Psychoanalysis*. Ed. Teresa Brennan. NY: Routledge, 1989. 206–23.

Straub, Jean-Marie, and Danièle Huillet. Directors and Producers. *Too Early, Too Late* [*Trop tôt, trop tard*]. 1981. Film.

Steigler, Bernard. *Technics and Time, 1*. Trans. Richard Beardsworth and George Collins. Stanford: Stanford UP, 1998.

———. *Technics and Time, 3: Cinematic Time and the Question of Malaise*. Trans. Stephen Barker. Stanford: Stanford UP, 2010.

Stoekl, Allan. *Politics, Writing, Mutilation: The Cases of Bataille, Blanchot, Roussel, Leiris, and Ponge*. Minneapolis: U of Minnesota P, 1985.

Strosser, Margie. *Rape Stories*. Women Make Movies. 1989. Video.

Suleiman, Elia. Director. *Divine Intervention*. 2002.

Taylor, Mark C. *Nots*. Chicago: U of Chicago P, 1993.

Ulmer, Gregory. "Abject Monumentality." *Abject, America* (Lusitania) 1.4 (1993): 9–15.

———. *Heuretics*. Baltimore: The Johns Hopkins UP, 1994.

———. "The Object of Post-Criticism." *The Anti-Aesthetic*. Ed. Hal Foster. Port Townsend, Washington: Bay P, 1987: 83–110.

———. "One Video Theory (Some Assembly Required)." *Critical Issues in Electronic Media*. Ed. Simon Penny. Albany: SUNY, 1995. 253–74.

———. *Teletheory*. NY: Routledge, 1989.

———. "The Euretics of Alice's Valise." *Journal of Architectural Education* 45.1 (November 1991). 3–10.

Vattimo, Gianni. "Nihilism: Reactive and Active." in *Nietzsche and the Rhetoric of Nihilism: Essays on Interpretation, Language, and Politics*. Ed. Tom Darby, Béla Egyed, Ben Jones. Ontario, Canada: Carleton UP, 1989. 15–22.

Ventura, M. "Peter Weir's State of Emergency" *LA Weekly*, 4 March 1983. 5–39.

Vernant, Jean-Pierre. "Feminine Figures of Death in Greece." *Mortals and Immortals, Collected Essays*. Ed. Froma I. Zeitlin. Princeton: Princeton UP, 1991. 95–110.

Vidler, Anthony. *The Architectural Uncanny*. Cambridge: MIT UP, 1992.

Virilio, Paul. *Open Sky*. Trans. Julie Rose. NY: Verso, 1997.

Vitanza, Victor J. "The Hermeneutics of Abandonment." *Parallax* 4.4 (1998): 123–39.

———. *Negation, Subjectivity, and The History of Rhetoric*. Albany: SUNY, 1997.

———. *Sexual Violence in Western Thought and Writing: Chaste Rape*. NY: Palgrave, 2011.

———. "Threes." *Composition in Context*. Ed. W. Ross Winterowd and Vincent Gillespie. Carbondale: Southern Illinois UP, 1994. 196–218.

Vonnegut, Jr., Kurt. *Slaughter-House Five*. NY: Dell, 1971.

Waters, John. *Crackpot*. NY: Macmillian, 1986.

———. *Director's Cut*. NY: Scalo, 1997.

———, dir. *Multiple Maniacs*. VHS. 1970. Film. Can be viewed on YouTube. Web. 21 May 2012 <https://www.youtube.com/watch?v=tm2PPPKlX8Y>.

———, dir. *Pink Flamingos*. VHS. New Line Cinema. 1972. Film.

———. *Hair Spray, Female Trouble, Multiple Maniacs*. NY: Thunder's Mouth P, 2005.

———. *Shock Value*. NY: Thunder's Mouth P, 1981.

———. *Trash Trio*. Second Edition. NY: Thunder's Mouth P, 1996.

Weber, Samuel. *Theatricality as Medium*. NY: Fordham UP, 2004.

Weir, Peter. Director. *A Year of Living Dangerously*. MGM. 1982. Film.

Weiss, Allen S. *The Aesthetics of Excess*. Albany: SUNY UP, 1989.

Weiss, Paul. *Cinematics*. Carbondale: Southern Illinois UP, 1975.

Wells, Pamela Caragol, dir. *24 Hours After Hiroshima*. National Geographic Video. 2010. Video.

White, Hayden. *Tropics of Discourse*. Baltimore: The John Hopkins UP, 1978.

Wittig, Monique. *Les Guerilleres*. Trans. David Le Vay. Boston: Beacon P, 1985.

Wolf, Christa. *Cassandra*. NY: Farrar, Straus, Giroux, 1992.

Woolf, Virginia. *Jacob's Room* and *The Waves*. NY: Harcourt, Brace and World, 1959.

———. *Mrs. Dalloway*. NY: Harcourt, Brace and World, 1953.

———. *Orlando*. Herfordshire: Wordsworth Editions, 1995.

Yuknavitch, Lidia. *The Chronology of Water: A Memoir*. Hawthorne Books and Literary Arts. Portland, OR: 2010.

Zinn, Gesa. "Gender, Germans and Men in Helke Sander's *Die Deutschen und ihre Manner*." *South Atlantic Review* 64.2 (Spring, 1999): 20–36.

Žižek, Slavoj. *Organs Without Bodies*. NY: Routledge, 2004.

———. *The Sublime Object of Ideology*. NY: Verso, 1989.

———. *Tarrying With the Negative*. Durham: Duke UP, 1993.

———. *Violence*. NY: Picador, 2008.

———. *Welcome to the Desert of the Real!* NY: Verso, 2002.

———. *The Year of Dreaming Dangerously*. NY: Verso, 2012.

Zupančič, Alenka. *The Shortest Shadow: Nietzsche's Philosophy of the Two*. Cambridge: MIT P, 2003.